JOHN SELLERS

HOW INDIE ROCK SAVED MY LIFE

SIMON & SCHUSTER

NEW YORK   LONDON   TORONTO   SYDNEY

SIMON & SCHUSTER
Rockefeller Center
1230 Avenue of the Americas
New York, NY 10020

Message board postings and lyrics from "I Am a Scientist"
by Robert Pollard used by permission.

For information about special discounts for bulk purchases,
please contact Simon & Schuster Special Sales at
1-800-456-6798 or business@simonandschuster.com.

Designed by Karolina Harris

Manufactured in the United States of America

10   9   8   7   6   5   4   3   2   1

Library of Congress Cataloging-in-Publication Data
Sellers, John, date.
    Perfect from now on : how indie rock saved my life / John Sellers.
        p.   cm.
    1. Sellers, John, date.   2. Journalists—United States—Biography.
3. Alternative rock music—History and criticism.   I. Title.
PN4874.S4258A3   2007
070.92—dc22
[B]   2006052284
ISBN-13: 978-0-7432-7708-2
ISBN-10:   0-7432-7708-2

To my dad, Mark Ashley Sellers Jr.,

for APBA, Magic, and the sounds of spring

"Life was something you dominated if you were any good."

—F. Scott Fitzgerald, *The Crack-Up*

"You're stupid, Sellers. Sellers, you're stupid."

—Mildly retarded kid on the author's school bus, 1982

1

MY IMPRESSION NOW

"You're finding out that it's way too late to be happy around your friends."

I hate Bob Dylan.

Not with the kind of white-hot anger reserved for the asinine personalities of *American Idol* or the talk-to-the-hand disdain whipped out for the guy who replaced Michael Hutchence in INXS. This is no ordinary hate.[1] It's primal. It's absurd. It makes me look bad. I mean, who doesn't like Bob Dylan?

Only a fool would resist the notion that Dylan might be a genius, would be reluctant to praise any of the 450-plus songs he's written, would fail to recognize that taking potshots at someone almost universally regarded as a living legend is a waste of energy. But until very recently, all of those fools were me. Every so often now, I find myself regretting my intense negative feelings toward him. There are times when I see images of him, especially as a young man, with his rat's nest hairdo and fluttering eyelids, and I feel bad not to be part of the club, many millions strong, that considers him a Martin-strumming Mozart. And then I imagine shaving off his hair and gluing his eyelids shut.

This is terrible, of course. But I've been moaning about Dylan almost since birth. Infrequently discussed, however, is the why. Why do I despise Dylan? Why do I want to press mute whenever I hear his incoherent bleating? Why am I tempted to

---

[1] Yes, an intentional allusion to Sade, whom I also hate. Please forgive me.

seek out and club defenseless old ladies whenever someone plays that song about shit blowin' in the wind? The reason: I was abused as a child. Not in a way that will make this book a best-seller. There are no touchy-feely priests here, no overfriendly clowns, no despotic transgendered soccer moms. What I can offer you is a dad who took whacks at me every single day for nearly two decades. Only his weapon of choice was Bob Dylan.

The next time you hear "Like a Rolling Stone," try to picture a man in his early forties with a Tom Selleck mustache, clunky metal-frame glasses, and tufts of curly brown hair sitting shirtless in a cigarette-tortured, baby-shit-colored rocking chair. He's perched Indian style, a position that strains his threadbare denim cutoffs beyond their limit, revealing areas of skin that no kid should be made to witness. Now crank up the volume: In a deeper voice and with far better enunciation than Dylan's, he's singing emphatically along, occasionally puffing on a Carlton 100 or suckling at the Jar of Death, which contains a lukewarm admixture of Sanka, curdled milk, diet cola, and Carlo Rossi Chablis.

This is my dad. Or at least the version of my dad that slaps me when Dylan comes to mind.[2] The image is seared into my brain: I saw him in this guise, or variations of it, nearly every

---

[2] My dad has many powerful quirks, each bearing its own image. There's the snake-loving dad who would leap from his Honda Civic to chase down slithering reptiles. (He used to store dead blue racers in the freezer, which made you think hard about going for that Fudgsicle.) There's the stuttering dad who'd get hopelessly stuck—say it! say it!—on words beginning with *f, s,* and *k* sounds; he combated this by creating a language consisting mostly of expressions that he had read or heard somewhere and that he felt applied to a given situation, such as "And the tar baby, he don't say nothin'," an Uncle Remus line pulled out when he was pressed on a subject he didn't want to talk about; "He is dangerous!" a snippet from *Jesus Christ Superstar* bestowed upon the person in a game of rummy who laid down the ace of spades; and "Prove it," Jack Palance's rhetorical dare in *Shane* that works in pretty nearly every instance I can think of. And there's the more re-cent dad, hunched like a vulture over a keyboard, hunting and pecking aphorisms pertaining to his disappointment that American society is not

night during my childhood. What I didn't realize then was that he was obsessed with Dylan. Totally. Actually, total obsession doesn't quite sell it. My dad was Bob Dylan's willing thrall. If Dylan had ever put a backwards message on one of his records urging people to take off their clothes, don their best blue bonnets, and skip like nancys across the Mackinac Bridge, my dad would have been the first to be arrested.

Sure, he listened to music by other artists—John Denver,[3] Jim Croce,[4] the Moody Blues[5]—but specific examples stick out only because of their rarity. We were force-fed Dylan at breakfast, lunch, and dinner, and when my dad really got going, there were Dylan aperitifs. My mom, a high school English teacher with a preference for Chopin, the Carpenters, and nonconfrontation, had long stopped protesting by the time my memories kick in; she retreated to safe zones out of earshot of the living room record player, the epicenter of the problem. She knew what my two brothers and I eventually learned: No matter how many times you ask for air-traffic-controller earmuffs, you aren't going to get them. Better just to run.

There was a time when my dad viewed us kids as potential converts, blank slates upon which to etch the scripture of Dylan.

---

where he thought it would be at the dawn of the twenty-first century. Each begins "It's already the year 2000 and we're *still* using ———," where the blank gets filled in with things like "pulleys" or "tires" or "sexual repression." I maintain that it would make a great gift book.

[3] During the John Denver craze of 1977, we heard his greatest hits album often, maybe every day; we also were dragged to see *Oh, God!* I could never get past the fact that, with his dumb bowl cut and wire-rim spectacles, Denver resembled a grown-up Oliver from *The Brady Bunch*.

[4] Or it may have been Harry Chapin or Cat Stevens. The three were interchangeable until I got it straight that Croce wrote that silly "you don't tug on Superman's cape" song and is dead, while Chapin did the even sillier "Cat's in the Cradle" and is also dead, and Stevens recorded the still more silly "Moonshadow" and isn't dead but converted, freakishly, to Islam.

[5] Only one lyric stuck: "I can see you, you can't see me, much to my delight." Goddamn voyeurs.

Starting first with my older brother, Mark, then with me, then with Matt,[6] he'd tell us, usually over marathon sessions of canasta or Yahtzee, about living in New York City in the mid-1960s and sitting in cafés where Dylan once performed. The lyrics of "Maggie's Farm" were explained. (Sticking it to the man, essentially.) There was a lot of "Listen to this next song—I think you'll like it." We never did. After a while, when the blank slates proved to be far more interested in Top 40 music, he just played the records as we rolled dice or bitched about magpies, and we limited the conversation to mutual interests like baseball and chili. He might have been more successful if he'd pretended to be really into James Taylor or something. I mean, next to the unparalleled earnestness of "You've Got a Friend," anything by Dylan would have compared favorably. After slapping us around for years with Taylor, he could have pulled out *The Freewheelin' Bob Dylan* and it would have sounded as enchanting as the coos of baby Jesus. But my dad is incapable of insincerity where Dylan is concerned. He is a true believer.

Now, I don't hate Dylan because I have anything against my dad—well, aside from being denied a childhood of telescopes and Lamborghinis, a financial impossibility due to the extreme lack of demand for unambitious freelance herpetologists in west Michigan during the late 1970s and early '80s. We still get along very well. No, I hate Dylan because the music was crammed down my throat. It's like a guy getting plucked off a desert island after twelve years of eating mostly coconut. There's no way he's eating that crap again. Instantly after my mom, in 1983, finally pulled the plug on the marriage—not even Stephen Hawking could have theorized a more unsuitable match—the absence of Dylan in our lives was gleefully apparent: We were four ship-wreck survivors gorging at a Chi-Chi's. Gorging, salsa-faced and

---

[6] My mom, always moderately pious, and my dad, a former Lutheran minister who lapsed (hard), named us kids after books of the Gospel. Fine. But it is lame that Matt, born in 1977 just months into the *Star Wars* phenomenon, isn't named Luke.

happy—that is, until an unfortunate incident a few days after we moved out. The four of us had driven back to the old house to pick up a television set, the last of my mom's remaining junk. The return trip was profoundly, disturbingly silent, apart from the sounds coming from the radio, which was set to a station that played a lot of Billy Squier and Styx. As if the deejay had conspired with my dad on a parting shot, the car suddenly filled with the opening electric chords of "Like a Rolling Stone," and we all—even Matt, age six—lunged for the dial before that voice could kick in. Minutes later, just after we stopped laughing, my mom barreled into a drunk jaywalker, causing ridiculous amounts of mayhem. (No one died, thankfully.) Although we didn't say as much to the policemen who arrived on the scene, it was the curse of Dylan.

Viewed from the minimum safe distance—five miles then, seven hundred now—my dad's obsession shifted from being weird and oppressive to being weird and mildly endearing. At age sixty-six, for example, he stays in touch primarily via e-mailed exclamations and forwards: "Dylan gets his own radio show!"; "Dylan documentary on PBS!"; "Conor Oberst: The New Dylan?" Not that anything has changed: Dylan is his and he is Dylan's. Which is why, even as my stance toward Dylan and his music slackens,[7] there is little point in giving in entirely: Since I can never hope to enjoy Dylan as fully as my dad does, why

[7] Until maybe 2002, the only way I could stomach Dylan was through a filtration process—that is, via covers or tributes by other artists, specifically: 1) the cue-card-flipping gimmick in INXS's video for "Mediate," appropriated from "Subterranean Homesick Blues"; 2) the Guns N' Roses version of "Knocking on Heaven's Door"; and 3) "All Along the Watchtower" as covered by Jimi Hendrix and especially U2. (Any cover by Peter, Paul and Mary, though, is to be hated.) But now I see the brilliance of "Like a Rolling Stone" and some of his other hits, and I love the humor of early Dylan, such as that in "Talking Bear Mountain Picnic Massacre Blues": The slack-jawed narrator gets trampled after a shipwreck and wakes up not only with various crippling injuries but also "bald, naked." He deadpans that he's "quite lucky to be alive though."

bother to get involved? Any effort to do so would feel as false as a former Lutheran minister listening to Black Sabbath simply because his middle child does. Of course, this stubbornness to embrace Dylan has perplexed dozens of total strangers and good friends; it has also prevented a closer relationship with my dad. It's impossible for us to talk about his one true passion in a way that isn't lopsided. Attending a Dylan concert with him is out of the question. As unfortunate as these things are, I decided long ago not to surrender completely. To do so would be an endorsement of my dad's puzzling behavior when I was younger. It would make three decades of Dylan-hate absolutely meaningless. Most of all, though, if I immersed myself in Dylan, it would suggest that I was okay with turning into someone like my dad.

And then two years ago I realized that, without warning, I had already turned into someone like my dad.

❖

A partial list of things music has made me do: fly overseas at considerable expense to see a live performance by a band I no longer liked, nurture a crush on a goth chick way out of my league, nurture a crush on an alternachick way out of my league, write a love letter to a German woman made up entirely of lyrics from my favorite synth band, reconsider fast friendships, get ticketed for doing 82 in a 55, drive around a remote area of England looking for a hero's grave, wear parachute pants without irony, perform the moonwalk in front of a crowded gymnasium, switch college majors, miss a final exam, shoplift (both successfully and unsuccessfully), dive to the bottom of a numbingly cold Scottish pond to retrieve my favorite T-shirt, stab my thumb into the back of a fellow concert attendee's neck to get closer to the stage, drink too much, lose my voice, stage-dive, cry, and regret. But it wasn't until I was thirty-three—on a Friday night in April 2004, to be more specific—that I found out exactly how important music was to me.

The evening began like so many others: the twist of a bottle cap, the first sip of beer, the descent of my buttocks into the swivel chair at my desk. My computer, a bulky eMac, still excited me a full year after I purchased it, in large part because it had completely changed the way I listened to music. Converting all of my CDs into searchable digital files had spoiled me. Gone were the days of hauling my carcass up to the wall-mounted CD rack to find the one disc that contained the one song required at a given moment. That song was now available with a click of the mouse—and it could be found while sitting down. Once again I fired up the iTunes program and within seconds a familiar song was dominating my apartment. As I scrolled through more than three thousand songs for the perfect follow-up, the value of iTunes as something other than a tool to organize and burn CDs revealed itself in a bang: play count. How had I failed to scrutinize this ingenious function before? Here in front of me was an unadulterated reckoning of how often I'd listened to each song in my collection since the uploading had begun nearly twelve months before—amazing. The frequency of seemingly uncountable thoughts and actions, such as the number of times I've said the word "awesome" or the sheer poundage of pizza I've eaten, has tantalized me for years, a desire that grew, most likely, out of a *Saturday Night Live* sketch from the late 1980s about a guy who arrives in heaven and proceeds to quiz an angel about all sorts of arcane trivia about his life, such as "What's the two hundredth grossest thing I ever ate?" (The answer: butterscotch pudding with a dead earwig in it.) Play count was offering up information that I wasn't supposed to have until death. It was a message from God. Or Steve Jobs, which is pretty much the same thing.

Okay, so the message wasn't divine; it wasn't even exact. Perusing the incredible totals, I quickly saw the problem. Take Outkast's "Hey Ya!" The single had been everywhere in recent months, and I had willingly submitted to it like everyone else in my age bracket. According to iTunes, the song, uploaded near the end of 2003, had been played just three times on my computer. Obviously I'd heard it many more times: at parties, on television, over the radio in the car, in a much-distributed Internet clip featuring dancing *Peanuts* characters, on a local tough's boom box outside my deli. "Hey Ya!" was inescapable. Exactly how many times I'd heard it was impossible to tell—twenty? forty? But as a new beer was opened, a new rule was considered: Whatever play count said was law. The totals were probably only slightly misleading. Very few appealing songs were popping up with the frequency of a "Hey Ya!"—it was an exception, and thus an outlier. Neither the radio nor video channels were major sources of musical entertainment for me anymore. My CD player was rarely switched on, and I did not own an iPod.[8] Couldn't nearly everything not heard on the eMac, my primary source

[8] I haven't bought one yet due to chronic laziness and stinginess, and requests for one have gone unfulfilled at the time of this writing. I'm a bit embarrassed about it. Any self-respecting music fan in 2007 should own an iPod, or another portable digital music player, because these devices represent a cultural shift in the way we listen to music. I have noticed, though, that the movement toward the downloadable implies that music is all about, well, the music. Mostly it is, of course, but not entirely. There are elements of the music-listening experience that I would sincerely miss if they ever disappeared for good. The act of storing and organizing CDs, be it in a teetering stack on the floor or alphabetically in a binder, feels necessary: It's comforting to have physical manifestations of the music you love. I also like flipping through the booklet that first time after a CD is purchased and staring at the cover art and scouring the liner notes to see what mysteries are revealed about various band members: Can they spell? Do they name-check any actors? Are they New Agey? Strangely, I might even miss the humbling process of opening a newly purchased CD, which has been sending me into Sam Kinison–like rages since about 1997, when packagers discovered the perfect conduit for expressing their wickedness: not just the shrink wrap but also that adhesive strip that says PULL on it, and which never comes off in one piece no matter how sturdy your fingernails. These things may well become extinct as more people embrace the practice of downloading full albums and as file sharing becomes more acceptable. (File sharing has led to at least one unintended problem: misidentification. Once, while browsing the old, illegal Napster, I saw a track by a group called the Foop Fighters.) Because of the iPod, CD collections are being viewed as mere redundancies, like when a friend of mine moved all of his music to his computer and then happily trashed his jewel cases, CDs, and liner notes because "they're

of music delivery since my collection was uploaded, be discounted? The stats seemed sacred enough. I chose to run with them.

Not surprisingly, the numbers, in aggregate, confirmed that indie rock is my favorite genre of music; it has been for nearly two decades now. Since I'll be using that term often here, it could use some clarification—in part because the phrase has become nebulous in this relatively recent era in which Borglike conglomerates have swallowed up labels once considered too insignificant to matter, and also because indie rock may be defined differently depending on whom you ask. Back in the early 1980s, when the term started getting thrown around, things were relatively simple: You were either on an independent label or you weren't—and if you weren't, then you probably sucked, at least to die-hard fans of the genre. But then R.E.M. got popular. And Nirvana. So now confusion reigns. Purists might disagree, but I think the term can now safely apply to anything that feels independent, whether

---

annoying." That kind of clutter will never annoy me, and in fact those tilting helixes of CDs around my apartment are a kind of sculpture. My biggest concern, though, is that iTunes and iPods will make it impossible to listen to albums straight through. Back when I started listening to music, mostly on cassette, it was a chore to constantly rewind and fast-forward to get to the parts of an album I wanted to hear. So I'd usually consent to sit through, say, "I'll Wait," when all I really wanted to hear was "Girl Gone Bad." But now it's way too easy to skip the songs you don't want to hear—far easier than in the days of CD players. Why listen to an entire, interminable album when you can so quickly organize your favorite songs using the "My Rating" function or a playlist? You can also search for tracks containing a random syllable, such as "bra" (I get twenty-two selections, including "Your Algebra" by the Shins and "A New England" by Billy Bragg), and that's diverting. Sometimes, though, it's important to hear a track like Radiohead's "Optimistic" the way it was intended: right after the noise that is "Treefingers." Not that you can't do that on iTunes or an iPod; it's just getting harder to consider it. But it would stink if "Treefingers" were permanently deleted from my digital collection. None of this means that I wouldn't accept a gift of an iPod for, say, my rapidly approaching thirty-seventh birthday. But I'm keeping my CD collection forever, no matter how much cash that record store on St. Mark's would give me.

published on an obscure label or something insidiously corporate, and it can include songs that many people associate more closely with another of indie music's many aliases and subgenres: hardcore, postpunk, grunge, shoegazing, lo-fi, emo, and stuff we older sorts used to refer to as college rock or modern rock. Such classifications, as you might expect, can be personal. Most indie aficionados—that moderately large listener base that has always been woefully underserved by mainstream radio and MTV— would probably consider Sonic Youth and Hüsker Dü and Dinosaur Jr. and Built to Spill and even Death Cab for Cutie to have retained their credibility after signing with majors. But what about the Smashing Pumpkins? How best to judge the case of Radiohead, which has always been on a major label? And what of Weezer, another major-label lifer—and one, in fact, that seems to be an independent band created in a major-label-funded laboratory experiment? I'll settle it: They're all indie.

However the genre is defined, I'm a fan. Well, mostly. Actually, lots of indie rock sucks worse than Dan Fogelberg. And just because I love indie music doesn't mean that it's all I listen to or that it's the only genre that matters. There is value in the Toto song "Hold the Line." I own every original studio album by Led Zeppelin, not to mention *Coda*. I will always possess the gene that makes some guys turn their vehicle into Neil Peart's ninety-nine-piece drum kit whenever Rush's "Tom Sawyer" comes on. But I'll get into all that later. What's at issue here is that, thanks to the play count discovery, my listening habits were now both quantifiable and sortable. It was thrilling even to look at tracks that didn't rank among my favorites. How many times had I played the Pixies' "Velouria" in the past year? Twelve times—a manageable once-a-month craving. I had failed to listen to any songs from Soundgarden's *Superunknown* other than "Fell on Black Days," which caused me to rock out unabashedly sixteen times. Songs by old favorites New Order and the Cure were played in the same moderation as those by newer go-tos the Shins and the New Pornographers. Van Halen's "Everybody Wants

Some!!" (22 listens) ranked ahead of anything by Nirvana, but the average number of times I'd listened to the first eleven songs on *Nevermind* (5.9 times)[9] greatly exceeded that of the eight songs on *Women and Children First* (3.8 listens). But obviously this is not the information that blew my mind.

No, what made me reconsider my place in life were the songs at the top of the list when sorted by play count. At 193 listens, the song I had played most often during the previous twelve months was written by a band that most people have never heard of. In fact, the top ten songs—and seventeen of the top twenty (and thirty-five of the top fifty, and sixty-three of the top one hundred)—were all by that same band or its offshoots. The facts told me what I had only just begun admitting to myself: I was obsessed with Guided By Voices.

Now there are a few ways you can give in to musical obsession. You can give in suddenly and briefly—such as when, over the course of a few weeks or months, you find yourself hooked on a particular album (especially a debut album or a breakout album) and start talking up the artist to everyone you know; but then, after seeing a boring live performance or hearing someone you don't respect gush about the music, you just as suddenly denounce the artist as being annoying or unoriginal.[10]

Or you can give in sporadically. This might happen if you are dealing with unfamiliar real-world concerns, such as a new job or mouth to feed, when you have neither the time nor the energy to satisfy the rigors of a full-blown obsession;[11] it might also be

---

[9] The album's finale, "Something in the Way," can't be counted reliably because it features a hidden track: Specifically, there is the familiar 3-minute, 48-second song of woe, then 10:03 of silence, and then 6:41 of dial-a-grunge. I'm usually long gone by the time it kicks back in.

[10] There is always a whiff of embarrassment in this kind of obsession. It might be better to pretend that it never happened.

[11] In other words, you have become totally lame.

that your passion peaked years ago and is only at the edges of your synapses now. But the mania is merely in remission; it is still there, waiting to flare up, much like herpes, at certain and often unpredictable moments: a release of a new bootleg, an anniversary of a hero's death, a reunion tour, a simpatico comment by a bartender, a delivery of killer weed.

Or of course you can go all in—and indeed, this is the most recognizable form of musical obsession. You let it dip into every facet of your life: your wardrobe, your hairstyle, the foods you eat, the drugs you take, the naming of your pets and children. Fanship of this type is generally expressed outwardly and unabashedly, and as such it tends to draw the bewilderment and ridicule of those who don't understand.[12] Not that you really care what those morons think. You may appear on an MTV program talking about your fanatical devotion; you will almost certainly blog about it. Tattoos are possibly involved, and in wacko cases, plastic surgery. If you observe a hero wearing a hearing aid or wielding gladioli, you will likely get an intense urge to be seen in public wearing a hearing aid or wielding gladioli. There is a sense of competition among your own kind to be known as the most dedicated fan. But you also feel most comfortable when among other faithfuls, and you may even have friends or a spouse whom you met at a show or through a message board. En masse, you and your brethren may be given a label by outsiders, usually derogatorily: Deadheads, Phishheads, Parrotheads, metalheads, goths, Elvis freaks, Teshies, Idiots Who Think That Michael Jackson Isn't a Child Molester. In other words, you are the Trekkies of musical fandom. But you are also that most loyal of fans: willing, in theory, to get beaten down defending the music you love.

I didn't intend for intense musical obsession to find me. Not

---

[12] Especially in those very rare, very extreme, very cinematic instances of musical obsession gone awry: stalkers, suicides, kids who shoot up schools, malcontents who commit murder because a message in a song told them to, loners who jump on stages to pump rounds into their heroes.

again. Not at the age of thirty-three. And especially not for the band Guided By Voices, which had been brought to my attention numerous times previously and summarily dismissed. It should have been too late. This was 2004, a decade past their heyday. The buzz was mostly gone. Their lead singer was forty-six. They lived in Ohio. But something stronger than reason was at work. A pleasant encounter with one of their albums had caused me to buy it on impulse. And then after a few listens a higher power assumed control. It made a Bloblike crawl through eBay and Amazon, eating up every CD in its path. But the music just kept coming: 252 songs on fifteen proper albums, hundreds more on EPs and compilations, and that didn't even begin to count the side projects, of which there were more than ten. A year and a half after that first listen, I had barely begun. Almost as compelling as the band's music (so familiar-sounding, with hints of the Who, the Replacements, and the Beatles—but also none of those) was its persona. These were hardworking Midwesterners whose collective genius had mostly been overlooked. Their lead singer and chief songwriter, Robert Pollard, had been an elementary school teacher. His brother, formerly in the band, worked at a General Motors parts plant. One of the drummers had been a male nurse. They wore sensible jeans, untucked cotton twill shirts, and high-top sneakers. They drank heartily. They loved sports. At last: regular guys who just happened to write transcendent songs.

Initially the iTunes totals made me proud. Puffed-out-chest, hands-on-hips proud. I'd listened to a song named "Game of Pricks" 193 times last year! But as the stats (and more beer) sunk in, it occurred to me that most people my age did not listen to music that way. With two or three exceptions, none of my friends seemed to listen to music anymore at all. Obviously they must have been doing so in moderation, and might have even been loving it, but not with the reckless abandon of youth. They were married, had tiny offspring, were focused on making money, on dinner parties, on breast pumps, on property. Somewhere along the line they had become adults. Adults do not spend thousands of dollars they can't really afford on paraphernalia relating to one band. They do not spend hours making wall montages featuring their new heroes in various comical poses. They do not plan trips around concerts—especially ones that involve air travel. Their biggest wish is not to meet a particular musician and get drunk with him. There seemed to be unwritten rules for people my age. Having diverse listening tastes: great. Going to the occasional concert: fine. Getting excited about one band more than others: okay, but watch it. Exhibiting fanboy behavior: embarrassing and not to be tolerated. Our differences in listening to music was a major reason I'd retreated from them, my best friends in the world. I wanted to hang out, hold court, and blare music, and they did not. I wanted to go to concerts, get drunk, and let go; they wanted to get up early. It was a drag.

Then again, I wanted money and property. I wanted to be taken seriously. And I profoundly missed my friends. The longing to mix with burgeoning adults but also the need to think and behave like a juvenile—these were conflicting, crippling desires. They seemed irreconcilable, too. To have fun, you couldn't go half-assed, but if you didn't go half-assed at my age, there were often severe consequences: increasingly painful hangovers, missed work and opportunity, a loss of interest in hanging out with more sedate friends, a frequently annoyed girlfriend. The warning signs were all around me. I'd seen how my dad turned out: Gollum, sitting happily in his cave, singing to his Precious. Did I want that to happen to me? Did I want to be a frothing man-child for the rest of my life? Over the next few weeks, with the obsession out in the open and my listening habits questioned, it dawned on me to conduct a low-level personal reckoning. Not in that Hollywood way parodied a few times on *Seinfeld,* in which George or Jerry would go to the pier at Coney Island, mull over his shallow existence, look around and see happy couples with kids, and finally run off, scuttling pigeons, determined to change his life. But I was experiencing relationship and career malaise—neither was very fun. My obscene musical devotion, and the lifestyle it espoused, didn't have everything to do with my stagnant reality. But it certainly had something to do with it. It was obvious that sooner or later some lifestyle tweaks would have to be made if I ever planned on having a cushy bank-account balance or a significant other who wouldn't tire of my frequently immature and obsessive behavior. Not that I had any intention of abandoning the music; I have always envisioned my eighty-five-year-old self as the scourge of the nursing home, blasting songs so loudly (theory: Frank Black is my generation's Tony Bennett) that my shriveled neighbors will be forced to turn off their hearing aids. Maybe, though, it was time to consider listening to music differently.

2

EVERYBODY WANTS TO RULE THE WORLD

"Welcome to your life. There's no turning back."

I should have been a meathead. That is, a wearer of too-tight, faded, and possibly ripped jeans who compounds the already unthinkable with a bleached jean jacket and a tank top bearing the expression ROOFERS DO IT HIGH. A dude with a bush of hair mown into an improbable topiary shape and the keys to a B2000 pickup—you know, to haul stuff—on a key chain also holding a bottle opener obtained at a regional Hawaiian Tropic swimsuit competition. In short, a guy whose favorite jokes involve the groin.

That might have been me had I never left the suburbs of Grand Rapids, Michigan, a city of roughly 200,000 that is a test-marketing hub for potato chips. As a high school junior driving around subdivisions in a silver Datsun hand-me-down with a hole in the floorboard, through which friends would hurl Burger King Whaler wrappers at cars foolish enough to tailgate, I thought little about personal evolution. Expectations rarely went further than next Saturday night. That's when we desperately searched for ways to amuse ourselves if no one could score Bartles & James or if there wasn't a new Sylvester Stallone movie out. Once, a decision was made to collect thirty FOR SALE signs from around the area and stick them in the lawn of the class weirdo, who, it turned out, was lying in wait for such shenanigans and who chased us to our cars shrieking like a samurai and brandishing a very real, very sharp ninja sword. Another time, we toilet-papered a cripple's house. These were the sorts of things guys like me did for fun in a town like Grand Rapids.[13] Not that it was an unpleasant place to grow up. There wasn't much crime, other than fashion-related, in the largely middle-class area where we lived, which was also home to the corporate headquarters of the legalized pyramid scheme Amway. The people were friendly enough, if a little too prone to hawking Tupperware knockoffs and soap products door to door. Besides the typical bullying by kids who needed to do that sort of thing to make themselves feel better about being ugly, or dumb, or poor, or all three, I was allowed to be me. The problem is, almost everyone was white. Almost everyone was conservative. But since this is a book about music, I'll put it another way: Almost everyone listened to Journey. Including me.

I liked "Any Way You Want It" and "Who's Crying Now" and "Faithfully" because I heard them all the time. Well, that's not quite it; I liked (and still mildly like) Journey because, despite the abundance of hair follicles and lyrics that were never more compelling than "lovin', touchin', squeezin'," Steve Perry's powerful, nuts-in-a-vise singing voice sounds good when paired with Neal Schon's spidery guitar licks. What I mean is that I was *able to* like Journey because I heard them all the time. It was the same with Foreigner, Styx, Eddie Money, and a lot of the other mainstream Top 40 rock that came our way in the early 1980s. Because this stuff—trash, really, but hummable and at times life-affirming trash—was being endorsed by the only decent radio stations in town, it appeared to be safe to consume. Then again, that's what Eve said about the apple.

There is nothing essentially wrong with being raised on a strict diet of pop music, and there were no complaints during my preteens. The act of listening to music in those early days was so pristine that it was hard not to embrace every new sound that came down the pike—well, except those created by Air

[13] Often referred to, with a sigh, as Bland Rapids.

Supply.[14] The first two songs I remember liking to the point of excitement were Queen's "Another One Bites the Dust" (perfectly acceptable) and M's "Pop Muzik" (not so much), and right there is the problem I faced throughout my musical nascency. Judging the quality of certain songs was often tough to do; a slipup could lead to playground humiliation in front of those whose opinions were more emphatic than my own. So many times I felt like the goon in the dunk tank at the county fair: Totally fine, even arrogant, when something I liked, even something so retroactively awful as Corey Hart, passed muster with my friends; but occasionally you'd mention a song in a positive light and—*ding!*— you'd get doused by dead-on put-downs.[15] It might have armed me with confidence to have known then that no one had any taste, that every one of us loved songs with insipid lyrics and big, cheesy riffs pulled off by big, cheesy rock stars—basically, anything that rocked, or ruled, or didn't suck. None of us, not even the vocal, taunting few, had any real concept of what music was all about.

And here is maybe the biggest limitation of living in a place like the Grand Rapids I grew up in: You weren't conditioned to seek anything out. You took what you were given and didn't think much of it. Who knew there was a bigger world out there? That just an hour away, at a college I would eventually attend, strange new music was readily available for consumption? As it was, I was stuck with whatever sprawling, constrictive suburbia had to offer, and the best it had to offer, tragically, was a venue in

---

[14] In particular, the 1983 song "Sweet Dreams" caused me severe distress. The lyric went "Close your eyes/I want to see you tonight in my sweet dreams." This did not compute. Why would the object of affection—and I'm guessing it's a man—need to close his eyes if the probably homosexual singer is the one doing the dreaming? Shouldn't the imperative be "Close *my* eyes"? Yes, it should. You also have to wonder about the title of their hit "Even the Nights Are Better." Wouldn't the nights be the first thing to improve? Shouldn't it be "Even the Days, During Which I Sit in a Tiny Cubicle and Pray for Death, Are Better"? But, yeah, that's a mouthful.

[15] Words of advice: Never admit to liking Mr. Mister.

the parking lot of a mall where Foghat and Spyro Gyra appeared almost bimonthly.

But somehow it worked out. Which is why, when examining my current preferences, I can scarcely believe that my second concert was Huey Lewis and the News.[16] That a considerable amount of time at the age of ten was devoted to creating a dance routine for Kool and the Gang's "Celebration." That I once shyly told someone that Bryan Adams was my favorite musician. I would pay a lot to go back and pop my younger self in the mouth.

---

[16] My two friends and I sat in the sixth row, mere feet away from a drunk pip-squeak in a jean jacket who hurled halfway through "Hip to Be Square." A reaction to the music?

3

THE REFLEX

"Don't want to be around when this gets out."

I feel sorry for anyone who wasn't born in 1970. What an embarrassment of riches we sons and daughters of that magic year lucked into, simply because Dad chose a timely evening to slip a mickey into Mom's Tab and have his way with her while she lolled on the couch. Or however that went down. The obvious advantage we hold over those born in the lesser years immediately before and after—I'm referring to the other denizens of an age bracket that would eventually, annoyingly, get branded "Generation X"—is the year itself:[17] 1970, an attractive, round number that has made life's mileposts so easy to calculate. But a subtler factor—and I suppose this part applies to most Gen-X kids, not just those born in 1970—is that we have been blessed with a prosperous shuttle run through pop-culture history. We have the good fortune of being too young to have any real memories of Watergate, Vietnam, and Tiny Tim, and too old to have been susceptible to Barney, New Kids on the Block, and the expression "gettin' jiggy wit' it." We vividly remember, with increasing wistfulness, the time before society's reliance on ATMs, VCRs, and computers—yes, we lived a chunk of our

---

[17] Forgive the ageism, but another advantage we 1970 babies hold over anyone born, say, pre-1966 and post-1974—i.e., non–Gen Xers—is that, since they did not overlap with our high school or college years, they are either too old or too young to matter, unless they have slept with us, bought us liquor, or let us bum rides off them.

years in that less lazy age in which you had to withdraw your money at the bank during business hours, handwrite letters (flaunting the soon-to-be-lost art of penmanship), watch television shows as they aired, and see movies while they were in the theater. But we also didn't live too long in those quaint, Amish-esque times, which would have rendered us too confused to embrace and master the new technology coming along[18] in that slow, sad way common to our parents' generation, which made them resemble confused baboons whenever we forced them to play Intellivision Baseball with us. (And, my God, wasn't it just awful when your parents finally discovered e-mail?)

What's most important to this discussion of Super '70 is that, unlike our Gen-X peers, our tastes and intellects began to gel in 1976, the bicentennial, with its strange quarters and un-trumpable Independence Day fireworks displays, allowing us—okay, maybe just me—to experience, at the perfect age, three life-sculpting events:

1) The King Tut exhibit (December 27, 1976): A sociologist might tell you that it was easier back then for us to have been collectively awed by this kind of pop-culture phenomenon—a Fonzie jumping the barrels, a potential panda pregnancy at the National Zoo, a royal wedding—simply because fewer media outlets were yelling, "Look at me!" All I know is that everyone in first grade loved the hell out of King Tut. To us first graders, that crazy Egyptian, "Born in Arizona, moved to Babylon-ia," as Steve Martin memorably proto-rapped, was a celebrity on the order of the Six Million Dollar Man or Evel Knievel. None of this explains why I fell asleep at the National Gallery next to the mask of Nefertiti.

2) *Star Wars* (August 9, 1977): I saw this just before my seventh birthday with a woman named Wendy Van Prooyen, the coolest friend my straitlaced English-teacher mom has ever had. Had the George Lucas gem arrived even a year earlier, I wouldn't

[18] Except instant messaging. What is the appeal?

have understood it, and would probably have been as scared as I'd been when my dad took me to see *Jaws* when I was five. (I quickly learned that when the ominous shark theme kicked in, I needed to haul ass to the lobby.) As it is, I remember a mock light-saber fight on the exit to Wendy's maroon Camaro, and having felt a great disturbance in an unmentionable force whenever Leia appeared on screen. Had I encountered the movie any later, I would have been too old when *Return of the Jedi* came out in 1983, or at least too old to pretend that the Ewoks didn't ruin the movie. Not that geeks born in other years don't love the holy trilogy just as much as I do. It's just that I experienced it better than they did.[19]

3) But it's the third event that truly sets the brother- and sisterhood of 1970 apart from our Gen-X peers: the debut of MTV in August of 1981. While all Gen Xers—and this is the last time I will use the term "Generation X" in this book, I promise—can legitimately feel proprietary about MTV, eleven seems like the best age to have discovered it. You're not old enough to drive or to have become overly concerned with the social strata of junior high or high school. Unless you're a genetic freak, you probably haven't yet hit puberty, which means you're not preoccupied with getting the opposite sex to like you. Yet you're not so young that your parents are constantly monitoring you. You're definitely at that age when, if left unprovoked, you have no qualms about watching television all day, every day. Time to an eleven-year-old is never an issue unless it's getting dark and you're playing baseball, or you need to be driven to the arcade, like, now. I vividly remember the afternoon our house evolved. I came home from school—this was late 1981, and I was in sixth grade—to discover a toothy guy in a Billy Sims jersey adjusting our television set. As nothing interesting ever happened around our small, rented hovel apart from intermittent rummy marathons and Hamburger Helper nights, my imagination was trained to go

---

[19] I fully expect this to be the single most hated sentence I'll ever write.

into hyperdrive: Apparently my mother, the ruddy harlot, had used her horizontal hold to get this unfashionable, burly man to fix our set's vertical, something my dad certainly wasn't taking care of. But when my mom, a first-rate prude and eventual Ph.D. whose dissertation was on nineteenth-century feminist writer Margaret Fuller, sighed and informed me that it was *just the cable guy, John,* I could hardly contain my disappointment—until it sank in that this meant we now had cable.

So began the slow decay of musculature.

After a few months surveying the newly acquired territories, something called MTV, or Music Television, emerged as the most suitable locale for encampment.[20] It's somewhat lost in the blight that is the current incarnation of MTV—which is too assured of its ability to connect with teenagers and is overly ambitious in its programming (a special about Holocaust survivors?), much of which has nothing to do with music (a special about Holocaust survivors?)—but the MTV that existed in the first few years after its debut was a gift akin to manna from heaven or a handful of Zagnuts from that old lady's house we hit every Halloween. At the time, the options for satiating one's budding interest in popular music felt insufficient: roller-skating parties, those forced marches with the school's ruling class, with their inclusion of "ladies' choice," code words for "sit dejectedly in the corner and watch better-groomed kids skate to 'Open Arms'"; television shows such as *American Bandstand, Soul Train,* and *Solid Gold,* all of which showcased the dancing more than the music and thus couldn't be taken seriously;[21] and of course the radio. I had

[20] It should be noted that in 1981, our cable service didn't offer much of a selection: TBS Superstation, CNN, ESPN, USA Network, C-SPAN, and some pay movie channels my parents were too cheap to shell out for, although this didn't stop me from trying to decipher the brief, Picasso-like shards of nudity that emerged from behind the squiggly lines that barred access to Cinemax, which everyone called "Skinemax."

[21] Really—it was like watching strangers have sex, a guilty pleasure at best, though admittedly I would have liked to play Twister with any of those Solid Gold Dancers, even that black woman with the freaky long hair.

only just started listening to the radio on my own, which is to say, outside of the car dominated by whichever parent was driving: my mom, who preferred classical, or my dad, whose dial was stuck on that granola college station that exclusively played folk.[22] And yet in many ways I was still a hostage. There were only two radio stations in Grand Rapids that played the Top 40 music deemed acceptable by my friends, and this meant I had to submit to the whims of stooge deejays. I would like to deny ever enjoying the music they were told to play by some Large Eastern Syndicate, but I loved "Queen of Hearts" by Juice Newton, "9 to 5" by Dolly Parton, and "You Make My Dreams" by Hall & Oates as much as anyone else. I'll even admit to feeling bodily pain whenever we couldn't talk my mom out of going to church, as Sunday school meant missing almost all of that week's *American Top 40* countdown ("America's coast to coast . . ." went the perky jingle), a must-hear even if it did mean sitting through Casey Kasem's treacly "Long Distance Dedication." It was too important for me to know how high that new song by REO Speedwagon had charted.

But here was a television channel that blended two of your favorite pastimes: watching television and listening to music. Now you could literally watch music! It was like that old Reese's Peanut Butter Cup commercial where an accident takes place and one guy's half-eaten chocolate bar somehow winds up in another's inexplicably open jar of peanut butter, creating lots of bewilderment and, ultimately, a new taste sensation. And the early MTV was startlingly fresh: video after video—at least a dozen per hour—by many of the same musicians you knew from

---

[22] Soon he bought a Civic with a tape deck, and even trips to Putt-Putt were Dylanized. Once, we cajoled him into coming inside to try Ms. Pac-Man. It was a pleasure to watch. He simply could not avoid getting killed in the first ten seconds. Contorting his lips in extreme concentration and confusion, he would attempt to guide the hungry heroine out of harm's way but his hand would slip, and *gotcha*. Afterward he clutched his chest and said, "I think I had a *thing*!"

the radio, plus some by unknown artists with vaguely sexual names like Krokus, Iron Maiden, and the Vapors. Because very few of my classmates' parents had yet subscribed to cable, MTV was not initially a topic of conversation at my school. This meant that I was free to take it all in on my own, without peer pressure, and without knowing whether or not it was cool. Well, not entirely on my own. I listened to the counsel of my new friends, the five MTV veejays (say them with me: Nina Blackwood, Martha Quinn, J. J. Jackson, Mark Goodman, and Alan Hunter), who helpfully offered up nuggets about some of the artists in the catalog—something Top 40 radio deejays rarely did. The fact that these people were flesh and blood and big, poufy hair, and not just fakey, disembodied voices, somehow made them more accountable for the music they played.

My older brother, Mark, and I watched MTV so regularly[23] that we created a game to see who could guess the video before its title appeared a few seconds in. This could be tough if the music didn't kick in right away. A dude getting out of a futuristic car in a *Mad Max*–like landscape? "You Got Lucky" by Tom Petty and the Heartbreakers! Some guy standing by a jukebox in a bar? "I Love Rock 'n' Roll" by Joan Jett and the Blackhearts! The videos fell into one of three categories: There was the performance video, in which artists would lip-synch for the camera while

---

[23] MTV contributed greatly to my legendarily short attention span. Our cable box, and I think it was a relatively common kind, was not technically operated by remote control. (Needless to say, our TV set, previously owned by cavemen, also was not equipped with one.) From across the room, you manned a flimsy, lap-sized control mechanism, attached by a wire to the cable box, that worked by sliding an arrow to a number that corresponded to the network you wanted. MTV was channel 22. I grew so skilled on this apparatus that, during the breaks in one of my favorite shows (permit me a quick shout-out to *The Greatest American Hero, The Fall Guy,* and *Tales of the Gold Monkey*), I could flick with the precision of a Palestinian stone thrower from the 4 of ABC to 22 to see which video was playing, rest there for maybe two minutes, and then, to my dad's eternal surprise, flick back to the program we were watching at the exact instant it was coming back from commercials as if divined by internal clock.

wearing song-appropriate threads (e.g., Hall & Oates dressed as gumshoes in "Private Eyes") or not (Flock of Seagulls in "I Ran"); or they'd stage a fake concert for a phantom crowd (Billy Squier in "The Stroke"); or they'd perform their song in front of a bona fide audience (Journey in "Don't Stop Believin'"). There was the concept video, where you had no idea what was happening because it featured heavy symbolism (David Bowie's "Ashes to Ashes"), bizarre camera work (Quarterflash's "Harden My Heart"), or crazy shit like drummers banging buckets filled with milk (almost every video made in 1982). And then there was the story video, which I'll argue contributed the most to MTV's success. While performance and concept videos could be compelling—see Talking Heads' "Once in a Lifetime" or "White Wedding" by Billy Idol, respectively—they could also backfire if the band was hideous (Blue Öyster Cult in "Burnin' for You"), bland (Air Supply in all of their lame-ass videos), annoying (Jethro Tull in "Aqualung"), or embarrassingly weird (ironically, the Buggles, who kicked off MTV with "Video Killed the Radio Star"). But a story video always helped. Say you're an artist with a terrible single. Let's use Pat Benatar's "Love Is a Battlefield" as an example. The video treats us to a vignette about a girl who flees her home ("If you leave this house now, don't you ever come back!" yells her pinhead of a father), becomes a prostitute, rallies her scantily clad coworkers to do a dance of defiance against their pimp (perhaps the world's first hooker union), and then slinks back home a more loving daughter. Benatar must have figured that if you offer viewers even a barely passable story, they'll become so invested that they'll ignore the putridity of the music for the length of the video, and possibly until their next trip to a record store. It even helped that Ms. Benatar and her costars were hams of the highest order and that the story is in dire need of a rewrite. Who wouldn't want to sit through something that unintentionally funny over and over again?

But if you were a marketable artist with a decent single, a story video could turn that sucker into napalm. It's not hard to argue that the band that figured this out first and best was Duran Duran. Something that felt as catchy as "Hungry Like the Wolf" did in the pop landscape of 1983 would have been at least a modest hit whether or not MTV had existed; success is almost guaranteed in pop music with a well-placed series of *doo-doo-doos*. Now tack on a slick video that showcases the charisma of early-'80s Simon Le Bon, a compelling quest in a locale reminiscent of the opening sequence of *Raiders of the Lost Ark* (Le Bon even wore a fedora), a helpful native boy who likes to point (okay, his inclusion made no difference whatsoever, but that kid deserves praise), and a rumble in the jungle versus a hottie who claws the fuck out of Le Bon's face. I don't know the precise calculation, but the song became something like seven times more listenable.[24] Indeed, when I think back to those early days of MTV, Duran Duran comes to mind more than any other artist. (A close second is Wham!, due to George Michael's insane, Reagan-era-defining cheesiness, or maybe Barnes & Barnes, who did that hilariously bizarre "Fish Heads" video starring Bill Paxton as a lover of "roly-poly fish heads.") They exploited the fledgling medium to its fullest, using their glammy, in-crowd looks and glimpses at their enviable lifestyles to sell their music, at least initially, to minors of both sexes, with a subset of the female gender loving them uncontrollably and a healthy number of guys begrudgingly fascinated by them.[25] The video for "Rio" found them cavorting on a yacht that's navigating waters teeming not with

[24] This came hot on the heels of "Girls on Film," the most important video to air during MTV's first two years. When the network banned it, largely because of parental outcry against its ludicrously lurid premise (sumo-wrestling models kick the crap out of and do unspeakable things off-camera to the Duran Duran waifs), "Girls on Film" achieved legendary status among newly hormonal boys, an unintended result that echoed Obi-Wan Kenobi's rebuke to Darth Vader: "If you strike me down, I shall become more powerful than you can possibly imagine."

[25] According to *The Rolling Stone Encyclopedia of Rock & Roll,* Andy Warhol once admitted to masturbating to their videos. I will take the Fifth on that one.

marlins or sharks but with leggy models. If you were a boy my age when that video came out, you may very well have concluded that the Duran Duran quintet[26] was living one of the twelve or fifteen kinds of lives you wouldn't mind having when you grew up. If you were a girl, well, I have no idea what you saw in them. I suppose they looked totally hot.

I'm bringing up Duran Duran here not because they're an indie band, or even because they provided a building block for the music I would later adopt. They were a mainstream band in every regard: propped-up, privileged, immediately popular, and never misunderstood, not to mention the product of a major label. But Duran Duran represented a turning point in the way I listened to music. Until they came along, my fixations were limited to individual songs, like Rick Springfield's "Jesse's Girl," Aldo Nova's "Fantasy," or the Police's "Don't Stand So Close to Me." The considerable love I'd feel for, say, Saga's "On the Loose" wouldn't automatically carry over to that band's (pretentious) next single, "Catwalk." A horribly written entry from a journal required by my seventh-grade English teacher indicates where I was during this period of musical infancy (and it also shows how feeble my twelve-year-old brain was):

ROCK GROUPS

My favorite rock group is Journey. Another good group is Def Leppard. They have been my favorite for the past few months. There are groups like Loverboy, Men at Work, ZZ Top, Men Without Hats, Asia, the Police and Planet P Project who are also good groups. My favorite video on MTV is "Sharp Dressed Man" by ZZ Top. My favorite song on the radio is "Foolin' " by Def Leppard. I think this is because it has rock and a good tune in it. My second favorite song on the radio is Quiet Riot's "Cum on Feel the Noize." I like this song because it is total rock and because of the guitar. I also like the lyrics of this song.

---

[26] Under no circumstances would I refer to them as "the Fab Five."

If that was difficult to read, I apologize. ("It has rock"? Planet P Project?) Anyway, the embarrassing entry shows that most of what aired on MTV in the early 1980s—an era when the network might play Lionel Richie, Devo, and Ozzy Osbourne in succession—seemed to be an entirely original and plausible source of entertainment to me, and yes, that included Kenny Loggins. My ears were just too stupid to latch on to one sound at the expense of everything else.

But I found myself getting swept up by the mania that surrounded Duran Duran circa 1984, despite the fact that I disliked the band's fondness for wearing caked-on makeup and what appeared to be pirate garb. This should not have happened to a heterosexual teenage boy, of course. It was obvious at that late date that the band, seemingly on the cover of every issue of *Tiger Beat,* was the domain of pubescent girls, and existed on the same testosterone-deprived plane of Hades as Wham! and Culture Club. What's more, I was entirely afraid of drawing negative attention to myself. Around this time, being cool was considered to be very important in the circles I traveled in, a problem, I suppose, shared by most eighth graders not looking to purposely alienate their peers. One uncool move, such as professing an affinity for *Hart to Hart* or donning the wrong brand of jeans (woe to the wearer of Wranglers!), could tarnish your reputation for life, or at least until you switched schools.[27] By the time *Seven and the Ragged Tiger* had entered the top five on the album chart, I'd heard enough chatter around my small junior high school to determine that liking Duran Duran as a teenage boy was decidedly uncool. So whatever moved me to scrawl "The

---

[27] Of course, nearly everything that was considered cool by the powers-that-were is the ultimate in uncool in retrospect, and vice versa. For instance, I earned social kudos for emulating the moonwalk weeks after seeing Michael Jackson perform it on the Motown Music Awards in 1983, whereas that brooding, slightly older kid on my bus who was into Black Sabbath was considered to be a freak—although for all I know he probably was.

Reflex" in large caps on my physical sciences notebook eludes me. I just know that I quickly found out why it wasn't a good idea.

Maybe I shouldn't have felt so insecure about my musical leanings back then. It's not like I was grooving to the slow jams of Spandau Ballet, which might have caused me to be pantsed on the playground. Rather, by the end of 1984, I had sizable cravings for edgy MTV artists like Billy Idol, Peter Gabriel, Adam Ant, Joan Jett, and the Go-Go's; was one of only two kids in my class exploring, via a late-night Sunday-night program on a local college radio station that you could never count on to come in because its signal was so weak, the realm of rap music outside of Blondie's "Rapture" and Chaka Khan's "I Feel For You";[28] and could talk the talk about the bands (e.g., the J. Geils Band, Van

---

[28] My first exposure to true rap ("King Tut" and "Rapture" don't count) came in early 1984 when MTV played, maybe twice, the video for Kurtis Blow's "Basketball." Because I was obsessed with the Michigan State Spartans and the Los Angeles Lakers at the time (and, sadly, probably *only* because of that), the song percolated my dumb-guy's interest. My friend Brian (an actually good basketball player) and I (a chucker) would joke about it, and this is how rap became an acceptable diversion in my little corner of Whiteyville. Rap felt like a personal possession, one of my toys maybe, even as it trickled into mainstream culture over the next few years via the unspeakably bad movies *Breakin'* and *Beat Street;* the number-three-charting Chaka Khan single (featuring Grandmaster Melle Mel); the spazzy *Miami Vice* character Noogie; the *Saturday Night Live* sketch in which Jim Belushi and guest star Alex Karras performed the "White Guy Rap" ("We're white guys, and we take no crap . . ."); a novelty song called "Rappin' Duke," in which impersonator Shawn Brown turned John Wayne into the illest mofo ever; and the big one: the Chicago Bears in "The Super Bowl Shuffle," which requires no explanation. While "Jam on It" by Newcleus (i.e., the one with the gibberish phrase "wikki wikki wikki wikki" in it), "White Lines" by Grandmaster Flash (which, coincidentally, Duran Duran would later cover on their unfortunate tribute album *Thank You*), and early stuff by Run-D.M.C., Whodini, and LL Cool J wowed me, I see now that rappers excited me most when they were intentionally silly: the Fat Boys, UTFO, the Beastie Boys, DJ Jazzy Jeff and the Fresh Prince, Young MC, Tone-Lōc. When Run-D.M.C.'s "Walk This Way" came out and rap irrevocably became mainstream, I gamely stuck with it a few more years; but it

Halen, Quiet Riot) that a pubescent boy was supposed to love. I mean, on a scale on which ten is perfectly cool and one is perfectly uncool, I would have placed somewhere between three and four. Not bad; I had friends who surely ranked lower. (And besides, the closest anyone in my insular school got to ten was maybe 5.8.) So I could have been subjected to a lot worse than a withering public putdown—"Hey, Sellers! 'The Reflex' sucks!"—by a popular, shaggy-haired classmate.

My yearlong Duran Duran phase pains me like few others I've gone through—exceptions being, obviously, the bed-wetting winter of '76 and the Morrissey-borne meat-free summer of 1990. How embarrassing that a band as breezy and candy-coated as Duran Duran was once so important to me! So embarrassing that I haven't, in fact, told anyone about this, even girlfriends, since maybe 1987, when I'd taken enough abuse on various fronts to learn that you need to keep your questionable musical infatuations a Ziplocked secret because, as Holden Caulfield said, "people are always ruining things for you." I won't go so far as to say that I was obsessed with them; that designation is reserved for bands that truly changed my life, and

---

became tougher than, well, leather for a guy of my hospital-corners upbringing to hold on to the genre as it turned increasingly explicit and gangsta. But it impresses me that I flirted with something as foreign to my world as rap, and not just because it led to my shining moment as a music shopper: A sibling, who didn't know that I'd already deemed Def Leppard's *Hysteria* the most disappointing album of all time (and it still might be: next to *Pyromania,* it is an overproduced, castrated, one-armed bore), had given the album to me for my birthday, and I'd sped off to the record store to return it. But this particular store only offered credit, which sucked because it was in the lamest of all Grand Rapids malls. To avoid another visit, I had no choice but to find a replacement then and there, even though nothing came to mind. Mildly panicking, I came across a display for a cassette whose cover depicted an unlikely scenario: a bunch of black dudes standing around a turntable looking about as badass as a bunch of guys standing around a turntable can possibly look. I had to have it. Little did I know that *Yo! Bum Rush the Show* was yet another Def Jam gem. Public Enemy remains the only group I've ever been ahead of the curve on.

Duran Duran lacked the grace and the talent to do that. (Even then I knew it wasn't going to last. The head-slappingly dumb "You're about as easy as a nuclear war" lyric at the center of their 1983 tootle "Is There Something I Should Know?" made me cringe.) So let's just say that Duran Duran was my first musical crush, which I think works because crushes are fleeting, hard to explain, and generally bad for you, and that pretty much sums up my relationship with the band.

When "A View to a Kill" came out in the spring of 1985, I was ready to leave Duran Duran behind. But I learned for the first time that it's not easy to ditch a band that once meant a lot to you. You cling to it well after you know it isn't useful to you anymore, and you soon find yourself buying Arcadia singles and Andy Taylor solo albums and handing over cash to see the overproduced, underwhelming *Notorious* tour. As if any of that could bring back that life-affirming rush you got when you were enamored of them. Even when I am confronted with a Duran Duran song now, a shocking twenty-plus years after I tried to sweep them under the rug where so many other inconsequential bands lurk, I don't have the backbone to dole out the tough love they deserve. I listen in, remember how many years have passed, and chastise the kid who spent all that time on Duran Duran instead of on a band with more proficiency. But there's utility in regret. In order never to repeat such an experience, I always need to remember that fourteen-year-old who did a David Lee Rothian scissors kick during the "fle-fle-fle-fle-flex" part of "The Reflex" in front of someone who wasn't a family member. I just don't ever need to hear that song again.

4

BAD

"If I could, you know I would let it go."

In the realm of comic books, the origin story is oblig-
atory and essential: The reader absolutely must know how the
hero came to be so heroic, why the villain is so villainous, and
whence all the kooky special powers. In real life, some things are
better left unexplained. For instance, if you are to respect me, I
shouldn't tell you that the climax of my indie-rock origin story
takes place in the back of a van with the fifteen-year-old protagonist wearing red-and-white Bermuda shorts, Docksiders, and a
light blue T-shirt that depicts a dozen sharks circling a scuba
diver whose thought bubble reads, OH, SHIT . . .

Like all stories from the mid-1980s, this one begins at a
shopping mall. They say that there's only one first person you can
sleep with, unless you're Caligula or Tommy Lee. Likewise,
there's only one first record you can buy. I'd love to announce
that my first purchase, at the fluorescently lit MusicLand near the
food court at Woodland Mall, was something remotely befitting
the subject matter of this book—maybe *Shake It Up* or *Combat
Rock* or *At Budokan*. This is not the case, even though in 1984
I liked songs and videos by the Cars (especially "Just What
I Needed"), the Clash ("This Is Radio Clash"), and Cheap Trick
("She's Tight"). "Wait," you ask, "it surely must have been
something by Duran Duran, whom you just finished telling us
was your first musical crush—right? Maybe their new-wave classic *Rio,* or even that live album *Arena,* which gave the world 'The

Wild Boys,' a song that now inflicts pain when you hear it on an '80s flashback hour?" No. The first album I ever bought was *VOA* by Sammy Hagar. At the time, I thought that the cover image depicting Mr. Hagar parachuting onto the Capitol lawn while wearing a red leather jumpsuit and clutching a sweet-looking guitar seemed entirely plausible. The album's hit, "I Can't Drive 55," was in heavy rotation on my favorite radio station, and its video prominently featured a Lamborghini. I wanted one of those. I also like how the storyline of the video playfully reenacts the lyrics: Sammy really does have "one foot on the brake and one on the gas," a judge really does threaten to "throw [his] ass in the city joint," and when asked if he gets the point, Sammy really does reply, "Yeah! (Oh, yeah!)" What's ridiculous to me about this purchase now is that I don't remember ever listening to the album. Well, I'm sure it did get thrown onto my mom's record player at some point (yes, a vinyl purchase, but only because our outdated hi-fi system didn't have a tape deck, and we hadn't yet splurged on the portable double-cassette dubbing unit that would propel me along the musical learning curve) because a song called "Dick in the Dirt" is passed out in the gutter of my memory. But mostly I feel the same way about *VOA* that I do about the first girl I ever slept with: huh?

I knew I'd gotten burned when T.Z., one of the more popular kids in my tiny junior high class, enthusiastically asked to borrow the album and then returned it the next day without a sound, not even a snicker about something as ludicrous as "Dick in the Dirt." I swore never to buy another album again, ever, even if it came with a guarantee that my mediocre social status would drastically improve because of it. It was easy to do. In ninth grade, too many leisure-time activities were competing for my hard-earned nut—that is, the five-dollar-per-week allowance I received for doing absolutely nothing. I had unhealthy addictions to video games (particularly Robotron: 2084), comic books (especially anything featuring Peter Parker, who was exactly like me, only with a girlfriend and superpowers), baseball cards (favorite player: Lou Whitaker), and Big League Chew (preferably grape). All of those pursuits cost money. Music could be gotten free via MTV and the radio. I was always pretty good at math.

In many ways, this perpetual lack of disposable income is the reason I never became a collector of music. If you're not wealthy, being a serious collector of anything, even if you have a regular income, is a prohibitive pursuit. Every iota of available cash has to go toward building your collection or it's money spent poorly. Sure, you could finally have those squealing brakes on your Cavalier fixed, but that would mean you couldn't get that Pete Rose rookie card that you've been eyeing at Argo's for only $100. The car hasn't killed anyone yet, has it? Even beyond the money, though, collecting has never seemed viable. To get the deals that are essential to amassing an enviable collection—the only conceivable kind to have—you have to hunt high and low, pillaging gems from dead people's relatives at estate sales and from your drooling neighbor Timmy. It involves more diligence and double-talk than I could ever muster. Worse, you have to befriend and trade with other collectors, people who are every bit as diligent and double-talking as you are, and who tend to be the sort who have mites in their hair. Where music is concerned, I have always been content to be a fan. And not an overly anal one, at that. This means that I have little desire to own or trade bootlegs of concerts I didn't attend. This means that I don't need every one of my band's albums in the factory-sealed packaging; used or dubbed will do just fine. This means that I will try to hear every song the band has ever recorded, but I won't go to great lengths to do so; it has always been my theory, misguided though it may seem (and it has, indeed, stunted my growth), that if a song is truly worth hearing, I will hear it eventually. The biggest difference between a collector and a fan is that the former will tell you that one of the B-sides to, say, "Panic" is the live instrumental "The Draize Train," while the latter will tell you that "Panic" is a really fucking awesome song. In other words, a collector would kill for the rarest release by a band; a fan would kill for the band.

But in my dotage, I do envy my collector friends because they have some pretty awesome shit and know way more about music than I ever will. (But do they know more about my bands? No, and that's all that has ultimately mattered to me.) Unfortunately, when it could have helped me the most, in my early teens, I didn't know a beneficent collector type or any kind, older, tapped-in souls, like an Annie Potts in *Pretty in Pink* or a Mr. Miyagi of rock, who, recognizing my interest in the Power Station, would pull me aside and say, "Hey, kid, I overheard you saying that you like 'Get It On.' That's cool, although I don't like glory-hog Andy Taylor's axe work on it. But did you know it's a remake of a T. Rex song?" and then hand me a copy of *Electric Warrior*. I probably should have told you this in the last chapter, but from sixth to ninth grades, I existed in the vacuum of a small Christian Reformed school, where the kids in my class of roughly thirty students were depressingly similar, except for that poor bastard who said he wasn't allowed to see the *Star Wars* movies because "they deal with forces." (Oh, and except for me: As a disenchanted Lutheran, I was the only student in my class who neither knew nor cared what "Christian Reformed" meant; though severely limited by a teacher's salary, my mom sent my older brother and me there, rather than to a public junior high school, to get what she viewed as a better education, although this turned out to be debatable.) At a school of that size and nature you almost have to conform. Individuality was tolerated if it pleased the group or your teachers: the guy known to be overly concerned about his hair, the girl with the endless supply of jelly beans, the boy who could moonwalk (for the last time, that was me). But any antisocial or disturbingly eccentric behavior would have got you singled out as a mutant by the kids you had to see in class every day, year after year, and, considering how pious the school administrators were trying to appear, it might have even got you expelled. Why make your time there even worse than it already was? (And this included interminable Bible classes and daily, kidding-but-not-really tauntings about personal grooming.) There were no rebels at the Christian Reformed school.

But there was my friend Dave. He was probably my best friend during those cozy, suffocating junior high years, although this suspicion was never confirmed by either of us because it would have seemed too, I don't know, gay. Dave had an older sister. As a kid I would have considered such a concept detestable, even gross, but now I think my life would have turned out better if I'd had one of those. Girls invariably discover the things worth knowing long before boys, who are way too into Asteroids and baseball statistics and their penises to get interesting until well into their teens, and maybe even their forties. Long before guys have gotten over their infatuation with the secretions of amphibians, girls have set up vast social networks that exist solely to pass around information about what's in and what's out.[29] Sure, their musical tastes often depend on whether the phrase "He's so cute!" applies or not. But I like to imagine that any sister of mine would have eliminated that part of the process and fallen on the cool end of the girl spectrum, where she'd have been prone to liking, say, Gary Numan instead of Corey Hart. As her lucky brother, I would have gladly endured the bras and nylons draped all over the bathroom to have access to the scraps of feminine wisdom she disgorged down the familial food chain. At least I think I would have. I have no real idea, though, because I was stuck with a big brother who liked Bob Seger and Madonna.[30]

If it's true that a culturally prescient older sister would have granted me a backstage pass to the world beyond mainstream bands at a younger age, then it seems fair to say that I would have encountered the music that matters to me now much earlier. I can only guess at how being introduced to something as seminal as

[29] Possibly using those folded-paper "mash squares" that both confused and frightened me.

[30] An aside here: Mark, I'm not suggesting replacing you. We'd merely add a big sister to the clan. So you'd still be there, and you'd still get the good bedroom, and yes, you'd still be able to pin me down, grab one of my wrists, and smack my own limp hand into my cheek over and over again while taunting, "Why are you hitting yourself? Why are you hitting yourself?" Relax.

the Velvet Underground or Big Star or the Buzzcocks at ten or twelve or fifteen would have paid off. Ticket to Harvard? Omniscience? Then again, as previously hinted at, the Grand Rapids of my youth was something of a cultural wasteland, so such bands would have been difficult for even a savvy female to sniff out. But not impossible. I recall a well-liked and surprisingly clean-cut punk at the large public high school that I began attending in tenth grade who'd stenciled CIRCLE JERKS and I'M A HEBREW (he wasn't Jewish) on his military-style jacket. I see a birdlike honors student with a new-wave hairdo who certainly must have been into the Cure and the Smiths. I remember my friend Tom's summertime transformation from a relatively normal teenager who liked the arcade game Bubbles into a guy with a Mohawk and a fondness for Black Flag. These people obviously picked this stuff up somewhere (older, college-attending siblings? a magazine? *Repo Man*?), but I could never bring myself to ask where. Being entirely invisible to potential tormentors was important to me, so I never cared to figure out where the most conspicuous students in school got their inspiration. I did envy them, though, even then: It was obvious that they were way more adventurous than I would ever be. Purposely sticking out, especially in a way perceived as negative by the powers that be, is punk rock; blending in to escape comments of "Move it, turd" is just sad. I listened to stuff like Sammy Hagar in part because I was too wimpy not to.

And here is where the origin story approaches its apex. In late 1985, in the middle of tenth grade, now attending a different high school but not quite at that imperceptible point of having fallen away from my life, Dave asked me if I'd like to accompany him on a family trip to Disney World over Christmas break. We were too old to show outward enthusiasm for such an obvious child's destination, of course, but I was pleased to be going places with Dave's family since mine rarely took me anywhere, a byproduct of my parents' marginally acrimonious and incredibly overdue divorce. We were driven to Orlando in a Chevy van, and

Dave and I sealed off the spacious, plush back-lounge area from "Chumper," Dave's seven-year-old brother, who was psychologically attached to a Cabbage Patch Kid that I would ungraciously heave across our motel room at a stopover in Chattanooga. It was in our secure mobile bunker that we played ironic Dungeons & Dragons, which we had put behind us a year back for different reasons: for me because the Detroit Tigers had taken over, and for Dave because he got into girls. But on that trip, Dave and I reverted to what we were like at thirteen, before life had been complicated by genetic and familial betrayal. Somewhere along the line we had procured a copy of the semierotic potboiler *The Ninja* by Eric Van Lustbader (this being the height of the ninja craze of the mid-'80s), and we took turns reading it in the rare moments twelve- and twenty-sided dice weren't being rolled. Whenever it was my turn to read, Dave put on headphones and listened to his fancy (read: primitive, freakishly large) portable tape player.

I should tell you that a few months before this trip, Dave had spent part of one of our increasingly infrequent phone calls singing Tears for Fears' "Shout" to me. This was odd for so many reasons, but the main one was that Dave had been regarded as happening at the Christian Reformed school, a member of that now-extinct race of young men who carried a comb in their back pocket to feather back their hair. It was an excruciating and bizarre couple of minutes that I'll never get back, during which I thought the following: *Is Dave actually singing to me over the phone? Really weird. Even weirder, he's singing that song by the band that Bry referred to as Tears for Queers the other day. Dave would get made fun of if I told anyone about this. Or would he? Is there something going on that I don't know about—again? Wait, maybe Tears for Fears is so damn awesome that I can't even comprehend what is happening here! Oh my god, Tears for Fears rules!* He'd also previously nudged me toward early INXS by loaning me his sister's copy of *Shabooh Shoobah* after hearing that I kind of liked the way the guitarist played the main riff in the video for "The One Thing." So he had a very short track record of turning me on to (then-) listenable indie-ish bands.[31]

Between hits from *The Ninja* I asked Dave what he was listening to—a question that I was always nervous to ask because it was sure to expose one of the many gaps in my knowledge, and it made me anxious when people found out that I didn't know everything. He said a tape he'd taken from his sister: U2's *War*. I knew what everyone knew about U2, of course. That image of Bono breathing out cold air, waving the Irish flag, and yelling, "No more!" at the rousing Red Rocks performance of "Sunday Bloody Sunday." That their song "Gloria" contained indecipherable Latin and was overtly religious but rocked nonetheless. That their scene-stealing set at Live Aid, the all-day, rally-around-the-hungry-Ethiopians benefit concert that would become the point at which MTV jumped the shark (or was it the day the network hired Pauly Shore?), blew away the recombinant forms of Led Zeppelin and the Who. But inbred laziness—my mantra, bequeathed to me as a native son of Grand Rapids, is "Let it come to you"—had prevented me from delving deeper. When Dave offered me the headphones, it was almost like that scene in the movie *Garden State* when Natalie Portman's character, a motor-mouth fan of the Shins, puts hers over Zach Braff's ears and says, "Listen to this: It will change your life." Only this wasn't the

---

[31] Tears for Fears most definitely does not rule, but *Songs from the Big Chair*—a title the juvenile in me has decided is an inside reference to lead singer Roland Orzabal's flatulence—was a favorite for much of 1986. That Orzabal dissed George Michael and Wham!, to whom Tears for Fears was bizarrely compared, endeared me to them all the more, and my minor infatuation lasted until their next album, 1989's *The Seeds of Love,* took the band's sound in the direction of a high school jazz combo doing *Sgt. Pepper's*. INXS, on the other hand, had those jangly riffs and charisma to spare (especially that Buddy Holly clone who played both guitar and sax), and I more than tolerated their existence for two full years until "Devil Inside," my least favorite track on *Kick,* became a hit and, shortly thereafter, Michael Hutchence exposed himself as a model-dating wanker.

most painful moment in the history of independent cinema. I knew that whatever I heard would be compromised by the fact that U2 had been pre-endorsed by Dave—which meant, of course, that I wasn't going to get made fun of if I admitted to liking them (unless I'd walked right into a particularly evil trap: "Sellers loves U2! I was only pretending to like such a hideous baby band! Ha-ha!"). But it didn't matter. I would have been into the music either way. The militaristic drumbeat and descending Edge riff that kick off "Sunday Bloody Sunday" trumped the live version on MTV, and the rest of the album got better from there.[32] I didn't know it then, of course, but this was the point of infection.

Okay, so it's not much of an origin story. It's not like I fell into a vat of acid in a German laboratory and emerged with the ability to decipher music reviews,[33] especially that particu-

[32] Exception: "Drowning Man," which gets my vote for the most annoyingly earnest song U2 has ever recorded—and that's saying something.

[33] I tried my hand at music criticism in college, but was terrible at it. Here's proof, in the form of the second (and last) record review I ever wrote, as a twenty-year-old junior at the University of Michigan (with annotations from March 2006):

I was going through that phase so many of us did where pretty much all I was listening to or talking about was Morrissey and the Smiths. Over the summer, while at home from college, I'd even tried vegetarianism, swearing off my mom's lasagna and meatloaf for cheese pizza and Prego-drowned pasta. But it's hard for a person raised on Manwich to abstain from eating meat for very long. After about six weeks, the stance fell, hard, during a household taco night, and I have never looked back.

The Michigan Daily
Tuesday, November 27, 1990
Manchester has spawned yet another monster, leading me to believe that Morrissey has gone and put an interesting drug in this northern English city's water. This time the Charlatans (UK) are the result. Following the mold of other northern English bands on their debut album, Some Friendly, the Charlatans have produced a sound that emphasizes guitar and

I understand the copyright laws that occasionally force bands to add that unwieldy "(UK)" appendage—Wham!, the Chameleons, etc.—but in this case, why not just come up with a different name? This was, after all, the band's first record. And, by the way, why don't bands from other countries ever have this problem? For instance, why is there no Soup Dragons (US)? Or the Farm (Ethiopia)? Come to think of it, maybe I don't understand the copyright laws.

larly virulent strain of rock criticism that attempts to compare the sound of a reviewed artist to as many obscure bands the reviewer can spit out before getting busted by the asshole

---

rhythm. But to differentiate themselves and promote their "flowered-up" image, they have included a very '60s-ish sounding organ which is used more in a "backbone" capacity. This lineup amounts to a refreshing mixture of old and new.

I was so infatuated with Manchester at this time that I should have hijacked this review space to discuss how a kid from Michigan could become enchanted with a faraway city based solely on the music that came out of it. I had even made my first trek to Manchester that August, so there would have been lots to talk about.

It's a Hammond—duh.

Wow.

The album showcases and seems to build on the outstanding single, "The Only One I Know." Almost all of the other songs seem to have elements of this single in them. "Then," the follow-up single, is not as good, but has its moments. Perhaps the best moments of the album come with the song "Polar Bear" when it sounds like someone is blowing in a conch shell. It creates a different sound that makes this track the best cut. Other songs, such as "You're Not Very Well" and "Sproston Green," are also exceptional, even though "Sproston Green" sounds a bit too much like the Stone Roses' smash "She Bangs the Drums."

Note: These are the only two entirely true sentences in this review.

I just listened to this song again, maybe for the first time since this review was written, and I didn't get this right. The faux conch is embarrassing, and "Polar Bear" sounds like it might have been written for or by the Information Society. It is in no way the best "cut" on the album.

Among them: a propulsive bass line and a groovy organ solo. But the virtually hook-free song was an unattractive choice for a single, and I should have called them on it.

No, it doesn't, but I wanted to throw in a Stone Roses reference because everybody loved them. Not too long ago, while going through some old college papers from this era, I found a note in the margin of a macroeconomics notebook that reads "'Fool's Gold' is the best song ever!"

After recently seeing an interview with this group on MTV, I concluded that the Charlatans are also distinguished from their competitors in another manner; they aren't arrogant (yet). They didn't move to cut down other groups and actually seemed embarrassed talking about themselves. But even though I have respect for them for this reason, that doesn't mean that they aren't another flash-in-the-pan group. If they play well live and if they can successfully follow up Some Friendly remains to be seen.

I saw them a few months later at Detroit's beloved St. Andrew's Hall, and was so drunk and excited that I consented, for the first time ever, to crowd-surf.

I should have invoked *120 Minutes* and Dave Kendall here.

The Charlatans (UK) are one of the few Manchester bands from this period still making music today. I wish I had predicted it.

police.[34] I wish for all of our sakes that Dave had been listening to the Smiths' *Meat Is Murder* or Sonic Youth's *Bad Moon Rising* or Hüsker Dü's *New Day Rising*. But everyone needs to start somewhere, even if it's at the relatively late age of fifteen. And the U2 that existed at the end of 1985—when they were still not fully into the mainstream, at least not close to where they were a year-plus later, after the release of *The Joshua Tree,* when even my mom knew who they were—was like marijuana to a crack addict: They were my alternative-rock gateway drug. For someone who was still hooked on Duran Duran, and who held Journey, Huey Lewis, and Whodini in high esteem, it's not a bad start.

And to continue the drug metaphor, I got stoned to the bejeezus on U2. A little while after returning from the trip, an ad for the RCA Music Service in an issue of *Rolling Stone* caught my eye, and I decided to break my Hagar-provoked vow of LP celibacy.[35] The offer was almost too good for a cheapskate with a meager allowance to refuse: six cassettes for a penny, with only three more tapes to buy over the next three years, at which point you would be given three more albums for free.[36] Five of the se-

[34] One of the worst I've ever seen—which I found reprinted in *Perfect Sound Forever,* a nicely assembled Pavement biography by Rob Jovanovic—originally appeared in the December 1989 issue of *Spin*. It goes: "Pavement's brand of string-churn is a lot like a hambone half-chewed by Ohio's Sister Ray, then rump-blasted into the gaping mouth of some revotard-pop cousin of Live Skull's girlfriend." I have no idea what this means, and they're just dicks for ever having published it.

[35] Actually, I'd already backslid once to buy the *Purple Rain* soundtrack—but only because, after a compelling lecture at Christian Reformed school about subliminal messages in the media, I wanted to hear what Prince was saying when you played "Darling Nikki" backwards. ("Hello. How are you? I'm fine 'cause I know that the Lord is coming soon, coming, coming soon." Gay.) And okay, because I loved, absolutely loved, "Let's Go Crazy."

[36] It seemed so cost efficient, until you were thwacked by an obnoxious $1.49 shipping-and-handling charge for each selection. Not to mention the considerable monthly hassle, to a sluggish high school sophomore, of having to mail back a cancel notice within ten days lest you get stuck with one of RCA's automatic selections, which was always something awful like Howard Jones or the Thompson Twins.

lections went to *Boy, October, War, Under a Blood Red Sky,* and *The Unforgettable Fire* (the last went to Van Halen's *1984*), and I would play these tapes so loudly on the Aiwa boom box we'd begged our mom to get us for Christmas that I'd miss shouts for dinner.

The word "obsession" is defined in *Webster's Ninth New Collegiate Dictionary* as "a persistent disturbing preoccupation with an often unreasonable idea or feeling." That winter my only obsession had been television. I knew every show that aired at every hour on every network, and had set about trying to rank them. A notebook contained a list of each prime-time television show I watched during a particular week. I would write a brief description of each episode, give it a placeholder rating based on its worthiness relative to similar fare, and then at the end of the week I'd rank the shows using various incredibly biased, though entirely consistent, criteria. The reason: I wanted to be able to say, using a kind of science, that my favorite show on television that season was X—and X, it would turn out, equaled *Miami Vice,* just ahead of *Moonlighting, Family Ties,* and *Magnum, P.I.* Does "unreasonable idea or feeling" apply to that? It was just a matter of time before I got persistently and disturbingly preoccupied by a band. And as much as it hurts me to resort to psychobabble, I was probably looking for something to keep me busy and to lift me up. My mom had a new boyfriend, the kind of guy who leaves beard trimmings in the sink and refuses to acknowledge that a woman with three children has three children. My dad's house was almost off-limits because of its clothes-adhering stench of cigarette smoke and wine, his brassy new wife (an industrial vacuum saleswoman), not to mention the persistent Dylan. And my brother Mark was now seventeen, had a car, and was as uninterested in hanging out with me as I was in playing Uno with eight-year-old Matt. At my new high school, few people talked to me, for the worst reasons. All the first month I'd had an acquaintance-stymieing pimple on my nose—no, not a pimple, an evil, overlord zit, one so scary that it cast a shadow: The big zit had little pimples on it, and those minion pimples were afraid, very afraid. Also, I was known by upperclassmen, derogatorily, as "that Sellers kid" because my mom taught English there, and until it could be proven otherwise, I was in league with her and her kind. So U2 (and TV, lots and lots of Friday- and Saturday-night TV) helped fill a void.

While I listened to plenty else in 1986—and in fact bonded over Van Halen and Ratt and Mötley Crüe with the geek-metalhead crowd[37] I was fortunate to have fallen in with—that calendar year was pretty much about U2. At least in secret. I fought hard to keep the growing obsession from my new pals, who seemed to be opposed to the earnest and the girly, both of which could be applied to U2. Outwardly I felt obliged to claim to be every bit as into Bon Jovi and babes as they were. But it wasn't really true, except the babes part. As conversations went on around me involving the gas mileage of cars or the hotness of

---

[37] We were one or two rungs up the social ladder from the true nerds. Oversimplified to the max, the hierarchy of our class might have been: good-looking, smirky jocks (football and basketball first, then soccer) → good-looking, cackling cheerleaders → ugly, thick-necked jocks (mostly wrestlers) → ugly cheerleaders → class clowns (especially the guy who, one Friday night, walked into the packed McDonald's, cruised slowly past the row of cashiers, turned like a supermodel, and strolled out, all without saying a word or smiling, and all while wearing a conehead) → that one egghead bastard who was heading for Duke but whom the jocks liked and who dated a hot cheerleader → those two sweet, smart girls bound for Michigan who got voted onto homecoming court based on their personalities → slick wannabe Kissingers with bow ties and floppy hair → nondescript athletes (second-stringers, benchwarmers, lesser wrestlers, track-and-field participants, and baseball players) → good-looking, smirky jocks who were the last to be cut from sports teams → mean girls who drank a lot → the valedictorian-to-be → sullen, pretty girls → skateboarders → new wavers, including those two probably gay guys → geek metalheads (so named because we were bound, mostly, for decent colleges, didn't do hard drugs, discussed pop culture too much, and loved metal as much as the actual metalheads, who were scary) → sullen, homely girls → true nerds → metalheads → goths → druggies → the cripple → the guy who wet his pants in sixth grade and never recovered socially → the guy who hung out with the kid who ambushed us with a ninja sword → the kid with the ninja sword.

freshmen, I would be thinking about the blast of guitar that follows Bono's statement "And this is the Edge!" on the live version of "Gloria," or about the frenetic outro of "Like a Song . . . ," or about the ease with which the Edge transitions, on *Boy,* from the stark, Germanic "An Cat Dubh" to the pretty, introspective "Into the Heart."

It was U2's music that was revelatory, not anything Bono was saying. His political hectoring may have played well in the United Kingdom and in the U.S. media, but it meant little to a shy, myopic fifteen-year-old dork from west Michigan whose biggest axe to grind was with the school board's decision to replace sides of macaroni and cheese in cafeteria entrees with fruit cups. And I reacted to the overt religious messages found on *October* the same way a wiry guy in my new clique had when informed about Stryper: "Jeez—just shut up and rock!" Mostly I ignored Bono's lyrics and focused on how everything sounded. It wasn't hard, given my penchant for hard rock, in which the lyrics were, by and large, so ineloquent that you were forced to focus on the music—and by way of example I'll cite Whitesnake's David Coverdale, who slobbered, "I'm going to slide it in right to the top/I'm going to slide it in, I ain't never gonna stop." What mattered was that Bono's voice fit the band's sound so well. His strained, pleading yelp mixed with the searing, esoteric guitar sounds made by the Edge to form a chilly, cavernous quality that no one could replicate, at least not until Coldplay came along.

An inordinate amount of time that year was spent alone listening to U2. And that's all I'd do—listen to the music. I don't mean putting it on in the background while doing my homework or cleaning my room, either. It was my boom box, my bed, and me. Sometimes I'd surround myself with balled-up tube socks and I'd shoot at a wastebasket that was just far enough away to make sock shots difficult. It became a prod. How many baskets could I make during side two of *The Unforgettable Fire*? Could I be perfect for the entire six minutes and eight seconds of "Bad"? Or I'd stare at the images of the band on the album covers, and critique. Judgment could be harsh. I liked the way Bono looked on the cover of *October*—fresh-faced, defiant, and tousled. But I hated him for wearing that stupid beret on *The Unforgettable Fire*. Larry Mullen Jr.'s wedge-shaped hair on that album cover: cool; Adam Clayton's bird 'do on *October*: goofy and ill-advised. Dave Evans's nickname: a big question mark. But I could kid because I loved—I had been hit by the "passionate flame that knows me by name," as Bono sang in "Surrender." It was clear that no band had ever meant this much to me before. INXS? I could not have cared less about who those guys were—they represented Australia, and that was enough. Duran Duran? I once paged through a biography that contained fragments of Simon Le Bon's pre–Duran Duran poetry—as my friend Deborah might say: I was embarrassed for Simon, and I was embarrassed for me. Tears for Fears? I still don't know for sure the name of the main guy who wasn't Roland Orzabal. (I *think* it's Curt Smith.) Journey? Huey Lewis? The Police? Van Halen? I just played their music and didn't worry about much else.[38]

Initially, I didn't care to know much more about Bono, the Edge, Larry Mullen Jr., or Adam Clayton than what each brought to the table musically. I'd zero in on certain vocal flourishes or Edge riffs or visual evidence, and I'd use these things to extrapolate who these guys were as people. They were angry and alienated; that kid on the front of *War* was the perfect model for what they were trying to get across. Videos suggested that the Edge was balding and a second banana. Was this hard for him?

[38] Well, Van Halen's persona was compelling because of David Lee Roth's smug gamesmanship (e.g., "Look, I'll pay you for it. What the fuck.") and Eddie Van Halen's marriage to TV darling Valerie Bertinelli. But the band lost its appeal on March 2, 1986, the day that *5150*, with my old pal Sammy Hagar on vocals, was released to the annoyance of everyone I knew. The first thing the listener heard upon popping in the tape was Hagar squealing, "Hello, baby!" This was not for me, and the rest of the album, bloated with keyboards and Hagar platitudes, followed suit. To borrow a Phil Hartman line, David Lee Roth had chunks of guys like Sammy Hagar in his stool.

Bono's spurts of enthusiasm (e.g., "With a shout! Shout it out!"—which was tolerable until a stain-remover slogan rendered it unintentionally comical) made me uncomfortable, as it meant that he was passionate; my high school had little tolerance for passion unless it involved grass stains, cheerleaders, and pain. First and foremost, though, U2 got the job done: These were guys who liked to rock out. Sure, they weren't the least bit playful in that endearing way that Cheap Trick or the Police or David Lee Roth or even Rush could be, and they may have even been overly serious, but their proficiency made that irrelevant. That was all I needed to know, for a while.

In fact, when more information about the band members trickled in, I began to pull away. Shortly after turning sixteen I scored a job as a bag boy at ShopRite, where I got reacquainted with a jowly, slovenly fellow who'd been a grade below me at my old school (and who always wore the same goddamn baggy green pants to work). Somehow he'd also developed a U2 obsession, only his was more advanced. It involved imports and singles. I dutifully dubbed copies of whatever he offered up, and we would unload arcane trivia on each other as we passed in the parking lot.[39] But it was a doomed friendship: Each of us thought his love for the band was greater, right or wrong,[40] and, almost overnight, the information exchange shut down. But not before he told me that U2 was working on a new album.

I didn't react well when the world discovered my band. Prior to the release of *The Joshua Tree,* no one at school was talking about them. You'd hear a lot about the rapid devaluation of the commodity known as Phil Collins,[41] about how insanely hot Su-

---

[39] For instance, he would call me J. Swallow, and I'd reply with, "Whatever happened to Pete the Chop?" Only U2 geeks know what the hell I'm talking about right now.

[40] I was right.

[41] For much of my adult life, I've gone back and forth on the usefulness of Phil Collins. Yes, he's wreaked as much havoc as anyone in music history. (A very short list of his crimes: "Sussudio," "Illegal Alien," the movie *Buster,* "Another Day in Paradise," that god-awful Oscar-winning song for

sanna Hoffs was, and about the proper way to have fun tonight (answer: Wang Chung tonight!). But zippo about U2. Then, in March of 1987, "With or Without You" launched its blitzkrieg on the airwaves, and it was as if everyone was the world's biggest U2 expert. Even the Poison fans I ate lunch with were saying how they'd always sorta liked "Sunday Bloody Sunday"—"but," they'd add, "Bono's still a fag." They had discovered my secret hiding place!

A lot of the hype had to do with Bono. He was everywhere—being interviewed on MTV,[42] giving that come-hither look while wearing a leather wifebeater in the slick video, and gracing every magazine you can think of. (THIS MONTH IN *Boating:* CRUISIN' WITH BONO OF U2! Okay, he was never on the cover of *Boating.*) In those months after the album arrived, Bono proved to be too theatrical and fame-hungry for a person like me to get behind completely. Even though he was given a lot of slack for being in my favorite band, and I loved it when he just shut up and sang, I began to resent him the more he commandeered the spotlight, the more interviews he'd steer toward a discussion of injustice, the more scaffoldings he'd climb. There seemed to be this growing general belief that he was the main factor behind the band's whopping success: Bono's so hot! Bono's so cause-conscious! Bono's such a rock star! But U2 would have gone nowhere without the Edge. (That Larry Mullen Jr. and Adam Clayton do their jobs competently and stay the hell out of the way is all I've ever needed from them.[43]) Yet my nerves were even being grated by the man I regarded as God's own guitarist. As quickly as that

---

Tarzan.) But he's also responsible for the awesomeness that is "In the Air Tonight." I don't know. I kind of miss the little guy.

[42] Possibly by mane-haired veejay Adam Curry, who later became a podcasting pioneer.

[43] My friend Rob Kemp, in a review of *All That You Can't Leave Behind* for *The New York Observer,* quipped that Clayton is the second-luckiest man in rock history, behind Van Halen bassist Michael Anthony. True! Would the third be Ringo Starr? Krist Novoselic? Andy Rourke?

May, when "I Still Haven't Found What I'm Looking For" was all over MTV, I began to question the cowboy getup and the Willie Nelson ponytail. That wasn't what I signed up for.

Disenchantment with certain nonmusical aspects of the band aside, the new songs awed me. There wasn't a bad track on *The Joshua Tree*—a rare example of a "dinger," a nonsense term I coined to describe an album that lacks a song (or more commonly, songs) that you tire of in five plays or fewer.[44] My consumption of it was constant, and a lot of that was because my older brother had handed down his Datsun beater to me when he returned to college that winter. The car became a sanctuary from the tedium of Grand Rapids. If there was nothing better to do, I'd often tool around doing a Spockian mind-meld with the music, rewinding certain parts to get them straight in my head, fast-forwarding to the song that I'd been humming during pre-calc. I learned everything about the album in that car, knew it better than any of their previous releases, thought it was the most important thing in the world, didn't feel let down. In the Datsun, U2 was still my band.

As such, I felt completely justified—but in the years since, sick in the stomach—at having to shoot down an acquaintance named Jim when he asked if I wanted to drive to Detroit with him to see the U2 show at the Silverdome. Later, I'd room with this same guy at college for three years, partly because we were so compatible musically. At the time, though, the known facts were as follows: He had attended a recent gig by Blue Öyster Cult, which he referred to as B.Ö.C.; he loved everything by Yes *except* "Owner of a Lonely Heart"; he knew the difference, sonically, between Emerson, Lake & Palmer and Emerson, Lake & Powell; and he had once expressed a desire to live in a school bus. Jim did not deserve to share U2 with me. Now, of course, I hate myself because the Silverdome stop on the *Joshua Tree* tour

---

[44] In fact, only eight rock albums are true dingers. The list can be found in Appendix A.

would have been, by three months, that all-important First Live Show. Instead, my first concert was Duran Duran. Worse, it was Duran Duran with only one Taylor. And a horn section.

Ironically, the kill shot came when I finally did see U2 live, in 1992. That might sound counterintuitive, considering that their stage show has always been a major selling point. But I watched, horrified, as Bono ordered Domino's pizzas to the arena and spent much of the evening pretending to be that impish, spotlight-craving character he referred to as the Fly. (There was no appearance by MacPhisto, thank god.) The man's ego had become untethered from all humility, and it made continuing on in servitude to U2 impossible to picture. Their music still spoke to me—and still does to this day, albeit in softer tones;[45] once you get a taste for U2, you will always hunger for it. But what was missing at that show can never return: that other Bono, the one waving the flag without irony in the Denver fog—the one that made the band complete.

[45] Ever since *Rattle and Hum,* which felt like a marketing ploy at a time when they were already overexposed, I've coached myself to be cautious during the hype surrounding the launch of a U2 album. With *Achtung Baby,* caution quickly gave way to optimism: It was undeniably a product of genius (especially "One," arguably the best song they've ever written, although there are so many contenders for that title that it's irresponsible to tackle the issue in a parenthetical aside). But then you had the mediocrity of *Zooropa.* And the thud of *Pop.* In 2000, when they returned with a vengeance, I checked my excitement, and I'm glad that I did. Other than "Beautiful Day" and "All Because of You," nothing I've heard on these two twenty-first-century albums has lived up to the critical praise. But they will always kick the shit out of Coldplay.

5

TEMPTATION

"I've never met anyone quite like you before."

I regret that I will be unable to join your revelry on the dance floor. There will be no Sellers, arms akimbo, doing a mock white-man's overbite during the deejay's ironic trifecta of Terence Trent D'Arby's "Wishing Well," Shannon's "Let the Music Play," and Poison's "Unskinny Bop." It's not that I can't bust serious, multiple, mind-bending moves, one of which faithfully reenacts the triple-take zombie strut from the "Thriller" video. It's just that I'm following my own marching orders, the ones that I've been operating under since the Great Dance Fiasco of 1991.

One fateful morning that spring I awoke reeking not only of rum and cigarettes but also of piteous failure. A hazy memory reminded me that I'd spent part of the previous evening on a dance floor with two of my male friends willfully ignoring multiple clusters of nicely packaged girls in order to do all of the following: 1) high-five one another at the start of every song we liked; 2) boo loudly at every song we hated; and 3) slam-dance to a song that no one had ever slam-danced to before (and certainly hasn't since): goth banshee Peter Murphy's violin-driven "Cut You Up." At some point during that strident modern-rock nugget, bouncers swarmed and, citing our extreme stupidity, picked us up like kittens by the collars of our loose-fitting T-shirts; very soon I was sitting on the pavement outside the club spouting impotent, drunken threats of legal action. Clearly rules were needed to ensure that I would never dance again just for the heck of it, and in bed that morning I decided that there are only two instances in which a man can be excused to dance: 1) He is an employee of Chippendale's; 2) There is a 76 percent or greater chance that he might score as a direct result of doing so—where "score" means making nonincidental contact with a female nipple, even if it's only through the clothing. I haven't danced in male company since, except at that recent wedding reception where I attempted to get airborne during the chorus of "Jump" and gouged a friend's left shin with the heel of my dress shoe.

This change of heart is relevant because I used to go dancing all the time. In fact, during college a shockingly large amount of time was spent willingly listening to dance music. Duran Duran was one thing. At least they were a real band. I'm talking here about Depeche Mode. Erasure. Yaz. Orchestral Manoeuvres in the Dark. Bands that replaced guitars with keytars. Bands that hoped to make you dizzy with a tsunami of synth. Bands that overemployed that fake clap sound. Here's something I'm admitting for the first time: I owned a Dead or Alive album. It's peculiar that a person who loved Guns N' Roses' "It's So Easy" could find any merit in a transvestite singing "Watch out, here I come!" I was like a driver who spins the wheel to get out of the path of a Mack truck, overcorrects, and crashes into a brick wall.

I blame girls. In the previous chapter, I spoke of my desire to have been blessed with an older sister to guide me on a path toward musical enlightenment. At a certain age, I discovered that any girl with taste will do. Actually, that's not precise: Any girl with taste *and* on whom you have a debilitating, soul-shattering, unrequited crush will do. There's an easy explanation for why significant advancement can occur under the influence of girls who want little or nothing to do with you. When you have a crippling desire to be around a particular, incredibly cute person, but you suspect that she is superior to you in mind, body, soul, and the ability to dance without looking like an epileptic heron, you are susceptible to the things she values. You think, If I can make

myself enjoy the stuff she's into, then maybe she'll like me! This
almost never works, of course, and it may even embarrass you if
she likes things that suck. Yes, I briefly flirted with objectivism
because a crush was once seen carrying an Ayn Rand book. Yes,
I sang "Hello" at a karaoke bar because that one girl told me to,
even though I knew my voice would crack when I reached that
"tell me how to win your heart" line and people would avoid eye
contact with me as I returned to my seat.

I've been fortunate, a few times, to fixate on girls who aren't
entirely devoid of taste. The only thing all of them seemed to
have had in common is that they baffled my friends. Most of the
guys I chose to hang out with in my late teens were gentlemen
who feverishly debated whether the mousse-happy woman who
humped a Jaguar in that Whitesnake video was the ideal mate or
whether those snooty groupies in the Cinderella video were.[46]
While I'm not pretending to have been impervious to those
women's hooterific charms, I've generally gotten more excited
about flustery, brainy, Mary Tyler Moore types. Librarians-in-
waiting. The ones least likely to. (Or, rather, the ones most likely
to, but whom you'd suspect the least.) I had a crush on the

---

[46] The scale is obviously tilted in Tawny Kitaen's favor here due to the
simple fact that she costarred in *Bachelor Party*. What did those Cinderella
sluts ever do? Besides sleep with the guys from Cinderella, I mean? Which
brings me to a subject that has never, to my knowledge, been broached before, at least not in mixed company: babes in indie-rock videos. Why are
there so few examples of this? (And the lovelies in Lush don't count. I'm
talking about babes who aren't in the band.) There's the beret-wearing cutie
in "How Soon Is Now?" and there are those earnest, topless models in New
Order's "Round & Round." And? Now, I'm not suggesting that it would
have been a good idea to throw a groupie with size 38DD casabas onto the
hood of the car Michael Stipe is driving in "Can't Get There from Here."
And I can see why bands whose looks factored into their success (e.g., Echo
and the Bunnymen) should have self-fellating videos. But did they really
need to train the camera on the guys in Ned's Atomic Dustbin? Or the
Hoodoo Gurus? Or the Smithereens? Or School of Fish? No. Sex it up! Give
me goth chicks with icy stares and scores to settle. Give me bespectacled
teacher's pets with perverse night lives. Or, you know, just give me the girls
from *Ghost World*. But I guess you can't have everything.

brunette in Bananarama, the singer from the Waitresses, Martha Quinn, and even Joan Jett, who I figured was probably a lesbian. Mousy, elfin Go-Go Jane Wiedlin did more for me than Belinda Carlisle, even after the latter cut out the booze and the Ho Hos and dropped thirty pounds. I went against these preferences when, in my senior year of high school, a bouncy thing named Leslie chose me over dozens of less pimply boys, possibly because she'd already dated all of them. We weren't exactly compatible. In my yearbook, she spelled "in a way" as one word. But she had a firm body, smelled nice, and, most important, showed actual interest in me. I went with her for a few months, until the millionth "irregardless" coming from her mouth pushed me over the edge. (Okay, there were other reasons, too.) Sadly, Leslie didn't broaden my musical palate, at least not directly. She liked the tuneless British band China Crisis and, well, I wanted no part of that. Her friend Holly, though—wow. She exhibited none of the traditional punk-rock trappings: tattoos, piercings, punishing hairdos, the words FUCK and OFF spelled out on her knuckles. But she hated everyone. Isn't that what punk is all about? She was a total bitch, the kind of girl who sassed teachers, including my poor mother, and who drank cheap vodka straight from the bottle. She scared the heck out of me. And of course that made her super hot.

One winter night in early 1988 the three of us were cruising around in Holly's boat of a car, and she popped in a tape that messed with my classic-rock-soaked brain. The music fused Jimmy Page guitars with Jim Morrison vocals and had a harder bite than the other Led Zeppelin clones floating around at the time.[47] The cassette cover featured a dude whose head was enshrouded by what appeared to be a sinister plush toy. It was the Cult's *Electric,* and I'm sure the word that came out of my mouth was "sweet."

The Cult occupies a curious place in the indie-music pan-

---

[47] Kingdom Come, anyone?

theon. Their first notable album was *Love,* which was adopted by goths and new wavers, mostly for the soaring dance hit "She Sells Sanctuary." Ian Astbury, with his ridiculous Native American fetish, was odd enough to have indie cred, and his ethereal voice attracted fans of darker, more depressing music such as Sisters of Mercy and the Cure. *Love* was a huge success in the United Kingdom, and Astbury, the ambitious whore he turned out to be, wanted to break into the U.S. market. The best way to do that circa 1987? Hire Beastie Boys producer Rick Rubin to make every song sound as grungy as Led Zep's "The Ocean." On its own, *Electric* didn't alienate all of the band's core fans (although it certainly must have pissed off the goths, since there wasn't anything remotely depressing on it) because even with the amps cranked way up, the sound was still punky enough to be embraced. (Plus the exuberant "Love Removal Machine" resembled "She Sells Sanctuary" just enough to get played in dance clubs.) But straightforward, AC/DC-style rockers like "King Contrary Man" and "Peace Dog" attracted a new fan base: guys even more into hard rock than I was. And that would soon become the band's downfall. Unlike most of its peers, the Cult *wanted* to alienate its smaller, quirkier fan base and go mainstream, and, it being the late eighties, this meant emulating a hair-metal band.[48] The 1989 follow-up, *Sonic Temple,* might as well be retitled *Shit Temple* because it was an offense to anyone who didn't invest heavily in Aqua Net products. Seemingly overnight, the Cult had moved from the hearts of alternative-music fans to the Walkmans of Warrant disciples—completely unacceptable. When the band toured Europe that year with Aerosmith, the deed was done. Former fans rejoiced when almost everything after *Sonic Temple* bombed, especially that Doors revival with Astbury on vocals.

Of course, when *Sonic Temple* came out during my freshman year in college, it wasn't dismissed as quickly as it should have

---

[48] Fun fact: Guns N' Roses, just before the release of *Appetite for Destruction,* opened for the Cult on the *Electric* tour.

been. I was guilty of wanting to like it a little too much. And so the horrid "Fire Woman," featuring guitarist Billy Duffy's standard-issue hair-band riff[49] and Astbury's intolerable caterwauling, was frequently jacked at full volume in my dorm room, even though it wasn't exciting me like the stuff on *Electric* had. But that's what you have to do when a band you like puts out a monumental turd. Since you've already made a personal commitment to like them, you have to try and fight through it, even if you suspect it's futile. The alternative is to admit that you have poor judgment. And so you give the sludge that extra chance to lose its stink. But I wonder: Why did the *Sonic Temple* debacle cause me to lose interest, very quickly, in the album that got me there? Did I dump *Electric* from the rotation because I was too craven to be associated with the new Cult? Probably. But did *Electric* suddenly become terrible? No—the band did. I lost my copy of the album sometime in the last decade and have failed to upgrade to CD. Which is unfortunate, because I would kill to hear "Lil' Devil" right now.

Soon I'd broken up with Leslie, Holly had gone with her, and a new cultural guidance counselor was needed. Enter a bleach blonde named Tanya. She couldn't read to herself without moving her lips, but I was intrigued by her desire to become a model and by the way her scrawny, TanFaster-embossed looks seemed to defy this aspiration. We'd both signed up for a history class with the excellently named Mr. Pupil, and on the first day of class he assigned our seats in the most boring way: alphabetically (as opposed to the best way: first come, first served). I ended up with the other S students at the back and left side of the classroom; as a C, she was perched up front and to my right. I noticed that the seat immediately behind Tanya's was empty—a C had dropped the class—and, in a spark of decisiveness I've never again duplicated, I raised my hand and told Mr. Pupil that the board looked fuzzy. To my surprise, he said, "Sellers, either get glasses or just

---

[49] Second fun fact: Duffy, who hails from Manchester, played in a band called the Nosebleeds with Morrissey. I have nothing against Duffy; he was always the best thing about the Cult.

sit up front in this empty desk." I told him that glasses were really expensive.

Tanya and I became friends, which is to say she ignored me most of the time and I read undue meaning into her frequent borrowing of my four-color pen, which she used to triple-underline portions of her notes in green ink. One snowy evening her Pinto fishtailed and hit a tree. When she returned to class a week later, her left arm was in a cast and she had the kind of scabs on her face that model scouts frown upon. A window inside my demented brain creaked open. "Do you need a ride home?" I asked. She looked at me like a kitten eyeing a ball of string. "That would be nice," she said.

My days became defined by whether she needed a ride home or not. I knew that this was an unreasonable feeling: She didn't know who John Hughes was, and she cared more about lip gloss than the virtuosity of Eddie Van Halen.[50] But having her riding shotgun in my car made me feel vaguely important for the first time in my life, she the cosmetic-counter beauty to my beast with a Carl Lewis flattop. If I had to listen to her babble on about the cute twenty-four-year-old guy she met last Friday night at the skeezy dance club known as the Top, it was a moderate price to pay. At some point in our unhealthy arrangement, Tanya brought along her neighbor Sarah, who must have been instructed to be friendly to me in order to earn repeated rides. Sarah looked good too, of course, because pretty girls travel in packs, but she had the girl-next-door thing going on. She was the

---

[50] Of all the hard-rock acts I listened to in high school—and there were a lot, ranging from traditional favorites Led Zeppelin and AC/DC on down the food chain to Winger and the Vinnie Vincent Invasion—the one that gets played the most in my apartment nowadays is Roth-era Van Halen. Especially the power trio of "Ain't Talkin' 'bout Love," "Unchained," and "Everybody Wants Some!!" That Halen wasn't elected to the Rock and Roll Hall of Fame in 2003, its first year of eligibility, and didn't score a nomination until 2006, is as good an example as any of why the Hall's voting process needs an enema. Oh, but Jackson Browne is in there. Great job, voters! (See Appendix A for other reasons why I'll support any campaign to boycott the Hall—unless, somehow, the powers that be grant me a vote.)

Joyce DeWitt to Tanya's Suzanne Somers. It wasn't long until Sarah supplanted Tanya in the crush department, in part because Sarah helped me realize that Tanya had questionable musical preferences, which manifested themselves in dance-oriented mix tapes that were lousy with Stacey Q, the insipid Madonna wannabe who unleashed "Two of Hearts" on the world. I didn't know it then, but Sarah would become the first of many, many indie-rock crushes I'd develop over the next two decades. As a rule, indie-rock girls—and their sisters, new wavers, alterna-chicks, mods, and goths—are the most delicate flowers known to humankind, even the ones who hold punk goddess Exene Cervenka up as a role model and who'd kick you in the nuts if you looked at them the wrong way. I love them all, even the ones who would have nothing to do with me. *Especially* the ones who would have nothing to do with me. I know what you're thinking: Isn't this just as shallow as getting aroused by a Rolls-Royce hood dance? Yes. But at least the girls I've liked wouldn't stick their tongues down David Coverdale's throat. Well, maybe Tanya would have.

On the rare occasions in my teens when I'd encounter a girl who exhibited the right mix of these cute but quirky qualities—flesh-and-blood versions of Watts from *Some Kind of Wonderful* or Samantha from *Sixteen Candles*—I'd find my face getting hot and itchy: I was Hive Boy. This begins to explain how a guy like me, then an active listener to Mötley Crüe and George Thorogood, could have got caught up in a band like New Order in 1988. On paper, this group should have done nothing for me. New Order's music, at least what they were churning out at the time, was predominantly synthy, which went against my theory that if the most noticeable instrument was keyboards, it didn't get played.[51] Synth pop, that genre dominated by melodic, computerized keyboard sounds, was the domain of meaningless, wimpy artists like Animotion, Human League, a-ha, and Howard

---

[51] Concocted, in large part, to combat the infidels who attempted to play Van Hagar in my car.

Jones. It was not for me. Plus MTV was running a New Order video that consisted of little more than whimsically costumed dancers, one of whom disturbingly resembled Prince, jumping up and down and bumping into one another.

But Sarah liked them. My crush had gotten large enough that I sometimes let her have control over my tape deck on after-school drives. She had an older brother in college who was into indie music, and she would occasionally pull out a tape he'd dubbed for her, and I'd allow her to eject my Van Halen or U2 cassette to play it. Without fail it turned out to be new-wave hooey: Bronski Beat, Erasure, Depeche Mode—things I'd seen and spurned on MTV because they had way too many pale, skinny guys playing electric pianos and acting campy. Depeche Mode in particular bugged me: That song "Just Can't Get Enough" sounded as if it had been composed by a two-year-old, and their radio hit "People Are People" contained that embarrassing lyric "I can't understand what makes a man hate another man—help me understand." [52] And yet I asked to borrow all of Sarah's tapes just to indicate that I cared. (And, all right, I liked, for a chunk of time, Depeche Mode's "Never Let Me Down Again" because, for reasons that escape me now, I thought it sounded ominous.)

One day she put in a tape full of electronic noise that had no discernible tune or lyrics. I remember thinking: *Christ, who would willingly listen to this?* Oh, right: Sarah. She said that it was New Order's *Substance*. The next day I bought my own copy at Believe in Music and forced myself to listen to it straight through in one sitting as if shotgunning my first beer. And it was like drinking beer for the first time.[53] You feel as if you need to

---

[52] In 1990, when they crossed into the mainstream with yet another plainly dumb song, "Personal Jesus," I thought the world had gone to hell. "Ooh," people cooed, "Is Depeche Mode using guitars?" As if! Depeche Mode is the most overrated band in alternative-music history.

[53] Natural Light, with two geeky friends, in early 1987. It involved drunkenly making snow angels.

like the taste, so you keep drinking it: Maybe it'll get better. Amazingly, it eventually did. Once New Order's music had taken hold of me, it was hard to recall why I'd ever thought it was the musical equivalent of hail hitting a tin roof. At first I preferred the hits "Bizarre Love Triangle" and "True Faith"—partly because girls with angular hairstyles would stampede the dance floor when the deejay at the all-ages club Electric Avenue played them. But soon I was primarily listening to the stuff that kicked off side one, songs that took it easy on programmed keyboards in favor of actual guitar, drums, and bass. While the spare, muted "Ceremony" didn't fit my definition of what rock was supposed to be (and rock was supposed to induce the formation of devil's horns with your hands), the song sounded like just about the greatest thing in the world—although I didn't exactly know why yet. See, I had only started to enter the ugly depressive phase that would last all through college, during which perfectly informed, thoroughly morose songs—"the songs that saved your life," as Morrissey memorably refers to them on "Rubber Ring"—guided me through a string of unrequited crushes like the one I had on Sarah. It wouldn't be until a year later, when New Order and other introspective bands were sounding way better than Guns N' Roses and Van Halen,[54] that I realized that what you listen to can greatly affect your outlook on life.

Nearing the end of the crush, I would do drive-bys of Sarah's house on the off chance that I might glimpse her emerging. I had no real clue of what would have happened if this had occurred, though a perfect scenario would have involved tooting the horn playfully, stopping the car, and watching her run at me with arms outstretched. (More likely it would have involved an insane panic, the putting of the pedal to the metal, and the squealing of tires.) While on these missions of longing—which now would be called stalking—I took to playing the most consoling songs I had

[54] Even as New Order reeled me in, I went to a Monsters of Rock show. Dokken ruled!

on hand, and "Ceremony" was chief among them. In fact, I would get so caught up in the music that the drive-bys became almost secondary. One of the most comforting places for a teenager who knows deep down that he has zero chance to make meaningful contact with the girl of his dreams is alone at the wheel of a car, with his favorite music turned up loud.

It felt strange that first time I popped in my New Order tape with Sarah in the passenger seat. Showing a crush that her music has affected you is a risky step. Doesn't it belong to her, since she found it first? Maybe. But what if you suspect, as was the case here, that you care more for the band than the person who made the introduction, that you alone understand what the music is trying to say? Sarah let my overture go without comment, which I took to mean that she knew of my death-defying crush and just wanted to get home without seeing me embarrass myself further. But maybe she didn't say anything because she'd learned from her relationship with her brother that it's okay to let people influence your tastes. You take what you can from your friends and your family and run with it.

But just before leaving for college, I was again left to fend for myself. I made the young man's mistake of revealing my feelings, late one night at a party while drunk on vodka and orange Fanta. When I came to, that first month at college, I realized that Sarah had given me a musical STD—an interest in something regrettable. While I will always be thankful that Sarah introduced me to New Order, which in turn led me to discover songs that indeed saved my life, she also left me with a mean case of Erasure. It turns out that there is a cure for "Oh L'amour." But as I can tell you from gross, painful experience—namely watching Andy Bell flit around a Detroit stage in gold lamé hot pants on a night when I could have seen Ministry instead—it leaves lifelong scars.

6

DON'T LET'S START

"Everybody dies frustrated and sad, and that is beautiful."

Give a man a fish, they say, and he'll eat for a day; teach a man to fish and he'll eat for life. Well, I don't go in much for manual labor. And I don't often crave the taste of fish. But luckily, a similar sentiment applies to music. Give a man one alternative-music cassette and he'll listen to it for a little while; teach him how to discover alternative music on his own, and he'll listen to it forever.

My first moments at Michigan State resembled Charlie Sheen's arrival at the base camp in *Platoon,* only without the threat of a napalm attack or a Tom Berenger glare. On that nerve-racking initial foray down the hallway of my assigned dorm I looked inside rooms whose doors were open, and each appeared to be occupied by a crusty vet so confident that I figured they must have been living there for years, even if it had probably only been since that morning. In one room, a shirtless guy was aggressively pacing across the tile floor and smoking a cigarette and, as I passed, he nodded his head at me and grunted, "What's up?" I was almost bowled over by two curly-headed ruffians engaged in a Nerf basketball death match. Another door revealed two longhairs playing Nintendo. All of these people were blasting music without shame: The shirtless guy was rocking out to *Appetite for Destruction,* the Nerfers [55] were listening to rap

[55] Nerfists?

(Eric B. & Rakim, I think), and the headbangers had on, improbably, Tom Petty. Forget those university-made signs taped to every door that announced the names and the hometowns of the guys who lived within. The best way to introduce yourself to your floormates, it seemed, was to keep your door open and put on music. It went a lot further in telling a stranger what kind of person you were. And the music could help you make friends. You could walk down the hall and pick out acquaintances as if they were items at a supermarket: guy listening to the Ramones—get in the cart!; dude blasting Poison—next!

In those first lonely minutes in my sweatbox of a room, I decided to play New Order. It was a questionable selection to say the least. Once, over the summer, I had tried to sneak *Substance* by my friend Brad [56] as we were driving around. With the volume turned low, I inserted the cassette into my car's tape deck and then, as he launched into a rant about the idiocy of an acquaintance, I gradually increased the sound. This worked for two songs. But when "Temptation" faded in with its fey "ooey-ooey-oo, ooey-ooey-oo," he was nonplussed. And by nonplussed, I mean that he asked, "What is this gay shit?" and then ejected the tape in favor of the BulletBoys. I was relatively sure that a total stranger wasn't going to barge into my room and complain about my choice of music. But after so many years of having to hide my musical crushes from friends, putting in what I really wanted to play still felt risky. Nevertheless, I popped in *Substance* and cranked it up.

Nothing happened. No one came rushing in to ask, "Is that modern rock? Well, turn it up, dude!" But the music might have had a welcoming effect. I was a half hour into the unpacking, and

---

[56] This guy was a five-foot-nothing repository of white-hot rage. One time after school, he leaned out of the window of my car and flipped off the assistant principal, hollering, "This is for you, Mrs. ———!" Another time, while we were circling the mall, he became incensed by a pokey pickup in front of us and screamed, "Get your ass in gear, B2000!" It was never quiet when Brad was around.

worrying about the arrival, the following day, of my roommate—who had called to introduce himself by saying, verbatim,
"Wussup, homey! You miss me yet, homey?" (he was white)—
when a tan, well-groomed neighbor stuck his head in. "I'm making a liquor run," he said. "Want anything?" Other than various
forms of "What's up?" these were the first words uttered to me at
college. I was psyched. Or possibly stoked. I put in an order for a
pint of Popov vodka and waited for the evening to unfold. Much
later, on the way to getting incredibly drunk with three guys from
the floor, the subject of music came up. Phil, a small Asian guy
with a mushroom cloud of hair and a low alcohol tolerance,
asked what I was currently listening to. I confidently stated: New
Order's *Substance.* "That's pretty good," he said. "Do you have
the Joy Division compilation?" The which? And that's the way it
would be all freshman year. I'd mention New Order and some
guy would stick a Joy Division cassette in my hand. I'd admit to
liking the Cure's "Just Like Heaven" and the alt-music know-it-
all down the hall would inform me that a raucous cover of it had
just been released by a band called Dinosaur Jr. Where were these
people in high school?

Within weeks, Phil had introduced me to *120 Minutes,* the
Sunday-night alternative-music showcase on MTV.[57] As the network had soared in popularity and its library of videos had
grown exponentially, it had herded music by less mainstream
artists to the fringes of its schedule.[58] While you might very rarely
still have seen Hüsker Dü during daylight hours in late 1988, the

[57] MTV's once-a-month indie-music program *The Cutting Edge* pre-
dated *120 Minutes,* although I was too deep into my pop phase to notice.
Airing from 1983 to 1987, the show was produced by IRS Records (then
R.E.M.'s label) and hosted by Peter Zaremba, the lead singer of the Flesh-
tones, a band whose music I have felt guilty about not exploring ever since
the late 1990s, when he and I wrote for the same magazine and would run
into each other at parties.

[58] Other than *The Wonder Years, 21 Jump Street,* and *Late Night with
David Letterman,* MTV was the only thing I watched that year. This was
the era when MTV first began to experiment with nonmusic programming.

only time you could have been assured of seeing videos by artier, edgier musicians like Siouxsie and the Banshees, the Sugarcubes, and XTC was from midnight to two a.m. on Sunday nights. And so a subset of the video-watching public, which included Phil and me and anyone else on our floor who wanted to spend two hours in musical bliss, turned *120 Minutes* into appointment viewing.[59] The format was perfect: just enough borderline mainstream bands (such as R.E.M.,[60] Midnight Oil, and the Psychedelic Furs) and intriguingly obscure artists (e.g., Public Image Limited, Love

---

The early results were mixed. On the bad, pointless side of the coin: *House of Style*. On the great: *Remote Control*. Best game show ever, hands down. Not only did its theme song ("Kenny wasn't like the other kids/TV mattered, nothing else did") neatly sum up my childhood, the trivia questions were inspired. (Sample category: "Inside Tina Yothers.") Plus it featured the early comedy stylings of Colin Quinn and Adam Sandler, and had excellent eye candy in the shapely forms of hostesses Marisol and Kari. Reruns, please.

[59] I transferred to Michigan my sophomore year and tried to establish a *120 Minutes* ritual in the TV lounge on my floor. But I'd been assigned to a section of the dorm crammed with football players (including eventual Heisman Trophy winner Desmond Howard, who used to give his friends haircuts in our bathroom and not clean up the mess). The first few weeks, the TV was unoccupied and I watched in peace, although once I was joined by a sullen black guy with a sprig of bleached hair who professed a fondness for the industrial outfit Meat Beat Manifesto. Soon, however, a particularly gargantuan lineman began to show up; he would lope in at around twelve thirty a.m. carrying a large pizza and a two-liter of Dr Pepper. As he slowly but steadily worked his way through his bedtime snack, he'd stare, like a bored zoo gorilla, at the videos. While he never specifically requested that the channel be changed, I could acutely sense the disdain emanating from his shaved pate. After a few weeks of that, I had no choice but to set off in search of a more optimal TV lounge on a different floor, and miraculously I found one, in which two black-garbed girls sat petitely watching the show. My sophomore year improved exponentially.

[60] R.E.M., in April 1989, holds the distinction of being the first indie-rock concert I ever saw. The second: New Order. The third: the Mighty Lemondrops, with the Ocean Blue and John Wesley Harding as openers. I have absolutely no recollection of that particular show, and I couldn't pick a Mighty Lemondrops song out of a police lineup if it was holding a bloody knife.

and Rockets) to hold your interest if the show's loopy host, Kevin Seal,[61] introduced an intolerable video (anything by Kate Bush) or something too dull to make an impact (e.g., Transvision Vamp); plus musicians would stop by, who could either up the wow factor (guest host: They Might Be Giants) or give you enough time to run down four flights of stairs to the lobby soda[62] machine for a Slice (special live performance by the Godfathers). The opportunity to see your favorite musicians and to discover new ones was the main attraction, of course, but there was also something appealing about being one of the few people in my dormitory who cared. It was like joining an exclusive club—a club whose members often wore floral-patterned shirts, sang about unrequited love, and starred in videos in which everyone seemed to be suffering from a stomach virus.

The me of just a year prior wouldn't have approved of the person I was at the end of 1988, and to be honest, the me of 2007 doesn't much approve of him either. Being surrounded, at last, by sympathetic viewpoints had endowed me with musical confidence—but it was a narrow-minded and ill-informed confidence, as if I'd just attended a freaky cult's recruiting seminar and couldn't stop telling people about it. I was very "for" or "against"

---

[61] *120 Minutes,* first hosted by original veejay J. J. Jackson, had debuted in early 1986. Kevin Seal quickly took over and brought to the proceedings a goofy nonchalance that nicely offset the general seriousness of the videos. But the most memorable host—and really, the only one worth a fuller discussion—was Dave Kendall. Usually dressed as if he was heading to an S&M club, and possibly wearing a hairpiece, he gave Anglophile viewers what they needed: a weekly dose of the British way of speaking. Sure, he kept pushing Killing Joke and MC 900 Ft Jesus, but he would make up for such transgressions by pronouncing, say, Blur's debut album, *Leisure,* thus: "Bluh, *Leh-shuh.*" The bald, chunky, mid-1990s host Matt Pinfield was less interesting, and not only because he was from New Jersey. He seemed too smugly knowledgeable, and could be a suck-up to in-studio guests. It was for these reasons that he earned the moniker "Matt Pinhead."

[62] In Michigan, the word is "pop." So I'd run downstairs to the pop machine.

in those days, and rarely in between. I was for the Cure; I was against Warrant. I was for punk rock; I was against bubblegum pop. I was for plenty of reverb; I was against overuse of the whammy bar. But no matter what I was telling people, including myself, it remained the case that my genetic code, hardwired to find classic rock and blistering guitar solos attractive and to make me susceptible to some seriously questionable music, had yet to be overwritten by any newer influence.

Which goes a long way toward explaining this:

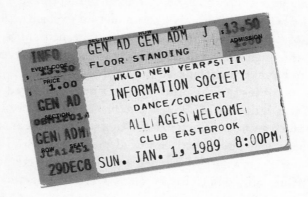

Still, I proudly called myself a fan of alternative music for the rest of freshman year.[63] I'd accumulated enough knowledge about

---

[63] In retrospect, that was incorrect procedure. I was *very nearly* a fan of alternative music during my freshman year. Van Halen, Duran Duran, Journey, Billy Idol, et al. were still getting plenty of play; a reasonable estimate of listening time allocated to alternative music would have been merely 60 percent. If you profess to be a fan of one sort of music, you are suggesting exclusivity, i.e., I am a fan *only* of alternative music. But that wasn't true yet. In order to be able to make that claim truthfully, the ratio has to be higher, definitely over 75 percent, and probably more like 90. And there also should be a watershed moment. It just so happens that I know the exact moment I became a true fan of alternative music. In July 1989, Phil and some other friends and I huddled on a grassy knoll to watch the excellent triple bill of New Order, P.I.L., and the Sugarcubes on their so-called Monsters of Alternative Rock tour. After the show my excitement was so great that I could not be stopped from playing Rush's "Limelight" a

the genre to see that there was no turning back. The stakes had been raised considerably. This was an art form that seemed tailor-made to awkward, sensitive, spineless guys such as I unfortunately was at that time.[64] It was a genre full of lead singers who didn't seem obsessed with sticking their groins in the camera. And it was blissfully free of songs whose choruses made unsubtle references to vaginas.[65] At home in Grand Rapids the following summer, my level of commitment only increased. The city had failed to grow with me.[66] There was yet another visit from Foghat. The only halfway decent radio station was still offering countless opportunities to "get the Led out." [67] Mullets abounded.

So I holed up, tuned into *120 Minutes* on Sundays (greatly enhanced by late-night snacks brought downstairs by my mom),

---

world-record twenty-three times in a row, despite numerous cries of mercy from my Geddy Lee–hating friends. But it was an exorcism. With that twenty-third play, classic rock was forever moved to the back burner of my preferences, and overnight I became a card-carrying member of the alternative-music tribe.

[64] And, goddammit, still am. But don't get me angry. You wouldn't like me when I'm angry.

[65] Exception: the tongue-in-cheek "Wynona's Big Brown Beaver" by Primus (the Rush of indie rock), until you listen to the lyrics and realize that it's actually about a big brown beaver.

[66] Well, there was a new club downtown, the Reptile House, that purported to have an industrial night, but it was 21+ and I was always too chickenshit to get a fake ID.

[67] At Christmas my senior year of high school, I received a crappy Kramer electric guitar. The first riff I asked my guitar teacher to show me was "The Ocean." While I can hold my own on songs that require almost no finger coordination, scorching riffs—that is, the stuff I was born to play, at least in my mind—will always elude me. If I could pull a *Quantum Leap* and "leap" into the body of anyone who was ever alive during my lifetime, and inhabit that person for a single hour of my choosing, I would pick Jimmy Page on stage, circa 1973. (The Beastie Boys: "If I played guitar, I'd be Jimmy Page!") Or maybe Eddie Van Halen in 1982. Actually, I'd probably go with Magic Johnson in the 1979 NCAA Championship Game first, then Kirk Gibson in game five of the 1984 World Series, and then Tommy Lee anytime after a Crüe show in 1983. But then Jimmy Page. Or Eddie Van Halen. Or, ooh, Tony Iommi in 1970. Yeah, Tony Iommi.

and ignored the future. Meanwhile I made lists.[68] Lists of my favorite songs. Lists of my favorite bands. Lists of my favorite songs by British bands, and lists of my favorites by American bands. Lists of the most rocking riffs. Lists of the coolest videos.

---

[68] Have you noticed yet that I've managed to go 70 pages without resorting to lists? Here are the top three reasons why I'm bringing this up:

1. I'm impressed with myself. I still come up with lists all the time, like it's a kind of mania. Some people knit. Some people make ships in bottles. I devise lists. Lists regarding the most overrated birds (1. the hummingbird; 2. the ostrich; 3. the ptarmigan; etc.), the best words beginning with the letter z (1. zygote; 2. zither; 3. zounds; 4. zebu; etc.), the nicest people I've ever met (1. my mom; 2. John Ritter; 3. the Parry family of Alsager, England; etc.). In fact, I originally conceived of this book as a series of annotated music lists that would somehow be worth your cash. Even after I was told that the idea "needs more meat" by a person way smarter than me, I figured I'd still be able to sneak in lists everywhere, just to spite him.

2. Lists are the backbone of present-day music writing. They appear regularly in most music publications; they are also all over VH1 and MTV, in books, and on the Internet. And they're becoming more prevalent. I believe that I have seen a new list every single day for the past year. The Top 40 Most Awesomely Bad Videos. The Top 50 Singles of All Time. Year-end lists. Amazon consumer wish lists. Even though music lists have been around longer than Casey Kasem has, we're just now reaching the saturation point. And how. Still, I can't help but think that maybe the creators of these lists know something I don't.

3. I'm lazy as hell. And of course that's ultimately why music magazines and cable networks put them out there so often: They're exceedingly easy to produce and they take up a lot of space. You come up with a topic and run with it—no sweat. Lists are also sure to titillate; editors and television producers prey on the fact that music fans will take issue if their personal opinions aren't reflected in a magazine or on a program purporting to be an authority on their favorite subject. Actually, they prey on the fact that people love to take issue, period. Personally, I think people take issue too often nowadays. The top three reasons why I think they do: 1. People are assholes; 2. People are increasingly smug about their right to express their opinions; 3. People think other people care about what they have to say. Take it from a part-time blogger: They don't. No one cares what you have to say. I'm surprised anybody's even reading this sentence.

The problem with most lists, of course, is that they become irrelevant the second they're finalized. (Except the preceding list: that one's pretty solid.) Here is a random example—My Top Five American Presidential Candidates of All Time:

Lists of the worst videos. Lists of the best drummers. Lists of the ugliest guitarists. Lists of the best songs that happen to appear last on albums. Lists of the funniest Morrissey lyrics. Lists of the

---

1. Gerald R. Ford
2. H. Ross Perot
3. Bill Clinton
4. William Taft
5. John Anderson

But see, the trouble with that is that I don't really like Ford the politician. I have always put him first because he grew up in Grand Rapids, and because of Chevy Chase's impression of him, and because he was in office during the bicentennial, and because he is somehow affiliated with Squeaky Fromme. If pressured to make a serious list, I'd cave quickly and Clinton would be at the top, followed by no one. Because Bill Clinton is really the only politician I've ever cared about, unless Mayor McCheese counts.

But a list can't have only one item in it. You have to fill it out, or else it's just a statement (e.g., my favorite American presidential candidate of all time is Bill Clinton). And a big problem that arises when you attempt to round out music lists, especially the long ones, is that the process itself is almost always compromised. Let's use a list from a magazine as an example, for the simple reason that it is currently sitting in the rack in my bathroom. What we have here is *Spin*'s 100 Greatest Albums 1985–2005, a list celebrating the alternative-rock-lovin' publication's twentieth anniversary. It's actually a pretty good list, with well-written tributes to all of the included albums. I guarantee that thousands of passionate e-mails were sent around while the staff argued out the list, and no doubt there was a heated debate about which artists needed to be included and in what order the albums should be listed. Which is why I feel bad about having to slash it up.

I'll start at the top of the list. Is *OK Computer* really the best album of the past twenty years? It might be—it's probably Radiohead's best album, and they're definitely one of the best bands of the past two decades. But is it really better or more relevant or more important than Nirvana's *Nevermind*? You can make a case either way. Is it even more listenable than *Kid A*, which shows up at number forty-eight, or *The Bends*, which doesn't even place in the top one hundred? Yes, but only a little. But these questions don't matter. This is because the editors were all but forced to select *OK Computer* as the magazine's top choice, for two reasons. First, unlike we normal folks who make lists, the brain trust at a magazine (or a network or an Internet concern) has to consider its audience and its advertisers. The advertisers want a younger audience always, and the audience wants to think it is

best songs phrased in the form of a question. By the end of the summer the lists were writing themselves, each one a totem of my boredom. But they stood for more than that. Compiling the lists

---

younger always. That's just the way it is. So as much as they discussed putting other albums at the top of the list, *Spin* couldn't sign off on one by a band that's not still churning out music—Nirvana, the Smiths, etc.—or one by a band that their target audience/advertiser base might consider to be too old, such as U2 or R.E.M. In fact, despite this being the Greatest Albums 1985–2005 list, *Spin* almost certainly had to go with an album from the past ten years or less, because that magazine in particular needs twenty-one-year-old readers in order to thrive. At the time the issue came out, twenty-one-year-olds were born in 1983 or '84. While they might like, even love, *Nevermind* or *The Queen Is Dead* (which, let's face it, is the real best album of the past twenty years, hands down, and even the guys in Radiohead would probably say so), twenty-one-year-olds would prefer to have something from their own coming-of-age years validated, and the editors know that.

Second—and this is the more relevant reason *OK Computer* was chosen as number one—the album at the top of the list had to be slightly unconventional. If they had picked Nirvana's *Nevermind*, everyone would have yawned and canceled his or her subscription. In fact, enough surprises have to occur throughout a list this long to ensure that readers won't fall asleep. And the unorthodox choices will goose readers into writing letters saying, "Wuzzat? How the hell did the Afghan Whigs make this list?" Take the issue of U2: *The Joshua Tree,* which is almost certainly the band's best and most important album (and it's not hard to argue that it's the best and most important album of the past twenty years), didn't even make the list. The only U2 selection is *Achtung Baby,* at number eleven. *Achtung Baby* should be on the list, but certainly not higher than *The Joshua Tree,* and I don't think that's a personal opinion; it's almost irrefutable, because *The Joshua Tree* fits all the criteria: Its emormous success took the industry by surprise, the album sold tons of copies, and it catapulted U2 into Biggest Band in the World status, which in many respects they still hold. Plus it didn't have anything to do with Bono's ironic phase, in which he pretended to be a character named MacPhisto. But selecting *Achtung Baby* is a less boring choice. (And is it really? What about the age-old practice of outfoxing the reader: *Oh, we know that you know that we don't want to pick* The Joshua Tree *because how boring would that be? But since we know that you know, we're going to do it anyway, and we're going to put it at number four, where it belongs. Gotcha!*)

Of course, both of these issues arise due to the nature of this particular list. I daresay that if *Spin* cranked out a list of the 100 Greatest Albums Ever,

was a first stab at quantifying my musical judgment. It was an important quantification. In the fall I would be transferring to Michigan, where access to my network of trusted tastemakers

---

they might very well go with *Nevermind* at the top spot because they'd be stacking Nirvana up against the whole of rock history, and in that case *Nevermind* would both feel like an unconventional choice (over, say, *Revolver* or *Blood on the Tracks*) and be relatively recent (sixteen years ago, as opposed to, say, twenty-eight years ago for *London Calling*). The magazine's 2004 list 50 Greatest Frontmen of All Time bears this out, as Prince took the number one spot: He's more recent and way, way more unconventional than the choices that immediately follow—Mick Jagger, Robert Plant, and James Brown (who, it must be noted, Prince kinda ripped off). To reverse the conjecture: If *Spin* had done a list of the Top 20 Frontmen of the Past 20 Years, they might very well have selected Karen O (who placed an unbelievable number twenty on their 2004 list—ahead of Ozzy Osbourne. This isn't possible. Ozzy bit the head off a bat. What the hell has Karen O ever done? Besides stealing her shtick from Siouxsie Sioux?).

A lesser reason why a list like *Spin*'s 100 Greatest Albums 1985–2005 could have been problematic is that list makers rarely duplicate artists when citing top songs or albums. The *Spin* top album list mostly avoids the problem by allotting two positions each to Radiohead, Public Enemy, Nirvana, Pavement, the Pixies, the Beastie Boys, Outkast, Beck, De La Soul, and Sonic Youth. The other eighty spots are taken up by eighty different artists. But it still makes you wonder. Sure, by including *The Bends* you'd have to boot something else off. But *The Bends* is better than at least ten of the albums that made the list. But could they really have put three Radiohead albums on the list without being accused of favoritism or single-mindedness? Obviously they think that there's a fine line. You can duplicate, but you can't duplicate too often, even if the duplication is deserved. But come on, *The Bends* is unconditionally one of the best one hundred albums of the past twenty years; it should have been on the list anyway. Maybe kick off the Afghan Whigs? Please? Because it sounds like I'm bashing *Spin,* here is where I must restate that the magazine did a superb job on the list overall, and performed a great service to its readers by including albums by Pavement, the Smiths, and the Pixies in its top ten. And besides, nothing on their list (or, rather, not on their list) was remotely as anger-inducing as the time *Rolling Stone* published its list of Top 100 Guitarists Ever and didn't include Johnny Marr, the man who wrote "This Charming Man," "How Soon Is Now?" and "The Headmaster Ritual." (Not to mention they put Pete Townshend at number fifty. The dude who perfected the windmill move! And Eddie Van Halen was at number seventy!) But see, both *Rolling Stone* and *Spin* got me. I've been titillated. And ultimately that's why you read

would be limited to infrequent weekend visits and the even less frequent receipt of personal letters. On my own, would I be able to ascertain whether something I'd seen on *120 Minutes* or read about in *Melody Maker*[69] was worthy of adoration or not? Would I stagnate? Would I miscalculate and leave myself vulnerable to nothing bands like the Smithereens, the Church, and Toad the Wet Sprocket? In order to meet and impress the sort of people I wanted to meet and impress at my new school, it felt necessary to put to rest that era in which unworthy bands excited me, stole months and years of my energy, and made me look foolish in the eyes of people who might otherwise respect me. At the advanced age of nineteen, it was high time to know for certain, without anyone having to tell me, whether something I was hearing for the first time as well as the one hundredth time had any real merit. Past history, with all those failures, could be used as guideposts, but to hone my assessment skills—with a secondary goal of becoming a tastemaker myself—considerable fresh analysis would be required in every case. Lists, then, were a means to an end. They allowed me to order my preferences. I postulated that those preferences, as long as they were sound, could be used to create an algorithm that would guide me in all future judgments. It was obvious: Only mathematics could crack this code.

There is a formula out there that will allow each and every one of us to determine the value of a particular band. Of this I am certain. Coming up with the one that will work for you is another matter entirely. Despite dozens of attempts during the summer of 1989 to create the ultimate bunker buster, I just could not

---

other people's music lists: They can make you really mad, and it's fun to get mad about things like this. For plenty of lists, see Appendix A.

[69] Preferable to *New Musical Express,* and only one of the tabloid-sized publications could be purchased every week due to the lofty $2.95 import price. In those days before Pitchfork, the weekly gossip that *Melody Maker* served up about indie bands was invaluable, despite occasional lapses in editorial judgment such as a two-page 1990 interview with Bret Michaels of Poison.

figure out a working solution, one that resulted in the Smiths, Joy Division, New Order, and U2, among other favorites, appearing at the top of the list, and nonsense like New Kids on the Block and Paula Abdul way down at the bottom. So that endeavor had to be set aside. But seventeen years later I'm as convinced as ever that a magic formula does exist, and I will find it eventually, and that first Nobel Prize will be mine. In fact, the calculation seems incredibly close at hand. Every potential formula must follow the same three ground rules:

1. The quality of music, based strictly on personal preference, is the most important factor in determining the value of an artist. It must count anywhere from 60 to 75 percent of the final score.
2. Image is worth at most 40 percent, and generally diminishes the overall value. A band with an absence of image (e.g., the Replacements) is vastly preferable to a band whose image borders on the gimmicky (e.g., the Hives), and will be rewarded accordingly. Since most bands are annoying as hell, the image portion of the equation should often produce negative results.
3. A band's X factor can be worth a considerable amount in extra-credit points. Intangibles make or break most bands, and this must bear out in any respectable calculation.

If figured correctly, the final value will determine how much I should like a particular band at that particular moment in time. And with a few minor tweaks allowing for changes in individual preferences over time, the calculation shouldn't waver much from day to day and year to year; that is, all things being equal, it will always be able to inform me using cold, hard science—okay, and a good deal of bias (though consistent bias)—what my favorite band in the world is. Pretty easy, huh?

Near the tail end of 1989, though, my confidence in musical

judgment had gotten so high that such a formula hardly seemed necessary. Besides, with my preferences still constantly in flux, any attempt at nailing down a precise calculation would have been a colossal waste of time (which, of course, would have been half the fun). No, a calculation wasn't needed after all.[70] By the time the 1990s began, there was one thing I was abundantly clear on: All of my favorite bands were from Manchester, England.

---

[70] It would be unprofessional to bring this up and not make another attempt at a working formula. See Appendix B.

7

SUFFER LITTLE CHILDREN

"Oh, Manchester, so much to answer for."

There comes a time in every music obsessive's life when he knows he has to prove it. The only solution: a pilgrimage. The idea behind the proud tradition of the pop-culture pilgrimage is that, by going to the places where one of your heroes grew up, achieved notoriety, died, or was buried, you can certify your fanship. Once accomplished, you can offer up quantifiable proof to the world that you love your idol entirely. You'll be able to say, "I just spent $1,200 to fly to Iceland to take a photo of Björk's childhood home!" Or: "I just drove fifty-seven hours round-trip to visit the college in Halifax, Nova Scotia, where Sloan formed!" [71] It gives you a trump card to play if another fan dares to question your obsession, especially if your retort is along the lines of, "Oh, yeah? Well, have *you* ever made out with a midget on Jim Morrison's grave?" The only thing is, many obsessives are preoccupied with very well-known icons, and the places famously associated with their heroes' names aren't exactly uncommon ground to tread upon. Think Graceland. Or Hemingway's residence in Key West. Or the Anne Frank house in Amsterdam. Places that have been turned into museums, in other words. It goes almost without saying that a pilgrimage doesn't have the same clout if people might be inclined to go to a place

---

[71] Why anyone would bother to take such stinky sojourns is another matter entirely.

after reading about it in a tourist brochure. A sensible rule to determine the excellence of your journey: If you show up and run into the sort of humans you dislike, you've actually accomplished very little. For example, say you're standing in front of Bruce Lee's oddly nondescript grave in Seattle. While you're paying your respects by recalling a few of the deceased master's quotes (e.g., "You have to feel it, like the sun and the moon"), two drunk guys in Chi-Delt caps, Ralph Lauren buttondowns, pleated shorts, and sandals walk up and start snickering beside you.

But something like that couldn't possibly happen in the city where I've made two of my most memorable pilgrimages: Manchester, England. Anyone who would go there as a result of musical obsession is a person whom I'd get along with. Unless the pilgrimage involved the Broadway musical *Hair* and that song "Manchester England." I probably wouldn't tolerate someone like that.

❖

On December 28, 1998, I arrived in Manchester having traveled more than 3,500 miles to witness New Order's first live performance in five years. This was a big deal: One of my favorite bands of the 1980s, whom I'd seen only once, a decade before, would be coming off a long hiatus to stage a single show on its home turf. When I first learned of the concert while procrastinating in my small office in Brooklyn, there was a great sucking sensation in my gut that meant attendance was mandatory. I had to represent. The compulsion arose from propriety. New Order has always seemed underappreciated, even at the height of their popularity; or more correctly, they have been appreciated in the wrong way. They are known, especially in America, almost solely for their synthesizer-programmed hits "Blue Monday," with its fake, staccato drum beat and peppy, makin'-popcorn keyboard line, and "Bizarre Love Triangle," which had the emotive but meaningless chorus "Every time I see you falling, I get down on my knees and pray." [72] If you went to a club's new wave night in the late 1980s and early '90s,[73] or if you attended a fraternity party,[74] you were bound to hear one or both of those songs. As an emerging fanatic, I was irked that most of the people dancing to these songs had no idea what my New Order was all about. They were as annoying as those fools who had adopted R.E.M. because of "Stand."[75]

Anyone who classifies New Order as the purveyors of synth pop might not recognize the forlorn "Dreams Never End" that kicks off their disonant 1981 debut album *Movement,* and might be surprised to learn that quite a few of their songs do not use synthesizers at all. You can only begin to hear the diversity of their sound on their hits album, *Substance,* the classic compilation that served as a launching point to my obsession with them. Their history can be broken up into three parts: their postpunk

---

[72] In general, the band's singer, Bernard Sumner, is a mediocre lyricist. A handy rule of thumb: The earlier he wrote the lyric, the better it probably is.

[73] Ann Arbor's only dance club back then, the Nectarine Ballroom, held its new wave night, I believe, on Thursdays. Mondays were industrial-themed, and it was the better night to go, because the music was more obscure and flat-out superior. But Thursdays had more and prettier women. A high percentage of them, for reasons unknown, were of Asian descent, and the event became known to some as "Asian Invasion." Even my Taiwanese hallmate Peter, who loved the The and the Smiths, called it that, and he refused on principle to go there with me, and rightly so.

[74] Even though we severely maligned frat guys, my small group of friends willingly mixed with them the first few years of college. The absence of fake IDs prevented us from drinking at bars, so fraternity parties were a necessary evil. We took the bad (frat guys, including one who said to me, "Man, you're *ugly,*" and another knuckle dragger who mistakenly thought my friend Jim was Jewish and punched him in the face) to get the good (free and limitless keg beer). It might be the case that they played New Order because they knew girls would dance to it, because, hey, dancing is a nice prelude to nonconsensual sex.

[75] As insipid as the song was, "Stand" was used to perfection in the opening credits of *Get a Life.* I think a number of R.E.M. songs would work well as sitcom themes. "Me in Honey": *Reba.* "Shiny Happy People": *Everybody Loves Raymond.* "Everybody Hurts": *Curb Your Enthusiasm.* This is not a good thing.

period, which ran from the band's inception, after the 1980 demise of Joy Division,[76] until 1982; their ecstasy period, which ran
from 1983 to 1989 and included their biggest hits but also subtle,
sad songs that get lost in the flurry of synth; and everything after,
when they were so well known in Britain that they almost became parodies of themselves, especially on their novelty single
"World in Motion," written in support of the English football
team heading for the 1990 World Cup.[77] Their minimalist period
is what has been disregarded, and that's a shame because their
music sounded more human back then: real people playing real
instruments. If only they hadn't gone and discovered happy pills.

Except for a few of those early tracks,[78] I had almost entirely
stopped listening to New Order's music long before the 1998
concert. When it did get played, the noise was processed in that
dismissive, guilty way you deal with your best friends from junior high after you've figured out you don't need them anymore.
Musically, New Order seemed a bit of a relic in the postgrunge
'90s; it wasn't at all clear when I went to the show that only a few
years later, musicians who'd grown up listening to their songs—
such as the Killers, Clap Your Hands Say Yeah, and the Postal
Service[79]—would be using New Order's pillowy, programmed
sound as a launching point. It's a telling sign that, aside from the
albums *Substance* and *Movement,* I hadn't felt compelled to upgrade anything else to CD. Yet here I was acting as if my life de-
pended on flying overseas to see them.

Truth be told—and it's tough to say this because of what
New Order has meant to me—I didn't much care for the performance. The band members had gotten old on me (they had just

[76] I will discuss Joy Division at length in the next chapter. Stay tuned!

[77] It may have succeeded as a motivating tool: England made it to the
semifinals.

[78] Most notably the 1981 B-side "Procession," the only New Order
song that still has the same impact on me today as it did in 1989. I pity you
if you've never heard it.

[79] None of whom I actually like. See Appendix C for my rulings on
more recent bands.

entered their forties—unthinkable![80]), their music didn't sound tight, and they weren't behaving how I wanted them to. The once-aloof lead singer, Sumner, who used to play his guitar in Joy Division with his back turned to the audience, insisted on leaping around the stage like a monkey in estrus. This didn't mesh with what I liked most about New Order's best songs: melancholy. The other pillar of charisma, Peter Hook—whose signature bass lines, played high and fast as if emulating a lead guitarist, have been co-opted by countless bassists including those in the Cure and Interpol—seemed to be on a different stage altogether, as if he suspected he could be doing better elsewhere. None of the fifteen or so songs the band played resonated with me, even three tracks pulled out of the Joy Division archives—which, by the way, they shouldn't have played, because Sumner's recently acquired giddiness goes against what that band stood for. And though the crowd was in a frenzy, it likely had more to do with a collective release of nostalgic (and, for some, ecstasy-fueled[81]) love for the band than the quality of the performance itself.

Seeing New Order live in such a far-flung locale, however, made me revisit how much influence they've had on my life. When I thought about it more fully afterward, I determined that their music has done more for me than any other band's—which surprised me given that I'd stopped listening to it. Because of New Order, though, I launched headlong into a still-thriving obsession with Joy Division. Because of Joy Division, I became enamored of all things Manchester and morose, which in turn brought me to a knee-buckling obsession with the Smiths and Morrissey. Morrissey sparked a momentary interest in Oscar Wilde, which mildly contributed to my decision to become an

---

[80] Now most musicians I like are this age or older. But at twenty-eight, forty seemed ancient.

[81] I have never tried ecstasy and never will. I also have never dropped acid, snorted coke, injected heroin, sniffed glue, done whippits, or eaten peyote.

English major, which informed my decision to become a writer, and so on. So you can blame New Order for this book. All right, just blame me.

❖

But the bigger reason I was happy to have decided to splurge on the trip to see New Order is that it allowed me to go to Manchester again. The last time I'd been there, in 1990, a few weeks shy of twenty, it hadn't ended well. I'd traveled to England with my friend Sauce. (Yes, this name has been changed to protect the mentally deficient.) We'd come up through the ranks[82] together, first in high school in Grand Rapids and then at the University of Michigan, and we were scarily similar: We agreed that humor could be derived from the misfortunes of others. We liked to drink in large amounts. We went to lame parties, ogled girls, but never scored. One night we drove around wearing Jason masks just to see the horrified looks on the faces of other drivers. I was the Beavis to his Butt-head, had those two moved on to alternative music. Our rationale for coming to England was similar too: We wanted to drink heavily in another country.[83] But something entirely personal was fueling my first trip abroad: I needed to conduct three distinct pilgrimages. They were, in order of importance: 1) to find the grave of Ian Curtis;[84] 2) to stand in front of the Salford Lads Club, outside of which the Smiths memorably posed in a photo taken for the sleeve of *The Queen Is Dead*; and 3) to see the interior of the Hacienda, the club owned by New Order. Oh, I had other goals in England: to drink my first pint of warm beer (check, taken care of at Heathrow), to snap a photo of Oscar Wilde's home in Chelsea (check, but it came out

[82] For some reason this word has brought to mind the sex-obsessed dancehall rapper Shabba Ranks. Note to self: Seriously consider Shabba Sellers as a name for any future offspring.

[83] To people who have spent a lot of time near Detroit, Canada doesn't count.

[84] Again, wait until the next chapter for my tribute to Joy Division.

fuzzy due to the cheap-ass camera my mom stuck me with), and to make out with a British girl (still not checked off as of this writing). But the Manchester pilgrimages were why my savings account was being depleted.[85]

With our high school friend Steve, an always grinning imp working at an air force base outside Oxford, we drove our teensy rented Vauxhall northward to Manchester. We were already a wreck from a week of alcohol abuse, British cuisine, and one another's company. On top of it—and, yes, this is sacrilege—I'd had enough of BBC Radio, with those chirpy deejays and their spot-on accents, yammering on optimistically about the gloomy weather and playing the same three songs: Betty Boo's "Where Are You Baby?" and trippy remixes of Suzanne Vega's "Tom's Diner" and Sting's "Englishman in New York." I was looking for nonstop wish fulfillment: music by the Cure, Lush, My Bloody Valentine, Ride, and the other British bands I was reading about every other week in *NME* and *Melody Maker*. (I listened hard for *The John Peel Show*[86] but we never seemed to be in the car when it was on.) The foul mood we were all in contributed to my initial reaction to Manchester: That's it? We drove through the ugly, drab, deserted downtown area and I silently fumed. Where was

---

[85] The trip had been funded entirely by a mind-numbing summer job in the car-loan department at a Grand Rapids bank. Advice to youngsters out there: Never work at a bank.

[86] Longtime BBC host Peel, who died in 2004, had more influence on alternative music than he has been given credit for, at least here in America—although the very fact that I view him as an icon despite having never heard his program (or "programme," as the Brits would spell it) suggests that maybe he has received proper credit after all. Nearly every indie musician I revere turned up at his studio, often at the foot of the uphill slope of their career trajectory (e.g., the Cure in 1978, Echo and the Bunnymen in 1979), to record one of his famous Peel Sessions; many of the versions of songs recorded there outshine their album counterparts. My personal favorite (although I have heard maybe only forty of the some two thousand Peel Sessions): Joy Division's second appearance, in 1979, with its unparalleled version of "Love Will Tear Us Apart." One that I'm glad never to have heard: the Farm, post "Groovy Train," in 1991. In fact, the Farm appeared a shocking six times on Peel's show. Nobody's perfect.

the sign saying THE SMITHS WALKING TOUR BEGINS HERE!? Where was the city's version of Mt. Rushmore, featuring the craggy faces of local heroes Ian Curtis, Morrissey, the Buzzcocks' Pete Shelley, and the Fall's Mark E. Smith? I all but needed Johnny Marr, Bernard Sumner, and the Happy Mondays' Shaun Ryder to be waving at us from the middle of a roundabout as we pulled in to town. But as Steve kept driving, looking for the B&B we'd reserved for the night, I noticed that we were on Rusholme Road, and that there were some possible ruffians walking along it. We passed a row of what might have been the "ugly new houses" that Morrissey talked about in "Paint a Vulgar Picture." A directional sign pointed out a road to Macclesfield, where Curtis had lived and died. I saw the gloom. I saw the futility. That was, of course, why I'd come: to see the squalor from which my favorite depressing musicians had sprung. Not only would it allow a glimpse into how they lived their lives, but secrets about their lyrics and music might be revealed only to me just by being there. At the same time, the visit might help to explain why their music was so important to a guy from a comparatively sunny and up-beat part of the world. Just maybe, my heroes were more like me than I could've guessed back home. At the very least, the city felt pleasantly familiar to someone who'd concocted an image of it from afar based solely on photographs, videos, and lyrics. There was beauty amid the colorlessness—or maybe because of it: the way the sunlight breaking through the overcast sky would hit and reflect off black Gothic churches, industrial buildings, and the gray stone town houses. Our spirits brightened considerably when we passed the only Domino's Pizza in northern England. Hungry, tired, and mildly homesick, we hooted in approval despite the consensus that Domino's tasted like cardboard. But the pizza chain, we knew, is a Michigan concern; it seemed perversely uplifting to have come all this way to get a few slices of something we rarely craved when we were at home.

After we'd found the B&B and scarfed the pizza, it was getting late. Actually, it was only seven p.m., but I absolutely had to be the first person in line at the Hacienda, because I am a goon. We hopped into a taxi and soon arrived outside a hulk of a building in an industrial area that resembled a location in a George Romero flick. There was no action at the club whatsoever. Even so, I felt torn by the pull of responsibility to my obsession (i.e., the need to be the first in line) and the camaraderie I owed my friends, who were compelled only by a general urge for good times. The compromise: relocating to a dingy pub across the street, where I could keep an eye on things outside the Hacienda. As we got totally shredded by Boddington's beer, I surmised that the pub had probably been there for years before the Hacienda opened in the early 1980s. Even though it was just across the street from ecstasy central, there were no signs of that culture. In fact, besides some baggy-pantsed kids who later destroyed us at billiards, we were the only people there who looked under forty. When the haggard bartender informed us that there would be an open-mike event later in the evening, I got my first sense that not everyone in Manchester cared about the music the city has produced. Excited, I asked him if anyone at previous open mikes had ever played any Joy Division.[87]

"Who?" he asked.

[87] Okay, apparently I can't wait until the next chapter. I'm writing this on May 18, 2005—an unimportant square on the calendar to almost everyone not born today or who doesn't own a calendar. There are no holidays to celebrate on this date, not even a Secretaries' Day or an equinox. It's just another Wednesday, it would seem, in a decade that no one can figure out how to refer to other than "the first decade of the twenty-first century." (Oh, wait: I am wrong. I just realized that May 18, 2005, is crucial to the people waiting in line to see *Star Wars: Episode III—Revenge of the Sith,* which officially opens at midnight on what is technically tomorrow. Please forgive me. Now put down your plastic Wookiee crossbows.) To at least one music fan, though, this day has considerable significance. Every year since 1989, barring the two times I unforgivably forgot to do so, I have reserved May 18 to remember Ian Curtis, the lead singer of Joy Division, who hung himself on his coatrack sometime in the morning on this date in 1980. Typically, my tribute has involved wearing my now-indecipherable and hole-ridden *Unknown Pleasures* T-shirt and playing any and all Joy Division music in my collection and thinking about what should have been; one year—and

Even so, dreams of local stardom began. In a reverie, I fig-
ured that if the pub had the appropriate instruments, Sauce and
Steve could be coaxed into playing bass and drums, respectively.
Sure, they weren't musically inclined and wouldn't in a million

---

please don't repeat this to anyone—it involved tears, although only a few,
and I had been drinking heavily.

I will admit, though, that May 18 has failed to deliver a heavy emotional payload in recent years. Over the past decade, my annual mental high
five to a fallen hero has gradually become a mere formality, like pouring
malt liquor on the ground and saying, "One for my homey." I still revere Ian
Curtis, but I can't remember now precisely what it was fifteen years ago that
made me lie on my floor and well up, laughably, at the beauty of that melancholy baritone chastening the world from beyond the grave. Today, as unbelievable as this sounds to my ears, is the twenty-fifth anniversary of his
demise. What follows is an account of what happens as I spend the day,
from morning until midnight, sitting at my computer, on my couch, and,
just possibly, in a fetal position in my closet, reflecting on what Curtis and
Joy Division mean to me now.

9:30 a.m.: Damn it. I overslept. I'm ashamed I couldn't wake up earlier
today. But it was tricky getting to sleep. Yesterday I thought a lot about Ian
Curtis in anticipation of today's task, and I carried a predictable unease to
bed with me. It occurred to me that England is six hours ahead of Eastern
time. According to *Touching from a Distance,* the biography by his widow,
Deborah, Curtis killed himself just after dawn on the 18th, which would
translate to around midnight in New York. So I lay there thinking, as I have
so many times before, about his final moments. I wondered if he'd considered other options—a door frame? a rafter?—before deciding to end his life
on a coatrack that reportedly wasn't even tall enough for him to dangle on
without bending his knees. I dredged up a familiar "what if?": He's hanging
there, expecting to die, and then the coatrack breaks; after the pratfall to the
floor, he is so moved with laughter that he decides not to kill himself. As
usual, this progressed to thoughts of the Bizarro World Joy Division, in
which they continue to release music, turning gradually into a keyboard-
heavy new wave band, until they achieve bloated elder-statesmen status;
later, Curtis, silver haired and pudgy, recalls the glory days on a BBC documentary about Joy Division, and his old bandmates jokingly reveal his
foibles, such as a ritual of consuming beef Wellington before every show.
And obviously I thought: It's good that Curtis killed himself after all. But
no, I quickly revised: Maybe Joy Division would have gotten even better
and fostered world peace. It wasn't until I thought about a rope squeezing

years get up on a stage without the prospect of money or naked ladies being involved. But their participation didn't matter, really, because all twenty wrinkly Mancunian eyes in the room would be fixed on me. Just before college my mom had bought me that

---

my own neck—not causing pain but euphoria, as I have heard is possible during strangulation—that I was content enough to fall asleep.

9:45 a.m.: The Sellers Notes for the uninitiated (which can be put to the tune of Falco's "Rock Me Amadeus," if you are punch-drunk enough): Ian Curtis is born in 1956 in Macclesfield, England, a small town outside of Manchester. In early 1977, with bassist Peter Hook and guitarist Bernard Sumner, both from Manchester, he forms a band called Warsaw; they recruit drummer Stephen Morris a few months further on and change their name to Joy Division in 1978. Joy Division records only two albums: *Unknown Pleasures,* released in June 1979, and *Closer,* released the following summer. Curtis kills himself at the age of twenty-three in his Macclesfield home, two months before the release of *Closer* and on the same day that the band is to fly to America for its first overseas tour. The surviving members, plus keyboardist Gillian Gilbert, meander on, at first morosely, kicking at pebbles, and then exuberantly as New Order—which, as you may recall, I discover through an unrequited crush at the end of my senior year of high school in 1988. That fall, during my freshman year at Michigan State University, my far more tapped-in dorm-hall neighbor Phil, probably disdainful of my repeated blasting of New Order's *Substance,* forcibly loans me the Joy Division companion compilation, also entitled *Substance.* An obsession is born. Rock me, Ian Curtis, Ian Curtis, Ian Curtisssss!

10:00 a.m.: I turn on and crank up *Unknown Pleasures,* an album I haven't listened to in its entirety since the late 1990s despite the fact that, for the umpteenth time, I've dug out my ratty T-shirt bearing its striking white-on-black cover image, composed as all Joy Division and New Order releases are by graphic design god Peter Saville, of radio waves from a pulsar. (Those jagged lines are not a mountain range, as they are sometimes mistaken to be.) The band's debut is the appropriate album to begin this day, of course, and I am pulled back to my late teens by the very first song, "Disorder," which could serve as the prototype for the Joy Division sound: a peppy, echoed drumbeat, an urgent bass line, and a simple, powerful guitar riff jamming under Curtis's haunting voice and confoundingly poetic lyrics. It's a perfect song in every single way that such things are judged. But it is "Insight," the fourth track on the album, that gives me hope of remembering what Curtis meant to me when I needed him most. "Guess your dreams always end," he croons softly over Hook's sad, meandering bass, and later

cheap Fender knockoff, and my first task upon getting into Joy Division was to learn as many of their songs as possible, if only because they weren't at all complicated. It was decided: I'd wail

---

adds, "I've lost the will to want more." Whoa. I remember communing with this song during a walk around Ann Arbor and realizing that I didn't have any dreams, other than silly ones like winning the lottery, playing third base for the Detroit Tigers, or holding the hand of that curvy brunette alterna-clerk at Wherehouse Records. This made me felt puny, which of course I was. It wasn't the first time a song had made me consider the world in a different way, but I reacted as if it were. I swore fealty to it forever, and hearing "Insight" now, I know that I would die defending the song—unless the challenge involved water torture. I'd cave if subjected to that.

As *Unknown Pleasures* plays to completion—I'll address "New Dawn Fades" and its other important songs elsewhere—I'm floored by simple nostalgia, the beauty to be found in something so bleak, and my dismay that it doesn't hold up as well as I'd imagined it would back when I'd pledged allegiance to it. I notice, maybe for the first time, that it's quite possibly overproduced, although saying that is a slight to Martin Hannett, the slave-driving lunatic genius who recorded most of Joy Division's music and helped coax the all-important ethereal component out of their savage, cacophonous, punk-influenced onstage persona. Even so, *Unknown Pleasures* is so familiar and comforting that listening to it is like returning to one of the houses I grew up in. Despite the obvious flaws, I feel guilty disparaging it.

11:32 a.m.: Mount St. Helens erupted twenty-five years ago, Pacific time. When I was twenty or twenty-three and learned of this fact, there was no doubt in my mind that the volcano exploded to protest the death of Curtis. Now I think it was just a coincidence that the two events occurred on the same day. Maybe.

12:12 p.m.: I'm a little disappointed I'm not feeling more depressed about Curtis's demise right now. After all, his is the one rock 'n' roll suicide that has ever truly affected me. Kurt Cobain's happened when I was twenty-three, my first year out of college, my craziest year, when nothing could spoil my desire to get drunk and have fun and become successful, not even the death of a musician who was a lot more inspiring than I gave him credit for at the time. That tragedy angered me more than anything else. I was mad that Courtney Love read, and added whiny asides to, his suicide note over a loudspeaker to those tearful fans who'd set up a vigil outside their suburban Seattle home. I was mad that MTV broadcast such a humiliating scene. I was mad that the media made the suicide seem as if the leader of my generation had died. The fact that I would never again hear any new Kurt Cobain

on "Shadowplay" or "Dead Souls" while singing exactly like Ian
Curtis, and the whole pub would recognize me for what I was:
the coolest guy on the planet. Then it hit me that I didn't know

---

music didn't hit me until many years later, when the excellence of Nirvana
had been magnified a hundredfold by an unending parade of worthless
grunge bands. It might also have been the case that Cobain was too famous
for me to have got grossly morose over his death. The premature demise of
an unsung celebrity is a far more romantic notion, probably because you
feel like you're the only one left to carry on the memory. This is likely why I
feel a kinship with the comparatively small group of torchbearers who sincerely miss Elliott Smith, who killed himself—or was it murder?—with a
kitchen knife in 2003. I can't claim to be a fan of his music, but I am a fan of
Elliott Smith. It just seemed like, despite his bizarre Oscar nomination, he
was a guy you might see standing quietly underneath a hanging fern at a
friend's party (and when I read in one of his obituaries that he drank and
wrote at the wonderful O'Connor's bar right near my apartment, this sentiment was further confirmed). That a larger group of people didn't discover
his music when he was alive made his death seem all the more sad.

I was too unattached to his music to consider Smith's suicide the end of
the world, however, and in fact I wrote it off, perhaps wrongly, as being just
one of those things that happen. But Curtis's suicide has always felt mythi-
cal, mainly because it happened so many years before I knew who he was.
When my friend Phil handed me the *Substance* tape, he said only that this
was the band that later became New Order after its singer, Ian Curtis, hung
himself. He told me nothing else about Joy Division, and because of that introduction, suicide is irrevocably tied to my perception of the band's music.
I have never heard one of their songs without knowing that the lyrics were
written by a man who killed himself. And this makes a big difference. In
those early days of listening to Joy Division, I would hear certain lyrics
("Strain, take this strain . . .") and construct fables from them about his
personal life: a miserable, solitary person, always dressed in earth tones, a
perpetual bummer. But I didn't really know. No one did. There was no Internet. There were no box sets with sixty-four pages of biographical liner
notes. There seemed to be very few people in the state of Michigan who
seemed to care much about him at all. It would have been wiser to maintain
the myth, I now believe, to have restrained from devouring the information
about Curtis's life as it became available. The basics that all fans knew
about him only helped the legend: He was an epileptic, he had an intense
stage presence, he hung himself. But the more I found out about him, the
more earthbound he became. I wish I didn't know, for instance, that in the
months before his suicide, Curtis had become torn between his wife and a

how to sing and play guitar at the same time. And that the pub almost certainly wouldn't have a guitar. And that I suffered from chronic stage fright. It was in this way that I was spared an unbelievable amount of public humiliation.

Belgian Yoko named Annik. That his wife filed for divorce against him shortly before he died. That he voted Conservative. That he was afraid to fly. These things helped to turn Curtis into a man who lives down the street.

1:33 p.m.: I am enjoying a ceremonial bowl of mopey Joy Division lentil soup. Ian Curtis probably wouldn't have wanted it this way, but what the heck—he's dead and I'm hungry. So tasty.

1:50 p.m.: If you somehow can avoid all of the biographies, articles, tributes, and the uneven movie *24 Hour Party People* and take only the music into consideration, Ian Curtis's artistic output, in terms of quantity, is quite slim. It's roughly fifty songs (forty-one by my cursory iTunes count, but I don't currently own a few songs that he recorded when the band was called Warsaw because they are terrible). The best idea you'd be able to get for what Curtis was like as a living, breathing person is by watching *Here Are the Young Men,* the 1982 Factory Records video featuring various live Joy Division performances, mostly from October 1979. What you'll see is a guy who threw himself so completely into a performance that it borders on being difficult to watch. During the chaotic thrash of "Dead Souls," for instance, Curtis skitters backward and forward at the microphone and flails his forearms around violently, as if he were a kangaroo on a leash. He has a completely blank stare. And he's doing this while wearing pleated slacks and a tucked-in, buttoned-way-up maroon shirt. He doesn't look cool at all, which of course makes him insanely, bizarrely, scarily cool, like a David Lynch character.

There are two other ways to get a sense of who Curtis was. First, a 2000 retrospective of the band's radio performances includes a three-minute interview with him and drummer Stephen Morris that aired on the BBC in August 1979. As Joy Division was notoriously media shy, hearing even an interview this short is a touch shocking. It's hard to tell which of the two voices is his, so it's impossible to quote him with confidence, but I think Curtis, in a polite Mancunian lilt, responds to a very tame question thus: "When you start a band, it's everybody's wild ambition to be the next Beatles or something like that." But then again, that might have been Morris. Either way: I don't like it.

You can also catch Curtis being himself in between songs on the three or four live recordings that have been officially released. On *Still,* the posthumous compilation of unreleased studio and live material, he says sar-

When we did gain entry into the Hacienda, it was a major disappointment. The interior of the club was too cavernous. In parts, it was pitch black; everywhere else was strafed by confusing bright lights. The deejay was playing trance and house music.

---

donically, "You should hear our version of 'Louie Louie'—whoa!" after the band's off-kilter cover of the Velvet Underground's "Sister Ray." Hilarious! On the 2001 reissue *Live at Preston,* he freaks out at the venue's shoddy equipment, saying that everything is "fucking busted" and that all of the sound is running through the bass amp. "I'd like to apologize for everything," he says slowly, almost tiredly, to the crowd. And then to the band, he directs, "Just play around a little while until the bass is repaired." A little later on, he's had it. "I think everything is falling apart!" he yells. A stern, world-weary taskmaster—that's the Curtis I want! One thing I wish I never heard him say, though, appears on the massive *Heart and Soul* box set before a live version of one of Joy Division's most danceable tracks. Curtis introduces the song by saying, "There are some things you'll never understand . . . 'She's Lost Control.' " That's just kind of dumb.

All of these things added up won't even come close to giving you an idea of what Curtis was like as a person. As the man said himself: There are some things you'll never understand. But the meager amount of primary information does offer up something not unlike an infrared image. Look hard enough at all the blues and the reds and the yellows, and you can discern how alive he really was.

3:07 p.m.: Sensing Curtis watching over me, I run across the street to the deli and purchase two lottery tickets: one for me and one for Ian. I also pick up a four-pack of Boddington's ale. Ian and I will be $14.4 million richer tomorrow, mark my words.

3:37 p.m.: I have always bristled when I hear "Love Will Tear Us Apart" in a public setting. It is undeniably pretty, and that keyboard riff is immensely whistleable, but I get annoyed for two reasons: 1) Most people can name only one Joy Division song, and it is "Love Will Tear Us Apart" (to me, that's like asking someone if he knows any Led Zeppelin and he cites only "Stairway to Heaven"); and 2) the prevailing opinion holds that "Love Will Tear Us Apart" is Joy Division's best song—it is not.

I am listening to the song now and see that what's behind my occasional resentment of it is that it sounds nothing like the rest of Joy Division's catalog. It is an anomaly—a wonderful one, but an outlier all the same. I could point out that Curtis's voice is actually his attempt to emulate Frank Sinatra, or the fact that a keyboard is prominently featured, which, based on a quick calculation, happens in precisely five other Joy Division songs. What

It wasn't what I wanted, although the club certainly can't be accused of false advertisement. But a part of me had hoped for something more like the Korova Milk Bar from *A Clockwork Orange*—a comfortable, trendy place to sit and shoot the shit in

---

I think separates it, really, is the notable lack of loud electric guitar. All narratives about Joy Division, including this one, tend to focus on its lead singer, and that's natural for a few reasons: He committed suicide, he was a little strange, and his bandmates seemed content to step back and let him do his thing. But how about we give it up for the other three guys for a change? Peter Hook—a complete original. He used a pick and played his notes quickly and emphatically; because of this, he's often the band's de facto lead guitarist (witness the chugging riff on "Love Will Tear Us Apart," for example). If I had to estimate, and I do, I'd say 27 percent of the band's success is due to Hook alone—more than his fair share. Stephen Morris (a winsome 2 percent)—solid. He banged on the pots as loudly and frenetically as you needed him to. Bernard Sumner (29 percent)—absolutely wailed on the guitar. Actually, he was horrid, at least technically, and he was easily addled. But I can't even begin to acknowledge my debt to him for giving us that simple, hopeful riff from "Transmission" (and it's safe to say that hundreds of emulous musicians couldn't either). You'd never guess by listening to, say, New Order's synthetic "Round and Round" that, as a power trio, they're pretty damn tight. In fact, I'd take the propulsive "Incubation" over every other rock instrumental I can think of, except maybe the Smiths' "The Draize Train" and Ride's epic "Grasshopper." And of course even without Ian Curtis (42 percent), the other three managed to make something out of their lives. They weren't able to avail themselves, however, of those desperate lyrics and that otherworldly voice, which is why, ultimately, New Order is less interesting. Come to think of it, maybe Curtis should be bumped up to the sixtieth percentile.

5:28 p.m.: Goths. What can I say about goths? I haven't run into that many lately, so I'll have to go back to 1990, when I would see them on Mondays during college at Industrial Night. Seemingly every one of these men and women was dressed in dark clothing and knee-high shit kickers, was wearing caked-on black mascara and red lipstick, was adorned with at least one religious symbol (ankhs were big), and was carrying around an almost liturgical devotion to Malcolm McDowell's anarchic character in Stanley Kubrick's *A Clockwork Orange*. They'd dance to music I'd never bother with out in the real world because it was either too aggressive or too absurdly arty. My Life with the Thrill Kill Kult, Skinny Puppy, Nine Inch Nails, Ministry, Front 242, Meat Beat Manifesto, and other bands that had vaguely spooky names. I absolutely loved to watch the goths work the

our strange dialect while drinking elixirs and listening to adrenalizing music. A few nights earlier in London, we'd had a blast at a massive club up in Camden that was having an indie-music night. People were relatively similar to us there, the vibe was

---

dance floor. (Note: Goths always dance by themselves.) Some would do this move where they'd clasp their hands behind their backs and angle their torsos toward the ground rhythmically while gently shuffling their feet. Others would attempt to bash their way to China by pulverizing the floor with their Doc Marten boots. My favorite part of any Industrial Night was when the goths would start circling one another ominously during a relatively slow part of a song (the verse portion of Ministry's "Stigmata," say), swinging their arms and quite nearly skipping; when the hard, fast part kicked back in (everything else in "Stigmata"), they'd slam repeatedly into one another like dipshits.

Anyway, the reason I'm bringing this up is that every week there were always one or two batches of songs that the deejay played that didn't quite fit the industrial mold—the true goth-music portion of the evening. A typical run might have the clackety first five minutes of "Bela Lugosi's Dead" by Bauhaus followed by a predictably awful Sisters of Mercy song (bathroom break!) followed by Siouxsie & the Banshees' ridiculous "Peek-a-Boo." Inevitably the deejay would play either "She's Lost Control" or "Transmission" (with its chorus of "dance, dance, dance, dance, dance to the radio!"), and, if I'd had enough to drink, I would enter the fray. Initially I didn't think Joy Division fit at all alongside the other bands being played. Now, though, I see why they skirt the fringes of goth culture. Their songs contain just enough of goth music's main ingredients—the pretty, the sad, and the eerie— and "She's Lost Control," with its echoing hammer beat, lyrics about a contorting female, and maudlin bass line featured them in abundance. There's the suicide, of course. But it's probably Curtis's voice that keeps the goths coming back for more. In fact, Curtis would fall fairly close to one of the two antipodes of goth culture: Bauhaus's Peter Murphy, the master of macabre mope (the Cure's Robert Smith, the king of gorgeous mope, is at the other end of the goth spectrum). Goths love Murphy because he was into vamp fashion, used words like "virginal," and would do incredibly theatrical and bizarre things onstage such as physically hanging upside down in front of the microphone like a bat. Curtis was nothing like that, but they had similar odd qualities. Ultimately, Murphy was harsh, morose, and macabre; Curtis was simply harsh and morose. After about a year of mixing with goths, I had warmed to much of their music, especially the beautifully moody Cure albums *Faith* and *Pornography,* which I find myself turning to with increasing regularity again. And to think, the main reason I decided to start going to Industrial Night was to be around women who dressed in black.

relaxed, and we got to watch cute British girls dance to the Pixies and Inspiral Carpets. But at the Hacienda it was ear-splitting techno accompanied by the enthusiastic whistle-blowing of

---

7:00 p.m.: This is *Jeopardy!* Against the spirit of what I'm trying to do, I turn on America's second-favorite game show (I'm kind of an addict) and take some much needed vegging-out time. But even *Jeopardy!* reminds me of something about Joy Division: I remember an episode from a few months ago that, without any explanation from Alex Trebek or acknowledgment from the contestants, featured three categories relating to the band: "Warsaw," "She's Lost Control," and " 'Joy' Division." A fourth might have been "Ian Curtis Rolls over in His Grave." I'll take that one for $200, Alex.

7:37 p.m.: I crack open the first Boddington's. So good!

8:10 p.m.: I crack open the second Boddington's. Even better!

8:13 p.m.: It is now time to play *Closer,* which is arguably Joy Division's finest hour (actually forty-four minutes, nineteen seconds). In college I preferred *Unknown Pleasures*—maybe because it's less discordant and contains "Shadowplay," a song that I learned on my electric guitar and would play loudly and awfully enough to cause neighboring doors to slam. But I probably liked *Unknown Pleasures* more because I heard it first. (Theory: When you fall in love with a band, you tend to elevate the album that made you obsessed with them in the first place above all their other releases.) But eventually I was won over by *Closer.* This is the sound of a band just beginning to near the summit; sadly, they weren't able to continue to the top. It's the final song, "Decades," that sealed Joy Division's—and Curtis's—legacy. You'd be hard pressed to find a weightier closing track on any album ever. Consider further that it's the final song on the final album ever recorded by the band, and it's practically a death march. Over a quiet guitar riff and spry keyboard pattern, Curtis moans over and over, "Where have they been? Where have they been?" His vocals are a six-minute, nine-second sigh.

9:05 p.m.: Boddy's number three. In remembrance of Curtis, I pour a bit of it on the floor of my kitchen. I don't like messes, though, so I wipe it up immediately.

9:12 p.m.: I put on *Still* and proceed to the first of two songs—taken from Joy Division's final concert on May 2, 1980—that kill me every time. "Ceremony" was powerful when I knew it only as a New Order single. But the live version on *Still,* with Ian Curtis rightfully on vocals, has always been mildly painful for me to listen to because it hints at how good Joy Division might have become had Curtis stayed alive, especially when he yells, "Oh,

some tranced-out, prancing boob in balloon pants and a neon tank top.

There were also no sightings of the members of the Stone

I'll break them all, no mercy shown!" above the fury that the band played with. And then it's once again to "New Dawn Fades." This song originally appeared on *Unknown Pleasures,* but its true menace is unleashed live. I've turned to this song more than any other in times of despair, primarily for the second verse (starting at 1:36 into the song and ending at 2:48). Over a descending bass riff that sounds as if Hook is headed into the mausoleum, and a guitar strum that suddenly wakes up in anger, Curtis bellows, "This strain's too much, can't take much more!" Even after hearing this for maybe the thousandth time now, I still can't believe that someone is using his voice to make this extreme a noise. Curtis finishes the depressing tale (in the first verse he'd already said, "A loaded gun won't set you free, so they say") by pleading for "something more." Maybe he found it two weeks later.

10:53 p.m.: It's getting late now, and to be honest, this has been getting progressively more difficult since I opened that first Boddington's. Maybe this account will prove that I love Joy Division as much as anyone in the world. Who else would do something like this? (And the thing is: I would do it again—gladly.) But as I sit here drinking my final beer, my thoughts return to that trip to England in 1990. Heading out of Manchester, I'd talked my friends into driving an hour out of the way to Macclesfield because of a searing desire to see Ian Curtis's gravestone, to prove that I cared. I had no proof that he was buried in Macclesfield; it was just an educated hunch based on where he'd hung himself. I figured, at the very least, I could see where he was born, lived, and died. The town itself has fled from my memory, but I do remember asking a broad-faced local manning a chippie van if he knew where Curtis was buried. He replied, in a thick accent I had considerable trouble understanding, that he didn't know the answer to that, but that he was acquainted with Deborah Curtis. "She lives just up the street there," he said, gesturing. "Eats here from time to time." I had no intention of intruding on Curtis's widow, nor did I have any intention of carrying on a futile search at my friends' further expense. I bought some chips and returned to the Vauxhall, and my friends were more than happy to hear that my pilgrimage was over. But on the road out of town, we passed a cemetery and I became far too excited for the size of car we were in. But the graveyard was too immense. No caretaker was around to ask. We had to drive on.

11:37 p.m.: It just took me all of two minutes and twenty-four seconds of Web browsing to find a site with a map detailing how to get to Curtis's Macclesfield grave site. (Actually he was cremated, so it's merely a memorial stone.) It turns out that we'd had the right cemetery after all.

Roses or the Happy Mondays. As much as I'd resisted, those bands had sucked me in a few months prior to the trip, after a few airings of their videos on *120 Minutes*. Initially I was annoyed by the one for the Stone Roses' "I Wanna Be Adored." With crinkled nose I thought, *Who the hell does this guy think he is, this singer who looks like Mickey Dolenz of the Monkees and who is wearing a silly Aztec print shirt and flared jeans? He's not even singing into the microphone in his hand!* But after seeing the video a few more times, and upon first listen of their eponymous debut album, I began to consider them the new Smiths. Which has always been a fun game to play over the years. In 1990 alone there were two other bands I referred to as the new Smiths: the Ocean Blue and the Sundays. Later it was the La's and Belle & Sebastian, and currently it is the Shins. But of course, there will never be a new Smiths. I initially preferred the Stone Roses to the Happy Mondays even though the latter was on legendary Factory Records and had at one time been produced by Martin Hannett, who'd helmed both Joy Division studio albums.[88] John Squire, the Roses' guitarist, had a unique sound. And by that I mean that he had managed to reinterpret the Byrds and Donovan via Johnny Marr and Will Sergeant from Echo and the Bunnymen more adeptly than any of the other 1960s-music-inflected English bands kicking around in the late 1980s and early '90s. With his guitar churning out immensely catchy psychedelic riffs and solos, the songs on that first album were electrifying, even if Ian Brown's indistinct vocals and schoolboy lyrics ("I'm no clown, I won't back down/I don't need you to tell me what's going down") threatened to ground them. In recent years, I have been surprised to find that the gems on that album—"I Am the Resurrection" and "Made of Stone"—have held up better than I thought they would in, say, 1994, when the Stone Roses finally

---

[88] Hannett had once produced the Stone Roses too, but only an early single. In the Roses' favor: Peter Hook of Joy Division and New Order produced "Elephant Stone," although it is among the wimpier tracks on the album.

issued their long-delayed and entirely soul-crushing follow-up, *Second Coming*. The layoff was too long, the ideas spread too thin. Forget what I said a few chapters back about *Hysteria* being the most disappointing album of all time. That dubious honor goes to *Second Coming*.[89]

The Happy Mondays didn't seem nearly as capable musically. Shaun Ryder, the crooked-nosed singer and chief instigator of the band's E'd-out-of-their-gourds public persona, enunciated poorly, had a gravelly voice, and sang off-key and out of time. The band's only assets, in fact, seemed to be infectious grooves and unbridled cockiness—two elements of rock 'n' roll that I have always been fine without. Oh yeah, and they had freaky dancer and spastic maraca player Bez. What a ridiculous concept![90] But the terrible catchiness of "Step On" got to me, and not only because when it was played at the club in Camden, every beautiful girl in the place went berserk. A man has to give in to a song like that, even if it is mildly repetitive and its singer can't even be bothered to whistle correctly. When another single, "Kinky Afro," and the album *Pills 'n' Thrills and Bellyaches* arrived shortly after our arrival back in the States, the Happy Mondays moved into heavy rotation. In a sad attempt at relevance, my exuberance over their and the Stone Roses' music moved me to pull the trigger on two flower-printed shirts and a pair of baggy Jean Paul Gaultier jeans at Urban Outfitters. Retroactively embarrassing to the extreme. But that punishing memory is a mere slap on the wrist compared to what might have happened

[89] This verdict should be backed up with a full list. See Appendix A.

[90] The following spring, Sauce and I carpooled with friends to Detroit to see the Happy Mondays. Drunk out of my tree and concerned about getting to the show in time, I hopped out of the car at a stoplight and ran across Woodward Avenue, the busiest street in Michigan, to ask a police officer how to get to the club. Somehow not killed or arrested, we missed half the show but worked our way up front anyway, where Sauce flipped off Bez for the entire length of "Grandbag's Funeral." Bez chucked one of his maracas at Sauce and nearly scored a hit in the left temple.

had I elected to accept Jesus Jones as my musical savior, like so
many of my peers had. I got off easy.

While scouring the Hacienda in hopes of finding a secret second dance floor that showcased only music by Manchester
bands, I began to feel bad. Physically. I had been scared of it happening since that first Boddington's had mixed with the lump of
consumed Domino's pizza in my stomach. It was clear that if action wasn't taken immediately, my jeans would be subjected to
an eruption rivaling that of Krakatoa. My strictest guideline in
life is to use public restrooms [91] as infrequently as possible for the
kind of business I needed to attend to. But leaving the Hacienda
before seeing how the night played out was hardly an option; my
fate was sealed. I entered what must have been England's small-
est, most crowded, and smelliest toilet since the Middle Ages and
took up residence in one of its two stalls. [92] Twenty minutes later I
emerged, sweaty and fatigued and a bit light-headed, but wholly
confident that my Hacienda pilgrimage story would trump anyone else's.

❖

To my eternal regret, the Salford Lads Club didn't feel like a necessary destination upon waking the next afternoon. I didn't even
bring up the idea to Sauce and Steve. Instead we stumbled
through a mall, hit a few more pubs, and spent more time than
we should have at the B&B taking naps. Almost immediately
after leaving the city, of course, it dawned on me that I'd failed
the Smiths. As they did for so many other people, the band meant
more to me, as the Morrissey lyric goes, than any living thing on
earth. I certainly cared more about them than New Order, the
Stone Roses, or the Happy Mondays—why the snub? Part of the
problem was that on the way into town we'd passed the Holy

[91] Funny word we'd started to call them: loos.
[92] All public restrooms should be required by law to have an odd number of stalls. At minimum, this allows for every-other-seat placement, crucial to maintaining a modicum of dignity.

Name Church, name-checked in "Vicar in a Tutu," and I'd snapped a photo of it, and that had seemed close enough. I was wrong.

Morrissey himself understood the importance of the pilgrimage. In his video for "Suedehead," he'd made one of his own, to Fairmont, Indiana—James Dean's hometown. The images of Morrissey driving a tractor, playing bongos amid cud-chewing cows, and reading James Whitcomb Riley in a hayloft are among the most rewarding in the entire Smiths canon. (My favorite: Johnny Marr showing Morrissey how to finger a guitar chord in the video for "How Soon Is Now?") That I didn't make more of an effort to have a proper take-home memory has always been a nagging source of shame: I cannot engage in Smiths pilgrimage braggadocio, other than the Holy Name Church sighting, and, let's face it, the song "Vicar in a Tutu" isn't exactly a fan favorite.

Then again, the Smiths shouldn't have been on my radar at all. The video for "Stop Me if You Think You've Heard This One Before," released during my senior year of high school, had quickly been written off as both unwatchable and unlistenable: this underfed, whiny, awkward, bespectacled guy in a cardigan pedaling around some dreary town on a bicycle that had a basket, with a bunch of scrawny, smiling lookalikes following in his wake. His moaning vocals: worse than a vomiting cat. That "Stop Me" had become one of my favorites just a year later illustrates a paradox in one's discovery of music: First you're outside a phenomenon and want it that way; the next thing you know, you're inside and shocked when people don't get it.

Even though I probably didn't deserve the invitation, being converted into a Smiths fan with the help of my freshman floor's resident alt-music know-it-all was a turning point in my life. This is not at all a unique sentiment, but Morrissey and Marr got me through college. I wasn't clinically depressed, at least not in a *Bell Jar* sort of way. But on nights when things weren't going right, I would lie on the floor of my room and think up ways to die: via a bear, confused and annoyed about being in a human's apartment, nosing open the door to my room and eating me alive; by a simple nail, propelled by an unseen and souped-up Black & Decker gun, flying through my window and piercing my right eyeball; or via my preferred form of suicide, kneeling in front of a train. Walking around campus, I would stage "Who's more depressed?" wars in my head. Seeing a mopey girl on the street would cause me to say to myself, "Oh, she thinks she's depressed. But, come on, I'm *really* depressed. And I can prove it!" The thing is, I couldn't. No one I knew had died. Enough people liked me. I had no serious medical issues. But when these depressive spells struck, which they did with the hushed certainty of an ice storm, it was almost a comfort: At least something interesting was happening. There was nothing for it but to sit in my room and play the absolute most depressing music in my collection and give in to the wallowing. Much of this music was culled from the Smiths catalog. Like most converts, I felt that Morrissey was speaking directly to me. Like him I, too, felt utterly out of step with the planet. Communicating with my peers on a meaningful level had always been difficult, possibly because the members of my family and the guys I hung out with, most notably Sauce, weren't big talkers. (My friends back then were very good at hooting and hollering, but they were the surface dwellers of conversation.) My incommunicativeness did not help me with the fairer sex, and it could be argued that it was from this perpetual lack of female contact that the brief bouts with depression originated. I was able to warm to such a foreign concept as Morrissey because he was offering up his worldview without filtering it through imprecise, emotive imagery like most lyricists. The guy had mastered the English language; my awkward existence needed to be addressed with earnestness, pettiness, spite, and wit, and Morrissey delivered on all four counts. I could whip out a lyric to solve any quandary or confirm any suspicion: "I've seen this happen in other people's lives/Now it's happening in mine"; "I wear black on the outside/Because black is how I feel on the inside"; "What makes most people feel happy/Leads us headlong into harm"; "Life is very long when you're lonely"; "I had a really bad dream/It lasted twenty years, seven months, and twenty-seven days"; etc. And these bon mots were accompanied by the perfect foil: Marr's signature, often jangly guitar swirl. As it has been for so many other lonely, desirous, self-pitying people, the song "How Soon Is Now?" was a double-edged dagger to the gut: Could there be a more painfully appropriate way to sum up one's blight of a Friday or Saturday night than the line "And you go home and you cry/And you want to die," and a better backdrop than Marr's masterpiece? But if I had to choose the song that summed up what the Smiths meant to me in my darkest hour, it was the one that began and ended like this: "Oh Mother, I can feel the soil falling over my head."

In *High Fidelity*, Nick Hornby's protagonist asks, "Did I listen to the music because I was miserable? Or was I miserable because I listened to the music?" During that period of my life, the answer to both questions was the same: yes.

But in my senior year (which turned out to be the first of two senior years) I had to get away from Morrissey and the Smiths. There was no time to spare on depression. Instead I threw myself into bands that conveyed their ideas with ironic lyrics or abrasive guitars or both—Soundgarden, Dinosaur Jr., Sonic Youth, and others that were rarely if ever maudlin. In fact, I even began to resent Morrissey's lyrics, and by extension Morrissey himself, for ever having had the power to floor me. When I did pick the Smiths back up again nearly a decade later, after a breakup (some things will always call for Morrissey), I knew that I'd never drop them again. Morrissey's lyrics from the 1980s are, when all else fails, still hilarious; Marr's guitar work is still an unreplicable mystery. In fact, Morrissey and Marr were the ultimate duo— take one away from the other, and he doesn't sound as good.[93]

Which is another reason why I ignored them for all those years. I don't like what's happened to these two people in the

---

[93] Oran "Juice" Jones: "You without me is like the cornflake without the milk."

years since the Smiths broke up.[94] So much was expected of them and so little has been delivered. Morrissey, for obvious reasons, has had the easier route: He was the face of the band, has that languid voice, and is the most concise lyricist in the history of pop music. He could have kept projecting his viewpoint at a high level of quality so long as he hooked up with the right collaborators. And he did, initially. Stephen Street, who coproduced the Smiths' final album, *Strangeways, Here We Come,* wrote the music that appeared the following year on Morrissey's solo debut, *Viva Hate.* He was the behind-the-scenes, low-profile collaborator that Morrissey needed, the Bernie Taupin to Moz's Elton John. Some of the tracks on *Viva Hate* are as complex and lovely as anything Marr ever wrote, and Morrissey seemed particularly inspired. It's hard to find a funnier, more self-deprecating lyric than on "Late Night, Maudlin Street," when he growls, "Me without clothes/Well, a nation turns its back and gags."

But he chose to ditch Street and part company with Rourke and Joyce, who, among other post-Smiths tasks, had played on and appeared in the video for the 1989 single "Last of the Famous International Playboys." Fine. I can understand wanting a fresh start. But why seek out collaborators with lesser talent? The Lads, as his new, youthful backing bandmates were dubbed almost immediately by the Morrissey faithful, are rightly beloved and have always performed their jobs more than capably. They add value. However, the creative prowess of Morrissey's longtime songwriting partners, Alain Whyte and Boz Boorer, just doesn't compare with Street's, let alone Marr's. Their glammy, hard-driving *Your Arsenal,* Morrissey's third solo album, a follow-up to the unbelievably dull *Kill Uncle* (another candidate for

[94] Mike Joyce and Andy Rourke get a free pass. Joyce deserves the royalty money he was granted in that nasty 1996 legal battle, and Rourke should have received his fair share as well. After all, they were full members of the band, and any replacements would have been cursorily dismissed by any true Smiths fan.

the most disappointing album ever), is considered by many to be among Morrissey's finest moments, solo or otherwise. Please. Maybe diehards regard the album so highly because they're comparing it to *Kill Uncle*. Or maybe they've downed the Kool-Aid. "You're the One for Me, Fatty" is just a silly, malnourished song any way you listen to it—and it's the best song on there.

Since his last shining moment, the pretty 1991 single "My Love Life" (cowritten by Mark E. Nevin, who was partly responsible for the *Kill Uncle* fiasco, and who was therefore smartly ditched), Morrissey has put out mostly good (not great) songs featuring good (not great) lyrics. People seemed to go a little too nuts over his 2004 album, *You Are the Quarry,* and I will readily admit to buying it with the hope that it would rekindle my love for solo Morrissey. But the best lyric I can find on it is "Close your eyes and think of someone you physically admire/And let me kiss you." And once again the music isn't addictive enough; in most areas it's boring. I did sigh, though, when he performed "Everyday Is Like Sunday" a few years back on *The Late Late Show with Craig Kilborn,* and felt a twinge of happiness during his 2005 concert film, *Who Put the "M" in Manchester,* when he and the Lads (though, really, no longer true lads at their current ages) trotted out some Smiths songs. And Morrissey still has that anvil-headed charisma. But mostly, hearing him now makes me wistful for how good he used to be.

For Johnny Marr, though, it just isn't working. Around the time that I started getting back into the Smiths, it was announced that Marr had formed a fairly standard five-piece band called Johnny Marr and the Healers. This was an idea that was long overdue. The man got a little session-happy there in the late 1980s and early 1990s, playing with Bryan Ferry, the Talking Heads, the Pretenders, the Pet Shop Boys, Billy Bragg, and Kirsty MacColl, among others. It was a waste of his unparalleled songwriting talent and guitar skill, the equivalent of Willie Mays, baseball's all-time greatest center fielder, deciding to become a full-time designated hitter in the prime of his career. (Theory:

Johnny Marr has become the Steve Vai of indie rock.[95]) Yes, he did have a productive stint in the The; the albums *Mind Bomb* and *Dusk* feature some smooth Marr action. But come on: The The has always been bristly, bald Matt Johnson's band, and everybody knows it.[96] I will say as little as possible about Electronic, the synth-heavy supergroup he formed in 1990 with Bernard Sumner of New Order: I think many alternative-music fans expected Jesus to walk out of the speakers the first time they put that record on, but of course the Son of God did not.

Through it all, Marr has steadfastly maintained that he has no interest in reuniting the Smiths. I might not have a problem if he and Morrissey never got back together, and in sensible moments I think that the Smiths probably shouldn't re-form. Maybe it could work if there was a very heartfelt, very public making-up period. But even then it might feel fakey to see Morrissey and Marr together on stage with all the baggage; it would be like attending a barbecue jointly thrown by the Hatfields and the McCoys. Most musical reunions, after all, are inevitably disappointing. Watching your heroes run through the songs that saved your life is nice in the immediate term. But what you really want is for new magic to happen. In the Smiths' case, you'd want them to hole up and create another masterpiece. But it wouldn't take; the outcome could only tarnish their legacy. The Beatles never reunited, and that worked out quite nicely for them.

Not that Morrissey would ever deign to reassemble the band either, and in 2006 he said, "I would rather eat my own testicles

[95] It was thrilling to learn, after months of listening to P.I.L.'s album *Cassette* (also known as *Album* and *Compact Disc*, depending on the format) during my freshman year, that the squealing notes on "Rise" were the product of Steve Vai, the noodler who also worked with David Lee Roth and Whitesnake. Roth, Coverdale, and John Lydon (aka Johnny Rotten): quite a trio. Vai more recently rocked out on the *Halo 2* score. Maybe Marr should check into video game work.

[96] Marr's obvious contributions to the *Mind Bomb* single "The Beat(en) Generation," though, lifted me. It's the only time Johnny Marr has truly shined, post-Smiths.

than re-form the Smiths—and that's saying something for a veg-etarian." But Marr should consider it realistically. It's not like he's setting the world alight with the Healers. That was obvious from their appearance in New York in 2004. Music aside, the concert was plain bad. The truth is that Marr isn't cut out to be a front man. First of all, he was chewing gum, which would be fine, barely, if he was just playing guitar, but in the Healers he also sings. Also, the band was very late to the show, which only be-came an issue when he didn't acknowledge that fact, and in gen-eral didn't speak to the audience at all. The house was packed, too, and it was likely filled with fans just like me, hoping against hope that Marr would make some reference, musical or other-wise, to the band he was formerly in. That's unfair to him and his new project, of course, but really: Get over it, Johnny. A single reference to his old band would have wowed everyone in the room and, by the way, would have greatly endeared the ticket-buying horde to the Healers. Or maybe not. The music was, to put it mildly, uninspired and even embarrassing, considering the source. None of his lyrics stuck out as being awful; none stuck out at all. His voice wasn't dynamic; it was whiny. A few of the songs sounded like Oasis. That was sad: emulating a band that emulates the Smiths.[97] But all of these transgressions would have been forgiven by everyone in the room had he done either of two logical things: 1) launched into his raucous 1986 instrumental "The Draize Train"—and this would have been fine because Morrissey didn't cowrite that song; or 2) played a supremely ca-pable cover of a Morrissey tune, possibly "Suedehead," as both a publicity tool and a demonstration of why Morrissey is worse off without him. Instead, all he accomplished that night, and pre-sumably every night on that tour, was to alienate a very sympa-thetic fan base. My friends and I were so crestfallen afterward

[97] And now Marr's gone and joined Modest Mouse. Egad. Not that Modest Mouse sucks or anything, but this is a bit like Olivier doing summer stock. Well, hopefully he's happy.

that we went to a bar, punched *The Queen Is Dead* into the juke-box, and bitched into our beers.

And yet I have hope that everything will turn out all right for everyone involved. Isn't it weird that two of your heroes can repeatedly disappoint you for more than a decade and you can still pull for them? It's almost like they are, in the end, your friends or members of your family. You might sometimes show them tough love, but overall you'll cut them a lot of slack. Electronic kind of slack. "Glamorous Glue" kind of slack. Sometimes, when I'm not thinking clearly, it occurs to me that they are bound to reconcile. One of these days, maybe soon, Morrissey will wake up and decide that it's time to ditch the non-Marrs he's been hanging with for the past twenty years; Marr will decide to spit out all of those non-Morrisseys (and the gum, please); and it'll just happen. I hope the first reunion concert is in Manchester.

8

GOLD SOUNDZ

"So drunk in the August sun."

In April 1992, I graduated from college in the worst possible way: as a possessor of a bachelor's degree in business administration. That's right. A guy who liked the literate music of the Smiths and Joy Division, who rocked out to decidely uncorporate bands like the Jesus and Mary Chain and the Replacements, and who had an intense lack of interest in supply-side theory and the behavior of organizations somehow emerged from the fog of college holding a diploma as if it were someone else's soiled underwear. And suits! I'm mystified that I had failed to consider at the onset of those two years of torture by Excel spreadsheet that business school could only end with the beginning of a very long life of suit wearing. I didn't like how I looked in suits, felt like a liar, wriggled through weddings and interviews in them, had to have my roommate tie my tie because it didn't interest me to learn how to do so myself. Near the end of that two-year sentence, I was telling anyone who couldn't have known otherwise that my major was comparative literature. I stuck it out in business school so as not to feel like a failure—which, of course, was its own sad failure. I should have bailed after that first Finance 101 lecture during which my Israeli professor repeatedly mangled the pronunciation of the words "zero coupon bond." What I did instead was use any elective space to figure out what I was missing: Italian, creative writing, Shakespeare, poetry. A few months before graduation, with only a single interview lined up and no interest in angling for more, my only option was to start over.

I didn't know it when I made the decision to return to school
as an English major, but my life was also in need of a new soundtrack. I'd gotten a lot of mileage out of the songs that had ushered
me through high school and the first four years of college—and
look where they'd got me. As previously mentioned, the lyrics of
Morrissey had ceased to have their former impact. I still winced
or nodded when I heard him singing, "I wear black on the out-
side/Because black is how I feel on the inside." But I no longer
wore black on the outside because I felt black on the inside; I wore
the color because a new wardrobe was too expensive. Listening to
the Smiths, Joy Division, the Cure, New Order, and U2 was like
trying to get one more wash out of a favorite concert T-shirt.

I tried and failed to latch on to grunge. The bands that made
up the genre—particularly Pearl Jam, but also its other heavy hit-
ters Alice in Chains, Soundgarden, and Nirvana—seemed to be
the province of backward-hat wearers. While they brought an
acceptable amount of guitar noise, the music itself seemed almost
cliché, mere rehashes of Led Zeppelin or Black Sabbath or the
Sex Pistols. I'd already done hard time with those seminal bands,
so it seemed okay to tune the newcomers out. Not that they
could be ignored altogether; you couldn't go anywhere in 1992
without hearing about Eddie Vedder doing this or Kurt Cobain
doing that. In fact—and I know this is shallow—I snubbed them
partly because of the hype. Due to exhaustion for hype, I no
longer felt compelled to listen to the things a person my age was
being told to listen to. Besides, I was listening predominantly to
shoegazing bands—Lush,[98] Curve,[99] My Bloody Valentine, and

---

[98] Ah, the double-barreled beauty of Emma Anderson and Miki
Berenyi. This is shameful, but at the 1992 Lush show in Detroit, I wormed
my way up to the front row and spent three songs trying to look up their
skirts. Soon the mosh pit behind me became too concussive and a retreat to
a safer region of the venue was necessary. Once again the snow flurries of
their interlocking guitars and vocals could be enjoyed without the annoyance of getting soaked in other people's sweat.

[99] Besides Anderson and Berenyi, two indie rockers battled it out in my
mind for Sexiest Hot Female Vocalist Babe: Toni Halliday of Curve and

Swervedriver—and they layered their sound to the point of ob-
fuscation. The lyrics of those favored bands were often impossible to decipher, and it fit a phase I was in. Lyrics had been getting
in the way because they further cluttered up my head. I required
complex, pretty, inscrutable songs turned up very loud to help
me avoid thinking that I didn't like myself very much.

❖

You read a lot about love at first sight. Not so much about love at
first listen. And yet it exists. Some sort of chemical interaction is
at play when you listen to music. Pheromones, I think, are coming out of the speakers, causing your body to react in a certain
way. Sometimes negatively. Take, for instance, the case of the
Dave Matthews Band. On paper, there's no real reason why I
should want to barf whenever I hear something from them: Dave
Matthews is young, he's personable, he's clearly more talented
than Richard Marx. Sure, he's got that warbly voice, employs too
much fiddle, and has about the same appeal as me playing a
recorder. But it is still enough to make me wonder: Why should I
want to vomit?

The answer: Dave Matthews has stinky pheromones.

Most artists do, I've found. But just often enough, the chem-
icals turn you on. But love at first listen? That's extremely rare. It
had only happened to me three times prior to 1993: with Kool
and the Gang upon hearing "Celebration" in 1981 (that crush
soured quickly and did not carry over to "Joanna"); with the
Stone Roses the first time I saw "Fool's Gold" on *120 Minutes* in
1990; and in 1991 with Sonic Youth, when I heard, belatedly,
"Schizophrenia." Only that last one has endured through the
years: true love.

Harriet Wheeler of the Sundays. Wheeler won because she was a chipmunk
to whom you might feed leafy greens. But Halliday, a vamp with lovely
cheekbones and baleful eyes, appealed to the frosted side of my Shredded
Wheatness and still does, even though the trampy, cold music of Curve says
nothing to me about my life.

But never before have I experienced a reaction as intense or immediate as I did on a drive down to New Orleans in February 1993. Three friends and I had decided to go to Mardi Gras; being twenty, twenty-one, and twenty-two, we needed to see firsthand if beads could really be exchanged for glimpses of women's bare breasts.[100] It was getting toward late afternoon, a few hours into an overnight drive, when Greg, the guy with the flannel jacket and the long hair, moved to put in a new CD. I was sure it was going to be Neil Young or one of his bleating alt-folk favorites. A protest formed in my brain, but as a denizen of the back seat, that thought was moot. Rule of the Road No. 1: A person not occupying one of the front seats must accept the musical selection of the pilot or copilot without comment. It would be my turn to drive soon and I'd get them back by playing Ride.[101]

For a variety of reasons, most of them relating to actual interest in my studies, my head was clearer. For one thing, I'd stopped indulging in depressing music—as if the depression of the previous four years was a disease in remission. I still occasionally turned to the old standbys, of course, because they were like phone calls home. But increasingly while getting ready in the morning before my literature classes, I was cranking early Sonic Youth and Dinosaur Jr.—two bands whose sophisticated, smart

---

[100] They can!

[101] Ride is maligned now as having been little more than a crew of pretty boys—an incorrect assessment. Sonically they were for a time quite interesting, with 1991's *Nowhere* being the high point. What drew me their way wasn't the floppy hair but their penchant for making a lot of noise, the best of which they'd acidified to the point where it came at you like a cool breeze. The Ride song remembered more than any other is "Vapour Trail," and that shimmering single still holds up despite exposing the group's biggest flaw: effeminate vocals. But iffy vocals aren't a problem on "Grasshopper," Ride's raucous twelve-minute instrumental epic (a B-side on the spectacular "Leave Them All Behind" single), with a crunch of guitar at each end and an echoing, emotive core that builds and builds. It is the ultimate car song, which seems appropriate for a band with a name like Ride. Please reunite.

music was best played at a high decibel level.[102] I was listening to
Buffalo Tom and Teenage Fanclub. There is virtually no chance a
person can get maudlin while listening to these sorts of bands;
they are like Mötley Crüe without libidos.

Those groups roomed with the Pixies in my heart—but I
was tired of the Pixies then. *Surfer Rosa* and *Doolittle* had been
played so often during the previous four years that the brilliant songs on them failed to do much for me anymore. Seeing
the band live, in 1991, was also a letdown: the feuding Black
Francis[103] and Kim Deal[104] did not seem to be enjoying the experience very much, and their animosity floated down to the sixth
row. But you can't give up on a band as perfect as the Pixies without finding a worthy replacement. The problem is, not many
bands can simultaneously melt your eardrums and make you
want to whistle, while also wielding slightly weird and highly
quotable lyrics.

Sitting in the back seat on the way to New Orleans, I heard
the future. After a grinding guitar intro—simple, grumpy, fun—a

---

[102] "Teenage Riot" is the perfect shower song, if you must know.

[103] When Charles Michael Kittridge Thompson IV, aka Black Francis,
changed his stage name to Frank Black when the Pixies broke up in 1993,
my annoyance knew no bounds. Later that same year, Prince reintroduced
himself as a retarded glyph and the media entered that ridiculous era of
referring to him as the Artist Formerly Known as Prince, or TAFKAP.
Memo to difficult "artists": Just pick a name and stick with it, please.
Thank you.

[104] Since I can't seem to restrain myself from discussing the hotness of
indie-rock women in this chapter, probably because I was at my all-time
horniest during my college years, please allow me to address the perplexing
case of Kim Deal. Back in college, my theory, which I unleashed on anyone
with ears, was that she'd actually be bordering on ugly if she wasn't playing
bass in the best band in the world. I was wrong, of course: Her smile alone
put Pixies-era Kim Deal well into the "hot" column, and that's before you
factor in her alluring vocals on "Gigantic" and her sense of humor ("All I
know is he was into field hockey players . . ."). Not that any of this matters.
Hot or not, Kim Deal is the coolest female rock musician ever, just a tick
ahead of PJ Harvey, whose similarly confusing hotness I will not get into at
this juncture.

voice spoke of a girlfriend who's "eating her fingers like they're just another meal." I had no idea what this meant, of course. None of us did. But it was as if I'd been invited into the house of someone I'd never met—a friendly, offbeat person who is offering me a beer and the good seat. The music was a surprise: It sounded like Dinosaur Jr. and Sonic Youth mixed with the Velvet Underground; underneath the blatant lack of polish in the singer's voice there was a mess of furious guitar noise. And then he screamed: "You took it all!"

I had to ask.

"It's this band called Pavement," said Greg.

Another song on the album began with a slow, sad guitar strum and the following statement: "I was dressed for success/ But success it never comes." Lyrics we would all understand eventually.

Every road trip needs a soundtrack. Mardi Gras '93 was all about *Slanted and Enchanted*.

When a new obsession kicks in (it'd been a few years; Ride or My Bloody Valentine, probably), it is a peculiar feeling. You have this sensation that the world is tilting, that the sun is a different shade of bright. It's a mix of feeling discombobulated and exhilarated—a ride with a particularly hellish cabbie. Another way to describe it is an itch that needs to be scratched. When we got back to Ann Arbor, I went to my favorite record store to buy *Slanted and Enchanted*. The "Trigger Cut" single and an EP entitled *Watery, Domestic*, with a painted rooster on its cover, were also gathered up and brought to the register. I asked the clerk if there was any more Pavement to be had. He said that a new compiliation of all of their early stuff would be coming out a few weeks later. Amazing! Just a month after hearing the band for the first time, I would own everything they'd ever released, meaning I would be in on the ground floor of what I now thought was the best new band in the world. That had never happened to me before in all my years as a music fan (and because I am chronically slow on the uptake, it would never happen again).

Watery, Domestic, released in November 1992, was immediately labeled the Greatest EP Ever Made, and it still holds that distinction. I will not take any alternate suggestions from the peanut gallery on this one: I am right and you are wrong. It was played so often in my room in those early days of the obsession that I thought of it as music being made solely with me in mind, as if whoever had written the songs had said, "Hey, guys—John's sick of 'Gigantic,' so let's crank this out and get it to him, pronto," or, "This one will be good for John when he's writing that Hemingway paper." Its four songs are "Texas Never Whispers," which opens with an overly distorted *ta da!* guitar riff before settling into a pleasing march; "Frontwards," pure slacker genius; "Lions (Linden)," a recap of a football game; and "Shoot the Singer (One Sick Verse)," a gem that Greg and I would play very loudly in his room at the tail end of nights out drinking. "Someone took in these pants," sang the voice. "Somebody painted over paint."

It occurs to me—though I wouldn't have thought this at the time, because I cared little about politics then—that there's something nicely coincidental about the fact that Bill Clinton had just been elected when *Watery, Domestic* came out. Here was a president who played saxophone on *Arsenio.* Who told an MTV audience that he wore boxers. Who said he'd never inhaled. Just the question about his marijuana use made him incongruous and refreshing as a politician; these things were not asked of George Bush or H. Ross Perot. Pavement was the right band for this new era. On *Watery, Domestic,* many of the lyrics have a playful, smarter-than-you, smirky quality—as if the singer doesn't think life is that big a deal. It's entirely Clintonian. Pavement's lyricist even riffs on Clinton's famous quote in "Frontwards," when he sings, "Now she's the only one who always inhales." If I had it to do over, I wouldn't have voted for Perot.

❖

I say "lyricist" and "voice" and "singer" above because, until March 20, 1993, about a month into my obsession, I didn't know the names of the men in Pavement, let alone what they looked like. (All three of the guys responsible for *Slanted and Enchanted* are pictured in the album's liner notes, but no IDs go with the photos. The only hints at the band members' names were on the sleeve: S.M., Stairs, Young.) So it was most joyous to see Pavement on the cover of *Melody Maker* that week to coincide with the release of their compilation album *Westing (By Musket and Sextant).* Mugging for the camera in a flannel shirt,[105] the lead singer, whose name turned out to be Stephen Malkmus, looked like this slightly loopy guy in my high school who was a star on our soccer team. Another band member was nondescript in an "I think that guy was in my chemistry class" sort of way. Although his name wasn't mentioned in the article (it was a terribly uninformative article, it must be said, as it assumed that you already knew everything about the band), I deduced that he must be the "Stairs" referred to on the back of the *Slanted* cover. (His full moniker was Spiral Stairs, aka Scott Kannberg, although I was still calling him Scott *Kannenberg* until 2004 because I am a moron.) The third member of the band was wearing a baseball cap and looked about forty; his name was Gary Young. The profile stated that Young did handstands during shows and sometimes made toast for people in the front row. This pleased me.

More press relating to *Westing* told me that there were two other guys in the band, at least for touring purposes: Mark Ibold, a frequently grinning bassist, and Bob Nastanovich, a rambunctious second percussionist. The more I read up on Pavement, the more it became clear that they were a lot like me. Other than Young, the guys were all my age, generally, and college-educated. Decked out in T-shirts, jeans, and unhip haircuts, they looked the same as I did, or people I cared about. They were sort of like a cluster of your friends who had improbably become a viable band—way better than you could have imagined when they

[105] Yes, even Pavement fell prey to flannel. When did that material become extinct? 1997? 1998?

wrote that first song about creatures living in the plumbing of your dorm. That couldn't have been said about Nirvana. I didn't hang out with anyone who had long hair or who was angry at the world or who was fucked up on heroin. As for Dinosaur Jr., the Pixies, Sonic Youth, the Jesus and Mary Chain, and My Bloody Valentine,[106] the members of those bands were considerably older than I was, came from parts of the world I couldn't relate to, and/or seemed unapproachably hip.

[106] It is time to take care of that open letter that should have been written five years ago:

Dear Kevin Shields,
Back in the days when it was customary to handwrite letters, I liked to open with a pointless anecdote, like that story about the time I cut my finger on the serrated lid of a can of cat food and how, as an unexpected result of that accident, I developed a fear of peeling potatoes.

But let's just do away with the pleasantries, shall we?

I think we both know why I'm writing. In 1991, your band, My Bloody Valentine, released *Loveless,* a work of unfettered genius. Your genius, mostly. I'm sure you've heard from other fans about how the album changed their lives, or at least improved their existences a great deal. To do so here would be tiresome to you. It would be old news to tell you that your album helped me get through that second year of business school—the year that I became convinced that my professors were speaking in tongues and that I discovered I was a butterfly collar in a class full of button-downs. I would sit on the floor of my apartment on Walnut Street, my first apartment, blasting your bleary song "Come in Alone" in an attempt to drown out a voice that I was hearing in my head, the prudent one, which was hoping to convince me that getting a job at the corporate headquarters of American Airlines in Dallas wouldn't be that bad. I've always thought it funny when people talk about *Nevermind* being the most important album that came out in 1991. I know which one was more important to me.

But I digress. My intention here is simply to ask: Don't you think it's time, Kevin? I mean, it's been more than fifteen years. Here's what's happened on my end since I last heard from you: I've gone from age twenty-one to thirty-six; I've voted for Perot, Clinton, Gore, and Kerry, only one of whom won, and he was a gimme; I have lived in thirteen different apartments and worked at sixteen different

I'm going to flash-forward eleven years to further my point. That I viewed Pavement as regular guys made it seem totally acceptable to accost Spiral Stairs at a bar in Seattle in early 2004. I

---

places of business, one of which was the game show *Who Wants to Be a Millionaire,* where I wrote 1,308 trivia questions, including one about *Loveless* that never aired: What album did *Spin* magazine name as its Album of the Year in 1991?: A. U2, *Achtung Baby;* B. Nirvana, *Nevermind;* C. Teenage Fanclub, *Bandwagonesque;* D. My Bloody Valentine, *Loveless* (answer: C—I know!); I've drunk roughly twelve thousand beers. In short, stuff has happened, not all of it good or important; in fact, most of it has meant nothing. But at least I've done stuff.

Here's what's happened on your end: ———.

Well, I'm sure that's not true. I bet you've done something. You've probably gone to the supermarket, for instance. I am well aware of the allure of the biscuit. And to be fair, I know you've been up to other, less mundane things. You spent five or so years draining the coffers of, first, Creation Records, nearly bankrupting them (luckily they'd signed Oasis), and then Island Records. At one point Island was reportedly paying you forty thousand pounds a month to produce your follow-up, which means you were receiving forty thousand pounds a month for doing absolutely nothing. Because, as we both know, there has never been a follow-up. After you'd frustrated them long enough for them to dump you from their rolls after a total expense of five hundred thousand pounds, you engineered and remixed a few tracks in your home studio for other musicians (e.g., J Mascis and the Fog, Curve, Yo La Tengo); contributed noise to a piece performed by LaLaLa Human Steps, a Canadian dance company (what the?); and went on tour with Primal Scream as a guitarist for hire. (Primal Scream? That's like Picasso offering his services to the creator of *SpongeBob SquarePants.*) But you released absolutely nothing of your own design until Hollywood came calling in 2003, when you contributed three instrumental trifles and one fleshed-out song (and of course, permission to use "Sometimes," the emotional center of *Loveless*) to the soundtrack of *Lost in Translation.* And then in 2006 you remixed two Bow Wow Wow tracks for use in Sofia Coppola's *Marie Antoinette.* I have no response to that.

I suppose there's little incentive, other than money, for you to put out another album. You're already considered a genius—a reclusive, slow-moving, rumored-to-be-bloated genius. I can see how your legacy might be ruined if you released something of nongenius caliber, you know, like the new stuff you did for *Lost in Translation.* I was out west on assignment to write about a big-budget Microsoft video game; on my last night in town, I went to a cherished bar from a summer spent in the city at the turn of the

---

am aware of how the thinking goes if the album were to tank: Well, maybe *Loveless* wasn't as amazing as we thought after all; maybe he just got lucky. The best example I can think of here is the Stone Roses, who released what a lot of people considered to be a gem in 1989, and then, after five years of nothing, returned with *Second Coming*. It was unutterably horrible. It made you wonder what the hell they were doing in those five years they weren't putting out music. Going to Ibiza? Hanging with Bez? It made you reconsider if they were ever good in the first place. And I suppose if you put out an album now, it would be regarded in the same way that something new from Salinger would be: It could only disappoint, because the expectation would be too high. Maybe it was better to quit at the top of your game, after all.

But you know what? Fuck that. I'd rather have a whole lot of stinky noise from you than endless nonsense coming from the direction of Moby. And anyway, I'm convinced that whatever you'd release wouldn't be terrible. It might feel dated, maybe, but it couldn't possibly be bad. Case in point: "City Girl," the only original song you've given to Sofia Coppola that has lyrics, sounds like something you might have written in 1990, and maybe you did. Even though no one would consider it your best work, it's decent stuff. I think we'd all love to hear more like that.

Here might be a good place to tell you that I went through a phase a few years back during which I described you as the Doug Henning of indie rock. I just got to thinking that all of these years of no Kevin Shields had to be an illusion. Or an ill-*ooo*-sion, as Henning used to say. I mean, you were at the height of your power. You could have done anything—hung out with Johnny Cash, ordered hookers like some people graze from minibars. Instead you chose to disappear. What chumps we were, buying your albums and falling in love with that way you'd layer a seemingly infinite number of sounds on top of each other, a rare example in rock music of addition by addition. What dupes we were to buy all the singles, especially "Tremolo," which contains one of my favorite lesser-known MBV tracks on it, "Honey Power," with its swirly, seesaw guitar action. And for latching on to all the shoegazing bands that rose up around you in the late 1980s, based almost solely on the release of your genre-defining 1988 album, *Isn't Anything*. I do want to make it known to you that I thought Lush, Ride, and Swervedriver were all amazing bands in their

century. It was a total dive, and they were having some weird, annoying, ironic karaoke night, so you had guys in fishnets and Doc Martens singing .38 Special and Eddie Money. At one point, I

---

time—but you were right not to want to be associated with them; they were lesser bands. But at least they attempted to follow up on their biggest successes (even if they disappointed, mostly). I guess what I'm trying to say here is that I've hated you because you left me hanging.

Okay, so I'm projecting. Maybe at this point you couldn't care less about putting anything new out. Maybe you've just had enough of the creative process, thank you very much, the same way I got fed up with the process of calculating prices of straddles in business school. People change. But I suspect that you'd have loved nothing more than to have put out an album that was even better than *Loveless,* possibly even sometime in the 1990s. I think you freaked out when it wasn't happening quickly, and it just kind of snowballed. Am I right?

But that's really not an excuse. In fact, you've been quoted as saying that you and your bandmates were at least working on *something* during those days of Island largesse—can't we at least hear that? I think what hurts most by your prolonged silence is that I know you're going to release some kind of album sometime. Maybe not tomorrow, maybe not this year, maybe not this decade. But if it's true that you're going to release something sometime—and it is inevitable, because I know you want to—you may as well make it happen right now. You can rest assured that all of us will shell out for it. In fact, you could price it at $100 a pop and everyone would still buy it with grins on their stupid, greedy faces. Personally I'd be willing to go much higher. In fact, I'll make you an offer, right here, between two gentlemen who presumably understand the extreme excellence of the song "What You Want." Here's the deal: If you e-mail me a digital file of what you consider to be the best tracks you recorded on Island's many dimes, or if you send me anything that you've written since then that did not appear on the *Lost in Translation* soundtrack, then I will give you everything I have in my bank account. At the time of this writing, we're talking only $1,677, but you know what? I'll work harder between now and when this thing is published to fatten that figure up. How does $2,000 sound? For maybe five minutes of your time? You're not going to get anything for free anymore, so this seems like a steal. Let me know.

At the very least, could you get back together for a few reunion shows with the old band? Since we've never spoken before, I'll assume you don't know that my friend Phil saw you guys perform in

looked at a man trying to navigate the crowd in front of the bar and thought, *Oh my God, that's Spiral Stairs.* What timing! I'd just had a conversation with a friend the other night about whether the guys in Pavement (and the Pixies and the Strokes) were millionaires or not. It seemed like they had to be, despite their indie roots and lack of smash hits. Really, how could the members of the band that wrote "Frontwards" *not* be millionaires? Lo and behold, not ten feet away from me was the horse's mouth. Like the asshole I most certainly am, I caught Spiral's eye when he passed by, burdening him with the international sign for "I'm going to bug you now and there's nothing you can do about it." He stopped, actually seeming not to be too put out by me, or anything else, really, including the bad karaoke. I informed him of my love of Pavement, we small-talked about what he was doing in Seattle (he lives there now), and he told me how to tune the song "Here" (drop D). Then I posed the money question. He laughed and said, "I've made enough to buy a house, but that's it." I asked if it was a million-dollar house. He told me that Steve West, the band's second drummer, was working in construction.

Detroit in the spring of 1992 and that he complained to me in a postcard two days later that his ears were still ringing from the thirty minutes of feedback noise you bestowed on the crowd—insane! On the same postcard he wrote that he'd taken a flight to D.C. the next day and summed up the experience using one word: "turbulence." I think that's a perfect noun to describe your music. I'd really like another chance to hear it live, because I wasn't around those two times you played in Detroit. I'm willing to go deaf. Think of the Pixies. Think of Dinosaur Jr. They reunited the right way. You guys could, too.

Anyway, I'll leave it at that. If I don't hear back from you, well, I guess that would be normal. Have a good one.

Sincerely,
John Sellers

P.S. That song "Cupid Come"? Everyone just calls it "Coffee Cup."

I asked if he was constructing buildings out of all the thousand-dollar bills he'd earned as a member of Pavement. Spiral's revelation about finances so confused and upset me that he managed to escape before I could ask him the hundred other fanboy questions in my head. If those guys aren't rich, I thought, what's the point of doing anything? To have total jerkbags bug you at dive bars for the rest of your life? And that's about when the drunk next to me, a fortysomething bike messenger at a Seattle law firm, started blathering at me, and I realized that Spiral Stairs's life could be a whole lot worse.

What I also discovered as I read more about them those first few months is that I was actually a good deal behind the curve. I'd missed a flurry of hype in the press all the previous year—*Spin,* for instance, had named *Slanted and Enchanted* its album of the year for 1992, over the Beastie Boys' *Check Your Head,* Rage Against the Machine's debut, and Sonic Youth's *Dirty;*[107] I also later found in my closet an issue of *Melody Maker* that I'd

---

[107] As sad as this seems to me now, I shoplifted music occasionally during college. Only the two times I got caught are worth mentioning. In London in the summer of 1992, I had a few hours to kill before hopping the train to Dover, where a friend and I were to take a ferry to travel through Europe. The best way to bide time when you're not ready to drink yet is to go to a record store. I saw that *Dirty* had just come out and decided it would be great Europass fodder. The problem was, all of my nonessential pounds had been spent or converted, and my credit card was nearly maxed out. An American tourist with big, important plans, I felt untouchable. I thought: HMV is a big place; they won't miss it. When the security siren went off, a beefy guard nudged me into a small cave of a room, where a manager gave me a firm talking to. When I stated for the record that I was very sorry (true) and had never done something like this before (not true), he gasped and said, "You're an American? I don't think we've ever had one of you back here. Usually we get Gypsies." So apparently he initially thought that I was a Gypsy. Luckily I had exactly ten pounds remaining in my wallet and it spared me further prosecution. And that's how I acquired *Dirty,* which neatly summed up how I felt on the way to Dover. Less than a year later I fucked up again. Only this time there were consequences. And would you

bought in England the previous summer that had an inset photo of Pavement (blurb: WHERE THE STREETS ARE INSANE . . .) right on the cover promoting a two-page interview with the band. How had I missed these things? Being clueless prevented me any chance of seeing the show or those shows in 1991 and/or 1992, when Gary Young had handed out toast to the crowd. In fact, I missed Gary Young, period—he either quit or was fired (depending on whom you ask) shortly after my relationship with Pavement began. While working abroad in the summer of 1992, I'd missed their first U.S. tour; one stop was in Kalamazoo, Michigan. It would have been wonderful to have seen Pavement in a place like Kalamazoo.

But none of this mattered because I felt I knew as much about them as anyone who'd been there from the beginning. By April I had become convinced that they were a radio-friendly band, that "Here" would sound more than okay right after "There She Goes" or "Friday I'm in Love." I'd call in to the only commercial station in the Detroit area that played alternative music (at the time this meant a lot of Depeche Mode and Red Hot Chili Pep-

---

believe it involved Porno for Pyros? I'd stopped off at a Tower Records during the hour between my final two exams ever at the University of Michigan and turned some built-up nervous energy into pure evil. The debut album of Perry Farrell's side project had just come out; as a slowly fading aficionado of Jane's Addiction, I was mildly curious. Suddenly, the cassette felt too hot not to take. I would be leaving Ann Arbor forever in two days! Still so untouchable! The tape went into the pocket of my German military coat and I started to walk out. A clerk hovered aggressively near the door, pretending not to be watching me, but it was obvious what was up. The culprit went quietly. Cost: untold shame, a hundred-dollar fine, and eighty hours of community service, which I eventually performed in New York City, partially at a soup kitchen on the Bowery and partially at a hospital. I was an hour late to my ninety-minute Shakespeare exam and wound up getting a C minus, the worst grade I ever received at any level of schooling. Getting caught that second time cured me. I haven't stolen anything since, other than hearts and, once, a turkey sandwich as I walked by a craft-services table on the set of a movie being filmed near my apartment—too much mayo. I never did hear that Porno for Pyros album.

pers) and request that song or "In the Mouth a Desert" or "Box Elder" or "Trigger Cut" and listen to a woman on the other end of the phone politely inform me that it wasn't going to happen. I'm not sure why it mattered. After all, I had these songs in my possession already; I could hear them whenever I wanted. But maybe hearing them over the airwaves would have validated my obsession to the world, or at least to a small subset of Detroit radio listeners. I wanted the deejay to say, "Thank John Sellers for this one. He's cooler than all of you are." Which of course only validates my dorkhood.

Around this time my friend Chris, who had been behind the wheel when I'd first heard *Slanted and Enchanted,* had scored a slot on the University of Michigan radio station. It was the first time, other than in the movie *Pump Up the Volume* (in which, incidentally, Christian Slater's character plays the Pavement song "Forklift"), that I'd ever been confronted by the idea that real people could be radio hosts. All Chris had done was go to the station and ask for a time slot: They were apparently handing these things out for free. It was too late for me, of course. My second and final graduation was just weeks away. And it's probably a good thing. I had come up with a format for my pretend radio show: a one-hour program where I'd play nothing but the same song over and over. The song would change from show to show, of course, but any given hour would consist of ten to fifteen spins of that song, interspersed with me telling anecdotes about why it ruled. The song I would have played the first time (the one and only show that any respectable station would have allowed to air) was "Frontwards." I considered hijacking Chris's show, but he began at three a.m. and that was usually my time to sleep off the beer.

❖

In August 1993, I moved to New York to discover that mine was not a unique passion. Everyone had heard of Pavement, loved them, knew one of the members, had recently seen one stumbling down Ludlow Street, or had inside information about their up-coming album, *Crooked Rain, Crooked Rain,* which was going to be released in early 1994. It pissed me off. The next album seemed earmarked for failure, at least in terms of what I wanted. I did not want this band to be lost to ubiquity. A moderate Pixies-sized following I could handle. But this was just after the alterna-tive-music land grab of 1992. All signs pointed to Pavement getting annoyingly huge, and to Malkmus's face showing up everywhere, and to me hating them and him and it.

It had happened with the Smashing Pumpkins over the sum-mer of '93. Their debut album, *Gish,* and the trippy low-budget videos for "Rhinoceros" and "Siva" had hit me hard the year be-fore. Billy Corgan inspired air guitar. Unlike so many other alter-native guitarists, he was comfortable embracing his inner Vinnie Vincent. Very few alt-rockers have ever delivered a proficient gui-tar solo—besides Corgan, we're talking Kim Thayil, J Mascis, and . . . who else?[108] (And no, Kurt Cobain's solo in "Smells Like Teen Spirit" doesn't cut it.) I bought *Siamese Dream* on the day of its release and still adamantly state that "Cherub Rock" is one of the best rock songs of the 1990s. But I didn't love that the album debuted at number ten on the *Billboard* chart. Or that you couldn't turn on MTV without seeing Corgan's round, ruddy face. While initially it was nice that something I listened to was getting airplay over Mariah Carey on mainstream outlets, I wanted the Smashing Pumpkins hype to die a quick death so that Corgan would go away. Maybe if he did, he'd revert to the guy that I liked in the first place. Major success magnifies both the good and the bad. In rare cases, the good outweighs the bad; one example is Radiohead, where the talent has always exceeded the ego, primarily because Thom Yorke isn't an insatiable camera hog. But success makes many artists irretrievably annoying. Billy Corgan relished the spotlight, and its glare exposed his flaws,

---

[108] I smell a list. See Appendix A for a rundown of quick-fingered alt-rock guitarists.

particularly the ego. And yeah, also the bald head. Corgan seemed less pretentious when he had that tuft of brown hair.

In the fall of 1993, I'd lie on the questionable futon assigned to me in my poorly lit living room sublet and repeatedly play "So Stark (You're a Skyscraper)" (a lumbering B-side on the "Trigger Cut" single) and none of the hype about Pavement would matter. I was interning at *Spy* magazine for fifty dollars a week, so there were a lot of nights spent in this way: listening to Malkmus and eating cheap pasta alone in a new city where millions of people lived. It was among the happiest periods of my life. Probably due to this isolation and contentment, I briefly lost track of the band's whereabouts. As a result, "Cut Your Hair" snuck up on me. I knew the album was due in February or March of 1994. But one afternoon I turned on MTV and saw Malkmus staring back at me. The video lampooned the stress of getting a haircut, and featured a guy in a gorilla suit sitting down in a barber's chair: funny. The song greatly disturbed me, though. It did not sound like Pavement. Where was the distortion? Why was it overtly catchy? Why were the lyrics easy to understand? As the buzz over the band swelled to what would later be seen as its high point, I started to lose my grip. I absolutely dug *Crooked Rain, Crooked Rain,* but I began to view Steve Malkmus as the prom king of indie rock.[109] For a guy who couldn't have gotten a vote for prom king if I'd handed out envelopes stuffed with joints, this is not a good way to view a musician you revere. That certain girls I knew began swooning over him only made it more troublesome. There is a healthy list of bands whose long-term success has been sparked by the mania of girls gone ga-ga (e.g., the Beatles, the Jackson Five, *NSYNC), and it disgusted me that the Pavement I already knew and loved might be entering that realm. Were they really growing in popularity because Malkmus wasn't hideous?[110]

And so I rebelled against "Cut Your Hair" and deemed it the

---

[109] Ah, but who was the prom queen? At the time: Juliana Hatfield.

[110] Sure, it's a nice bonus when your favorite musician isn't a disgusting bog beast. But when your interest in a particular band increases due to

worst song on *Crooked Rain, Crooked Rain*. I'd hit Skip on my CD player the second "Stop Breathin'" ended. What I didn't see was that "Cut Your Hair" being the first single off the album helped my cause. That it was the catchiest song in the band's arsenal ensured that Pavement wasn't going to linger in Smashing Pumpkins territory for long.[111] Take the Pumpkins' release strategy as a counterexample: "Cherub Rock" was the first single off *Siamese Dream* but probably just its fifth most radio-friendly track; the catchiest is arguably "Today," which, it turned out, was a much more popular song. The only other possibility for a crossover hit on *Crooked Rain, Crooked Rain* was "Gold Soundz." But let's face it: "Gold Soundz"[112] was too good for the mainstream.

The lack of a catchy follow-up, while surely a factor in Spiral Stairs's financial shortcomings, meant that sooner or later the band would be mine again. Not only did the "Gold Soundz" sin-

---

the floppy hair or soulful blue eyes or pouty lips of its lead singer, that's a little pathetic. Seriously. If this applies to you, you're just one step above those sluts who flash their ta-tas at Bon Jovi concerts. (Okay, maybe two steps.) Why is it, by the way, that few men get whopping crushes on female musicians and ramp up their interest in the music as a result? There's rarely any swoon factor, at least in the circles I've hung out in. I'm sure you can find countless guys who'd say that Harriet Wheeler was a chipmunk-cheeked cutie, or discuss their inexplicable attraction to Kim Deal, or utter the unspeakably dumb words "Liz Phair? I'd fuck her." But not one of these dudes would say that looks factored into their assessment of the music; music is either worth listening to or it is not. And they certainly wouldn't stoop, as one breathless female *Village Voice* critic did, to opening a review of a Decemberists album with four hundred words about her attraction to the band's frontman and other indie darlings just like him. Holy shit, that sucked.

[111] And Pavement—despite the war of words Corgan and Malkmus exchanged in various media outlets as a result of Malkmus's bodacious "I could really give a fuck" dis of the Smashing Pumpkins on "Range Life"— never was as popular. They'll have to settle for having been better.

[112] For a long time, *Gold Soundz* was the working title of this book. I changed it to the Built to Spill reference after a weekend of bingeing on the Idaho indie outfit's epic 1997 record of the same name. How ya like me now?

gle land with a wonderful splat, but in 1995 the band's difficult third album, *Wowee Zowee* (best song: "Black Out"), jettisoned lesser fans—and the group's following continued to thin throughout the 1990s due to unspectacular releases.[113] And so, with a promising new millennium looming, I declared myself the biggest Pavement fan in the universe. Well into the twenty-first century, I considered Pavement to be the best band of all time. Better than the Beatles. The Clash. U2. The Smiths. Nirvana. Radiohead. It

---

[113] Well, there are exceptions. Pavement's most deliciously Pavement-y song might be "Starlings of the Slipstream," off their durable yet undersung 1997 album, *Brighten the Corners*. (The killer lyric: "And I put a spycam in a sorority!/Darlings on the split-screen . . .") And the most listenable Malkmus material since '94 might have arisen from his sometime collaboration with college pal David Berman in the Silver Jews. While the Jews formed in 1989, they didn't approach anything resembling a serious concern until the release of *Starlite Walker* (1994), which nicely showcased the band's signature sound: deep, funny lyrics built around a stripped-down sound and Berman's monotone Virginia drawl. It's unfair to write off the Silver Jews as a Malkmus side project considering that Berman is the chief songwriter and because he's recorded and toured under the Jews name without the Pavement frontman. But so many Berman high points involve Malkmus, who always shows up with his full arsenal: unconventional tunings, slacker vocal stylings, and an enthusiasm for jamming. Their best team-up to date can be found on *American Water* (1998); it is here that Malkmus emerges as a guitar hero, a role he carried over to *Terror Twilight* (1999), the uneven final Pavement album, and to his three unjustly dismissed solo albums (although of late he's been sounding more and more like Jerry Garcia, that inveterate noodler). Berman also is at his most inspired here, as evidenced by the following lyrics: 1) "All my favorite singers couldn't sing"; 2) "I know that a lot of what I say has been lifted off of men's room walls"; 3) "And so the rent became whiskey/And then my life became risky"; 4) "I am the trick my mother played on the world"; 5) "In 1984, I was hospitalized for approaching perfection." There's not a bad song on *American Water,* and it could easily be argued that it is the most underrated album of the 1990s. As for Spiral Stairs, he puts out music now as the leader of Preston School of Industry, an inside reference to a song Pavement wrote on the fly while appearing on a Dutch television program. Neither of his new band's two albums measure up to Malkmus's post-Pavement work, but they're strong enough to make you forget that he's responsible for the very worst Pavement song, "Hit the Plane Down," off *Crooked Rain, Crooked Rain.* Man, what a boner that one was.

was my cocoon music. If the world were ever to have broken down around me, I'd have been okay if Pavement was on hand. In fact, until late 2002, I figured that Pavement and I would be joined together in matrimonial bliss for all of eternity, like my dad and Dylan. But then something better came along.

9

HOT FREAKS

"This one is on the house. This one is better than ever."

On a dreary Ohio morning in October 2004, I was banging on the steering wheel of a rented Hyundai and shouting the lyrics to the greatest song ever written. I am usually against displays of exuberance while driving in rentals, as I'm scared that a guy back at the agency is watching me on closed-caption spy-cam and laughing hard enough to make his Arizona Iced Tea come out his nose. I am also cowed by the potential scorn of other drivers. I know that whenever I look over and see some goon energetically mouthing the words to a song I can't hear, I assume the worst: Creed. But every so often I'll give in to a song entirely, and it will compel me, like the bug Khan put in Chekov's ear, to do its evil bidding, which in this case meant not only sincere air-guitar noodling and dashboard percussion, but also a move of my head I'll refer to as the Emphatic Chicken.

I've been blasting music in cars for nearly two decades now and these moments of total submission still deliver the same wonderful rush. It's like being on a narcotic, for two reasons: 1) You become delusional. You think you're a pharaoh at the reins of a chariot, or a near-god who, if offered the appropriate sacrifices, could clone Eskimos or beat Jesus in a thumb war. And yet it's obvious you should be wearing a bra on your head; 2) Your ability to operate potentially dangerous machinery is impaired by your reluctance to keep your hands in the ten-and-two position. If traffic cops ticketed for DWR—driving while rocking—my license would have been revoked long ago.

Like all transcendent music-listening experiences, the real thrill comes from the relationship you forge with what's emanating from the speakers. When you're completely possessed by a song, it has essentially become unique to you. You think you are the only person who has ever heard it or who really gets it. This phenomenon can occur even if you're listening to a cheesy song loved by billions of people. I once busted out in falsetto upon hearing "Ride Like the Wind" by Christopher Cross on the radio.[114] But as I've gotten older I have come to believe that the feeling is generally more powerful when the song is a lesser-known track by a lesser-known band. That's because you suspect, and probably correctly, that no one else on earth is listening to that particular tune at that moment. As a result you are able to claim it as your personal theme song.

On that day nearly a year ago, my theme—which I should repeat is the greatest song ever written—was "Buzzards and Dreadful Crows" by Guided By Voices. Its chorus goes:

> There's something in this deal for everyone
> Did you really think that you were the only one?

A little while later it hit me that, yes, I did think I was the only one—the only one possessed enough to have traveled nearly six hundred miles to the unlikely locale of Dayton, Ohio, because of songs just like "Buzzards and Dreadful Crows." In the car, though, nothing else mattered except proving my love for the raucous one-minute, forty-three-second gem by rocking out to it as hard as possible. And when it gave way, like an Olympic relay sprinter passing the baton, to the glorious shimmer of a song

---

[114] I especially love the Michael McDonald part: "And I've got such a long way to go/To make it to the border of Mexico." My issue with the song has always been its nonspecificity about the mode of transport being used. Is it a horse? A bike? A motorcycle? A bus? And if it's that last one, can a person truly ride like the wind on a bus? My best guess is that it's a horse, which makes the song all the sillier because Christopher Cross couldn't look any less equestrian.

called "Tractor Rape Chain," I had no choice but to submit all over again. Each subsequent Guided By Voices track that would come on during that drive into Dayton instantly became the new greatest song ever written.

The pilgrimage was long overdue. The birthplace of aviation might seem like a questionable mecca for a guy who's paranoid about flying, but of course this trip had nothing at all to do with Orville and Wilbur Wright. To me, the city matters only because it's the hometown of another man who should be recognized as an American legend: Robert Pollard, the genius behind Guided By Voices. To enumerate all of the ways in which I revere Pollard would exceed the contractual length of this book,[115] but here are a baker's dozen: 1) He and his revolving lineup of bandmates have persevered and even flourished for more than twenty years despite never having been in heavy rotation on MTV or mainstream radio. 2) He used to be a fourth-grade teacher and retained the job until he was thirty-six, well after his sell-by date as a musical commodity. 3) He received this note from one of his students: "Dear Mr. Pollard, thank you for helping me with my math. I didn't know how to do it at first but now I do. Thank you. Your [sic] the best teacher in the world. You are the best!" 4) He is now fifty years old,[116] yet still drinks as recklessly as kids half his age. 5) Even though he does favor Miller Lite. 6) He once pitched a perfect game in Little League. 7) He has written and released over one thousand songs—more than the combined output of Paul McCartney and Pete Townshend, two obvious influences. 8) So furious is his creative pace that a Dayton record collector once quipped that he'll write five songs on the toilet every day and "three of them will be good." 9) One of

[115] Technically 75,000 words, but it's going to the printer at a paltry 74,847. Sue me!

[116] Date of birth: October 31, 1957. Which means that he was busy celebrating his eighteenth birthday on that Halloween my mom put me in a ninety-nine-cent plastic costume inspired by the TV series *Kung Fu*, with a sad-sack rendering of Keith Carradine on its chest. Worst costume ever.

these songs is titled "Kicker of Elves."[117] 10) Another is "Navigating Flood Regions." 11) Another is recorded over the sound of a friend's snoring. 12) This lyric: "And now we see eye to eye that other men's trash is collectible." 13) Reacting to a Willie Nelson quote that lauded the songwriting of Matchbox Twenty, he said, "His grass is my ass, and he can eat it!"

To say that I'm merely a fan of his music wouldn't give my obsession the "Uh, you're scaring me" heft it deserves. Remember the totals on my iTunes play count? That's nothing. Not counting the Dayton trip, which promised to scorch my savings, I'd already spent more than one thousand dollars in the previous year on ephemera relating to the band. I have called one of my closest friends a dick for asking if Guided By Voices is a religious band. It has been suggested, by one of the few people who knows the depths of my fanship, that I've lost perspective where the band is concerned. To this I can only retort that I really don't care, Greg. Who cares that the best adjectives I can come up with when thinking about the band are "sweet" and "awesome"? Who cares that nearly every conversation eventually brings to mind something Pollard has said or done or sung? Who cares

---

[117] In October 2002, I took a northerly road trip with my girlfriend, a dyed-in-the-wool indie rocker and the cutest person I'd ever known. Various radio deejays were being unhelpful, so she suggested we put on a CD she'd brought along. With no fanfare, she selected Guided By Voices' *Bee Thousand,* an album I'd never heard of by a band that meant nothing to me. The first song mentioned UFOs. The second began and ended in less than two mile markers. The third sounded like the Replacements. Good stuff, made better through my affection for the person recommending it, but it went in one ear and out the other. We had been hoping to acquire cups of coffee, and near the tail end of the album we passed a worthy establishment. And so it came to be that in the drive-thru of a Dunkin' Donuts I officially became a fan of Guided By Voices. The song: "Kicker of Elves." The reason: I loved the semantics of the title. It seemed to me that it would be more apt to describe someone who kicks elves as an elf-kicker. The grammatical formality found in the phrase "kicker of elves" woke up the English major in me, and because I was raised on J.R.R. Tolkien and Dungeons & Dragons, the notion that some dude was going around smiting elves with his feet further increased its appeal. I listened more closely after that.

that I love many of his songs as much as my own family members? Nick Hornby has his soccer team. Ahab had his whale. I will not be denied my favorite band.

But, okay, I have lost some objectivity about Guided By Voices, or GBV, as the band is known to its hard-core fans. I can no longer understand why they've never been able to shed the tag of "indie-rock darlings" to move into the mainstream and beyond.[118] Or how indie-rock aficionados—that is, people who should know better—quite often don't know much about the band. And I certainly fail to see how a rational being who's heard GBV wouldn't immediately fall in love with them in the same way I have, which often involves inopportune humming.

Now, Guided By Voices isn't unknown, and may not even be obscure. In 1992, with only a quartet of poorly distributed, self-financed albums to their name,[119] the band mailed out its fifth full-length effort, *Propeller,*[120] to influential zines and music pub-

[118] Not that I'd ever want that, of course. I'd die if an ESPN announcer turned one of their lyrics into a touchdown call or if a GBV song were covered by an *American Idol* contestant.

[119] Pollard had been in various bands since high school, but it wasn't until he formed Guided By Voices in 1983 with childhood chum Mitch Mitchell that his knack for songwriting flourished. At first, GBV was little more than a hobby, something Pollard could do on the weekends and during his summer vacations. But by 1987 he and his bandmates—who also included, at various times, his younger brother, Jim Pollard, a former high school basketball star in Dayton, and local guitarist Tobin Sprout, who occasionally contributed his own songs to the mix—were pooling their money and taking out loans in order to put their songs on record. Due in part to the various career obligations of the band members, no live shows were played from 1987 to 1993; the gang would just get together in Pollard's basement (dubbed "the Snakepit"), drink unfathomable amounts of beer, and write music that few people outside their circle of friends ever heard. In 1992, as the fun of self-publishing vinyl records was being overtaken by the harsh realities of mounting debt, Pollard, already going on thirty-five, decided to put together one more album and then call it quits. He polished off his best unused songs, named the collection *Propeller,* and resigned himself to a not unhappy life as a schoolteacher.

[120] Only five hundred copies were pressed, each with a unique cover hand-designed by a band member or friend. One of these found its way to

lications. Very quickly this group of middle-aged men from the middle of nowhere became an underground sensation. *Spin*[121] and other mainstream publications picked up on it, and their fan base grew exponentially due to a glorious three-album run that began in 1994: *Bee Thousand,* the twenty-song masterpiece that best illustrates the unsophisticated, cost-effective recording technique that the band had begun using on *Propeller;*[122] 1995's mar-

---

Matt Sweeney, later of the indie band Chavez but then a struggling musician with good connections, who urged Pollard in a letter and subsequent phone calls to play a show in New York. In July 1993, GBV played an industry showcase at CBGB's, their first gig outside Ohio (not counting a date in Newport, Kentucky, a suburb of Cincinnati), and their first since the mid-1980s. Because many GBV songs clock in at under two minutes, they managed to bang out nineteen songs during their forty-five-minute set, and Pollard whipped out all of his favorite rock-star moves: Daltrey-style microphone twirls, high leg kicks, inebriated fist pumps. Record executives on hand, for lack of a more precise term, shat a brick.

[121] Jim Greer, then a writer at *Spin,* was an early adopter, leading to a friendship with Pollard. In 1995, when GBV's bassist left for a more stable career in law, Greer stepped in. The guy also dated Kim Deal, another legend from Dayton. Why doesn't this kind of stuff happen to me?

[122] Due to tight finances, Pollard and pals got in the habit of recording in the Snakepit on a cheap cassette deck and a four-track unit; tape hiss, sloppy edits, and volume issues proliferate on *Bee Thousand.* This budget- and user-friendly method of recording stuff is the chief characteristic of music in the indie-rock subgenre known as lo-fi. Guided By Voices led the lo-fi charge, but there were other indie outfits who got there first, most notably Daniel Johnston, Beat Happening, Pavement, and another of my all-time favorite bands, somehow heretofore unmentioned in these pages: Sebadoh. While a member of the highly regarded and highly volatile Massachusetts-based alt-rock band Dinosaur Jr., Lou Barlow had put out some of his own shoddily recorded sonic experiments under the Sebadoh name. It became a full-time endeavor in 1989 when the famously controlling guitarist J Mascis kicked him out of Dinosaur Jr., a clash that Barlow bitched about on "The Freed Pig," the angry, introspective opening track of the lo-fi landmark *Sebadoh III* (1991). Because home recording is so immediate, music in the genre tends to be quite personal, and many of Sebadoh's early songs are the equivalent of Barlow picking at scabs. Another seminal lo-fi record requiring mention here is *Exile in Guyville,* Liz Phair's frank 1993 debut. Despite, or maybe because of, lyrics as raunchy as anything penned

ginally more upscale *Alien Lanes,* their first on influential indie label Matador;[123] and the more traditionally recorded *Under the Bushes Under the Stars* (1996), some of which was produced by Kim Deal, then successful with the Breeders.[124] GBV played a few dates on the second stage on the 1995 Lollapalooza tour, later appeared on *Late Night with Conan O'Brien* twice, and had

---

by controversial rapper Luther Campbell of 2 Live Crew (on "Flower," for example, she sings about wanting to be a "blowjob queen" and trots out such tasteful lyrics as "I just want your fresh young jimmy/Cramming, slamming, ramming in me"—*yikes!*), the album, filled with simple guitar lines and Phair's quiet, deadpan voice, immediately turned her into the slacker indie-rock heroine du jour and went a long way toward rendering silly the (now very embarrassing) Riot Grrrl movement, which by 1993 had been run aground by growling, unappealing harpies, like that member of L7 who pulled out her soiled tampon while on stage at the 1992 Reading Festival and hurled it into the unlucky crowd. Can you imagine getting pelted by something like that? I would die a thousand deaths.

[123] *Propeller* was distributed through tiny, Cleveland-based Scat Records, which subsequently signed Pollard and co. to a two-record deal that resulted in 1993's super-lo-fi *Vampire on Titus* and their 1994 breakout, *Bee Thousand.* Matador Records, which struck up a deal with Scat to distribute the latter album, was founded in New York City in 1989 by Chris Lombardi; the following year he partnered up with Gerard Cosloy, a revered music zine editor who'd also signed Dinosaur Jr., Sebadoh, and Sonic Youth to short-term contracts while running Long Island–based Homestead Records. Matador quickly grew, in large part due to the surprise success of Teenage Fanclub's debut, *A Catholic Education* (1990), and Pavement's *Slanted and Enchanted,* and the list of bands signed to the label at one time or another is staggering: classic alt-rockers Yo La Tengo, Superchunk, Unrest, and many others, and more recent indie heroes the New Pornographers, Mogwai, and Interpol. GBV played at Cosloy's wedding in 1997. Wow. I don't ever want to get married, but if Pollard offered to play at my wedding, I'd seriously consider trying the knot, so long as the woman involved didn't totally suck.

[124] A few songs on *UTBUTS* were engineered in the traditional twenty-four-track style by prolific alt-rock producer Steve Albini (Nirvana's *In Utero* and PJ Harvey's *Dry* are arguably the most successful of the hundreds of albums he has helmed; he was also a founding member of the influential '80s Chicago punk band Big Black), but Pollard chose to rerecord all but two of them in a more familiar, lo-fi manner. The tour for this album was the last to feature Pollard (vocals), Mitch Mitchell (guitar), Tobin Sprout (guitar), and Kevin Fennell (drums), referred to by fans as GBV's

their Ric Ocasek–produced[125] 2000 single "Teenage FBI" included on a *Buffy the Vampire Slayer* soundtrack. All of which means that if you're the not uncommon sort whose collection of music includes Pavement, the Pixies, and Sonic Youth, you might very well own at least one of GBV's fifteen proper albums and have many passionate things to say about Bob Pollard and his music. But it's all relative. One of the band's bestselling albums, 2001's souped-up *Isolation Drills,* sold around one hundred thousand copies. Broken down, that's only two thousand copies per state, which isn't a huge amount, especially if you compare that figure to the number of people who, say, attend a U2 arena show.[126] I think it's safe to say that most people have never heard of them.

I can forgive the fans of Britney Spears and Clay Aiken for not tattooing GBV on their flabby biceps (they are still to be despised for liking Britney Spears and Clay Aiken, of course), but it's especially distressing when I meet a listener of indie rock who doesn't know much more about the band other than that they're one of the fulcrums of the lo-fi movement or that they appeared in that one Strokes video.[127] That's because, in so many ways, Guided By Voices could be the protagonist of the ultimate alter-

---

"classic" lineup because the foursome had managed to stay together since that fateful CBGB's show in 1993. When Sprout quit to raise his first child, Pollard opted to take the band in a different direction, severing ties with Mitchell and Fennell in order to hire what he has referred to as "professional musicians," most notably guitarist Doug Gillard, the one member of the revised lineup who would never be fired. The 1997 album *Mag Earwhig!* showed off GBV's new, not-unappealing loud-and-proud sound, but the lo-fi intimacy and addictive quirkiness of their previous five albums was mostly gone and would seldom resurface, for better or for worse.

[125] The Cars legend banned beer from the studio during the recording of *Do the Collapse* (1999), which could be a factor in the album being the least adventurous in the GBV catalog.

[126] I can hear Bono say, "Make some noise if you love Guided By Voices!" and only one sad section in the far back hollers. Then Bono adds: "Am I bugging you? I don't mean to bug ya."

[127] In the video for "Someday," the two bands squared off, for real, on *Family Feud.* GBV won!

native-rock story: Band toils in obscurity for nearly a decade in an unlikely locale, self-publishing catchy, quirky songs concocted in suburban basements and garages. On the verge of giving up, band mails out a handful of albums in a last-ditch effort to win over East Coast media types, gains influential supporters, and receives national attention. Band flirts with crossover success, doesn't quite get there, loses flavor-of-the-month status, gets taken for granted. Band is cited as an influence by a new generation of musicians. Celebrities start attending their shows.[128] Band calls it quits.

It's this last part of the story that brought me to Dayton. A few months prior, Pollard had announced (at a New York show I didn't attend because, hey, there'll be hundreds more, right?) that he was finally disbanding Guided By Voices.[129] I simply was not

---

[128] Drew Barrymore has turned up due to her romantic affiliation with the drummer of the Strokes. Other celebrities who have been spotted include Michael Imperioli of *The Sopranos* and director Steven Soderbergh, who commissioned Pollard to score the 2005 movie *Bubble*. Cue the sound of crickets chirping.

[129] Behold the contents of the least wanted Matador press release ever:

> **04/26/04—GBV call it quits**
> After almost 20 years, assorted lineups, and countless albums, EPs, singles, triples, stolen bases, misdemeanor convictions, and broken hearts, Dayton, OH's fortunate sons are taking leave of your senses. *Half Smiles Of The Decomposed,* to be released August 24 on Matador Records, will be the final album from Guided By Voices, one of the most acclaimed independent rock bands of all time. "This feels like the last album for Guided By Voices," explains Robert Pollard, GBV's lone constant member, lead singer, and famously prolific songwriter. "I've always said that when I make a record that I'm totally satisfied with as befitting a final album, then that will be it. And this is it." *Half Smiles Of The Decomposed* is the band's 15th full-length studio release, following 2003's *Earthquake Glue* and retrospective box-set, greatest-hits, and DVD releases. Although its tour later this year will be the band's last, Robert Pollard will continue writing, recording, and (possibly) touring as a solo artist. "I love the guys in the band, but I'm getting too old to be a gang leader," he explains. "There's a sense of maturity, and even integrity, I think, in continuing as one's own self."

prepared for the party to end: I hadn't yet talked to the host, the keg wasn't kicked, there wasn't any specific time I needed to be up the next day. Despite several opportunities to glom on to the band,[130] I hadn't listened to my first GBV album until 2002,[131] a good eight years after their heyday. I missed many chances to get wasted and climb onstage to man-hug Pollard, a near-ritual as GBV shows wind down, as if he were Michael Jackson or Morrissey; I squandered any right to say that I knew them when; I made my life immeasurably more boring. If you want to get technical, I was, until that fateful day in '02, exactly like all those clueless indie-rock fans I just vilified. My excuse (and my problem) is that, as a lifelong obsessive, I get far too attached to the bands and songs I love, and as a result am often reluctant to give new music a chance. Some famous person said that those who cannot learn from history are doomed to repeat it. I am forever stuck in a loop of missed opportunity.

[130] The two that have cost me the most sleep: In 1994, at the onset of their rise to power, they opened for Pavement here in New York City, but I lingered too long over Ballantine tall boys at my apartment and arrived after their set; and I possess a long-neglected *Under the Bushes Under the Stars* promo cassette from a 1996 fact-checking stint at *Details* magazine, where I'd ensured the accuracy of a review that rated the album an eight (out of a possible ten). Of course, when you first get into a band it is always distressing to learn about what you've missed out on. You want to be able to say that you're the biggest fan in the world, but how could you possibly be if you'd ignored them during their glory years, didn't go to that mindblowing performance in front of twenty people at that tiny downstairs venue, and never got to see them when they still had that cool, chain-smoking guitarist who'd play with a cigarette dangling from his lips?

[131] Yes, longtime GBV obsessives, I said 2002. I am one of those annoying latecomers who had every chance to be there from the start of the Matador years, willfully ignored them at their peak, finally discovered their greatness, and is now absolutely certain that he likes them better than you do. Feel free to flame me on the Disarm the Settlers message board. (FYI: I am a lurker; my screen name is Miller Lite Fan.) But before you do, please be aware that my pal Greg is to blame. Upon learning of my obsession, he informed me that he'd purchased *Vampire on Titus* back in 1993 and had instantly loved it. Nice. So why the hell didn't he force me listen to it in 1998 while we were working on the screenplay of our aborted teen sex comedy *Party Gras*?

Luckily, I play catch-up as well as anybody. Within six months of hearing *Bee Thousand*,[132] I had bought or borrowed all of their albums. I marveled at how drastically GBV's sound, if not Pollard's preference for daffy, whimsical lyrics (no doubt informed by so many hours spent with ten-year-olds), had changed over the years. One week I'd get an absurd thrill in discovering, on their 1987 debut album, *Devil Between My Toes,* which occasionally echoes early R.E.M. a little too closely, the hilariously weird lyric "No depth perception: Cyclops." Another time I'd blast their wistful 2001 anthem "Chasing Heather Crazy" so loudly that my bloodlusty downstairs neighbor, the dreaded Japanese cat lady, was inadvertently summoned to my door. And there was that day that I defied myself not to listen to "Blimps Go 90," from *Alien Lanes,* to hear Pollard poignantly recall "the sweet young days when I poured punch for the franchise/And thus was knighted, got so excited." What amazed me most as I went deeper was not only the many lyrics that seem to have been formulated after an intense D&D session, but that the music just kept coming: numerous Pollard solo[133] and side projects,[134] a

---

[132] Pollard has correctly pointed out that if you hold your tongue and say "Pete Townshend," it sounds a lot like "Bee Thousand."

[133] In 1996, Matador released *Not in My Airforce,* Pollard's sensational first solo album—solo, despite it featuring other GBV members and a lo-fi vibe. Pollard's subsequent solo albums were marginally more experimental than what would typify latter-day GBV. But really, any song on a Robert Pollard album sounds entirely like a GBV song, and vice versa. It can be confusing.

[134] Pollard started his own record label, Fading Captain, in 1999 and has used it to release every snippet of noise that he's felt doesn't belong on a GBV record. (I'll get into Pollard's quality-control issues in a later chapter.) His many side projects include Airport 5, Hazzard Hotrods, Go Back Snowball, Lexo and the Leapers, the Lifeguards, Circus Devils, the Takeovers, Psycho and the Birds, the Moping Swans, and at least five others—and that's not counting the hundreds of fake band names Pollard has devised and assigned to the throwaway GBV songs on the kitchen-sink collection *Suitcase,* or the time in 2000 that GBV performed at CBGB's under the alias Homosexual Flypaper, a show that I could have seen if I had any damn sense.

wealth of B-sides with songs better than the singles they supported, and *Suitcase,* a box set of one hundred discarded (and,
okay, largely unlistenable) GBV tracks. One hundred songs is
more than the total output of most bands,[135] even great ones, and
here GBV was releasing that number as if they were taking out
the trash.

Thus converted, I began spreading, near and far, the Gospel
of GBV According to John, which goes: "What? You've never
heard Guided By Voices? Wow! Well, they're from Dayton,
Ohio—yeah, I know!—and the lead singer, who also writes most
of the music, used to be an elementary school teacher. Crazy,
huh? Their songs sound like they were recorded in a submarine
or over the phone into an answering machine. Actually, most of
their stuff doesn't sound like that at all—the guy has written,
like, a thousand songs. I know I'm not describing them very well,
but man, they rock. I mean, they have a song called 'Gold Star for
Robot Boy'! They're so awesome. I'll make you a mix." My pros-
elytizing got to the point where my girlfriend, the very person
who'd first played GBV for me but who inexplicably owned only
one of their albums,[136] would put her head down in frustration
whenever I started to foam on about them, look back up at me,
and cover my mouth with her hand.

But at the New York City concert on April 24, 2004, just
eight days after I discovered the play counts on my iTunes, Pollard
lowered the boom. For a guy who once almost got into a drunken
fistfight with a fellow true believer after giving a point-by-point
argument of why *Bee Thousand* (my favorite GBV album and his
second favorite) is better than *Alien Lanes* (his favorite and my

---

[135] For example, the number of songs written and released by the Pixies
is somewhere around seventy-five.

[136] It vexes me when people claim to love a particular album yet never
bother to check out anything else by that band. My girlfriend, for example,
had never heard "Game of Pricks" or anything else on *Alien Lanes* (an
album that sounds very similar to *Bee Thousand,* only catchier) until I made
her a mix. Predictably, she loved it. Duh!

second favorite), this isn't news you process idly. It is a call to action. Calendars were brought out, dates were circled. August 17: A free concert on a pier in New York City, followed by GBV karaoke. December 3–5: three shows in New York City. And the big one, New Year's Eve in Chicago: GBV's final concert. At these events, I planned to say good-bye to a favorite band in a way that I'd never been able to before: on my own terms. This would mean a lot of beer and off-key singing. But I also suspected that these eight months of farewell would involve a personal quest. When your life appears to be in a premature downswing,[137] an unexpected announcement from your favorite musician—Pollard: "We are the kings of indie rock. When we quit, indie rock will die"—is a coincidence too important to ignore. I thought: *Let's see if this has anything to do with me.*

And then something incredible happened: I got invited to Pollard's house. My friend Cory Jones, the only person I know who loves GBV as much as I do,[138] was working as a writer and grunt monkey at the website of a men's magazine (one that publishes seminude photographs of the women of *Charmed* with regularity), and he had interviewed Pollard in 2003. In doing so, he struck up a fantasy-football-fueled e-mail relationship with Matt Davis, the publicist at Fading Captain. Commiseration

---

[137] Not that you care, but after nearly a year of problems, my girlfriend informed me in late March 2004 that a break was needed, one that looked to be permanent. So when Pollard's proclamation appeared in my inbox on April 26, it was as if I'd been dumped twice in the same month. On top of it, my career was stalled during this time and I'd just moved into an unexpectedly noisy apartment bedeviled by the constant *thud thud thud* of some rambunctious tot's feet on the floor above me. This period of my life is now known as the Era of Much Cussing.

[138] Cory is the guy I almost got in a fistfight with over GBV. We have also nearly come to blows at least two other times while arguing about our favorite guitarists, with him pimping Johnny Marr and me backing the Edge. These arguments are entirely moot, of course: The Edge isn't even close to being my favorite guitarist, and I love Marr as much as Cory does. But such debates help pass the time while we're drinking. What else are we going to talk about? Relationships?

over the end of GBV led Matt to invite Cory (and, by extension, an eternally grateful friend) out to Dayton to hang with Pollard and attend two farewell shows in the Midwest. I considered it divine provenance; so, apparently, did Cory. "It's like we got a ticket to heaven and we've been sinners our whole lives," he said.

And so there I was, cruising along a flat Ohio highway on a crisp October morning, past bingo halls and corporate parks, on my way from the airport to a chain hotel where I'd meet up with Cory and embark on the three-day bender that lay beyond.[139] I knew that I was about to be granted a privilege that thousands of GBV fans would buy off me for a lot of really useful cash. Quite frankly, that knowledge made me a person you wouldn't have wanted to know. As the CD player churned out one GBV track after another and I made a lot of noise in a small space, an unspoken thought separated me from the passing world: *You are nothing compared to me.*

And then came the worry. It had always been there, but in those interminable minutes that Cory and I sat on our beds at the hotel and waited for the phone call that was certain to change our lives, the cockiness deserted me. Just a week prior, at the Brooklyn bar we prefer because the jukebox has an acceptable ratio of Pollard music to non-Pollard music,[140] we'd gotten carried away with the excellence of our impending situation.

"So, do you think Bob"—I called him Bob, like all his fans do—"will volunteer to sing at my wake after I die?"

"No," said Cory.

"Why not?"

"He'll be too broken up."

"I can't wait for him to write a song about us."

---

[139] Again, not that you care, but after a hellish summer, my girlfriend and I got back together. Her sage advice as I embarked on the trip: "Don't drink too much."

[140] This is a major factor in where I go to drink. Every bar should have, at the minimum, "Tractor Rape Chain" on its jukebox, and if I worked on Capitol Hill, I'd lobby hard to make it a law.

"He's totally going to ask us to collaborate!"

But in the hotel room it was, "What happens if he hates our guts?" and, "What if I accidentally clog his toilet?" and, worst of all, "Dude, what if it's a trap? What if he lured us out here to get us drunk, make us have sex with Dayton hookers, and then call the cops?" We mapped out a game plan as best we could. Since Cory was the one who had gotten us invited and because he had talked to Pollard before, he would be the point man. My job was to keep my mouth shut, smile a lot, and not fuck it up.

I read an interview a while back in which Nick Cave said you should never meet your heroes. I suppose the danger is too great that either you will disappoint your hero or, more likely, your hero will disappoint you. One of you will not live up to expectations. In your case—or in my case—you will not meet the simple criterion that you should not make a nuisance of yourself. In your hero's case, he will bore you, or be a closet racist, or make you an unwitting stooge in private jokes that cause his hangers-on to refer to you as Scabies or Gonorrhea. In the line of duty as a writer of eight-hundred-word entertainment articles, I had met a few of my heroes, and except for that time when I tried to compliment Nicholson Baker [141] by saying that I like his books best when they're about things that don't matter, the interviews had been mostly rewarding. But there seemed to be more at stake here. If my opinion of Pollard was compromised by the experience—by guilt, regret, stupidity, or even friendship—how would that affect my perception of his music? In many ways, the consumption of art, whether done objectively or obsessively, requires a pure, one-way transaction: They produce it, you eat it up. How could I listen to *Bee Thousand* with reverence if Pollard turned out to be an asshole—like a friend accuses him of being on the DVD version of the GBV documentary *Watch Me Jumpstart*? Could a song as per-

---

[141] You should know that the footnote gimmick used in this book is an homage to my all-time favorite book, *The Mezzanine*. You should also know that Baker wielded footnotes far more adeptly; I'm just a remora trying to hitch a ride.

fectly cutting as "Game of Pricks" ever be taken seriously if he was too nice? And what if he was merely lukewarm, offering no hint of being either for or against us?

But in the end, there wasn't much of a choice. What obsessed fan would pass up the chance to drink beer at his hero's house? I decided to ignore all the risks, even the one in my head that had Pollard casting us out of Dayton and telling us to go and wander the earth for all our days.

10

BEE**R** THOUSAND

"Count the days that we have wasted from the start."

Whenever I go back to Michigan to visit family, I have to get into what I call "Midwestern mode." Primarily this involves pushing from my mind traumas born of bus fumes, summer trash odors, impassive deli clerks, panhandlers with painful singing voices, steep beer prices, lovey-dovey couples' public displays of affection in subway cars, close calls with rats and roaches, three-hour waits at the Department of Motor Vehicles, inane tabloid headlines, random jugglers and mimes, the word *schmear,* foodies, fashionistas, and yuppie stroller-pushing sidewalk hogs. When these things come to mind, I want to rage about them to anyone who'll listen. But it's become increasingly less palatable to complain about the negative aspects of living in New York City to the people back home. For one thing, the complaining just encourages them to bash New York, and that's reserved for people who are stupid enough to live in such a shithole. More important, bitching about living in New York makes them identify me as a New Yorker, a label that, as someone who proudly lived in the Midwest for his first twenty-three years, I still find completely unacceptable.

My complex about this began when I returned home one Thanksgiving a few years after moving to New York City and my brother's corncob of an ex told me that I was "edgy." In my mind, I was still a guy who stood *in line* instead of *on line,* who

expected supermarket clerks to thank me for my business, and who loved the Moons Over My Hammy at Denny's. That guy was hardly "edgy." But I knew that many of my signature Midwestern impulses had jumped ship somewhere along the way. No longer, for instance, did it seem perfectly natural to drive two hundred yards down the driveway simply to see what was in the mailbox. That alone probably meant that I was already a New Yorker, and it was true that moving back to the Midwest had ceased to be an option. Copping to my New York–centricism after only a few years out east was humbling, primarily because Michiganders stereotype New Yorkers two ways: 1) as cynical, pretentious, lox-eating money-grabbers who think they're more important than everyone who doesn't live in the big city, and who care way too much about Prada man-bags and the films of Werner Herzog; or 2) as amoral, drug-sniffing, whore-paying savages. I devised Midwestern mode to help me never be seen as one of those guys, at least outside the five boroughs. So far when the rule has been followed, it has mostly equated to the expression "When in Rome . . ." where the ". . . do as the Romans do" part has meant being preternaturally polite. When it hasn't, I've annoyed the shit out of people.

This is relevant because I slipped into Midwestern mode on the walk out to the car that was going to take Cory and me to meet Bob Pollard. In the days leading up to the excursion, I'd done a lot of fretting about whether we'd fit in, and had determined that the only way he'd like us was if we avoided sticking out too much. (Well, personality-wise. I could hardly do anything, at that point, about my New York City resident's standard-issue black-framed glasses.) And as a fan, I needed Pollard to like me, even marginally. There had to be some payoff for the heavy investment in Guided By Voices—those countless late nights spent rocking out to songs with provocative titles like "Perhaps Now the Vultures" and "Chief Barrel Belly," searching eBay for imports and concert T-shirts, surfing message boards to make sense of the comings and goings of the band's twenty-plus constituents,[142] and scouring liner notes and artwork to feel more attuned to the Pollard universe. Maybe, just maybe, he *owed* it to me to like me. This line of thinking is highly unfair, of course, for two reasons. First, a musician can't be expected to get along with all of his fans.[143] Some people are just flat-out jerky, no matter what kind of music they prefer. Second, I obviously knew way more about him than he knew about me, because unless pigs flew regularly over Dayton and he was familiar with the short entertainment articles I'd written or my book about classic arcade games, the only dirt he had on me was that I was a fan from Brooklyn being brought over by his friend-slash-publicist. And that meager information wasn't likely to lead to fruitful conversation, because it's tough to have a meaningful discussion with someone who clearly wants something from you—and I would most certainly want something: to prove to him that I understood. The entire evening would be a fight to refrain from being the Chris Farleyesque fanboy who says things like "Remember that time you wrote that song 'Pink Drink' and came up with the lyric, 'It's not who you blow but who you blow off'? That was awesome." Still, I had hope that we'd get along. When you're obsessed with music, you want to believe that you deeply understand the artists responsible for that obsession. And you want to believe they'd get you, too, if you were ever to meet.

I loosened up considerably after meeting Matt Davis, Cory's Dayton connection. Wearing a baseball hat, glasses, and a goatee, and in the vicinity of my age, Matt looked not unlike some of the guys I'd grown up with; plus he had a Midwesterner's default setting of friendly. It became apparent, as I listened to him and Cory have their first face-to-face conversation, that he was genuinely unaffected by his proximity to greatness. He may have

[142] This has proven impossible to do. I'll leave that part of the research to you. Suffice it to say that Pollard is the lone member of Guided By Voices to have appeared on every single release.

[143] And there was already a strike against me with Pollard: In a song called "Finks," he spoke of "city slickers, shrewd and untrustworthy."

been part of Pollard's inner circle, but that didn't preclude him from behaving like a fan—which is to say, like one of us. Without even asking, he threw on a GBV mix, cranked it up, and sped off toward our rendezvous spot. He made our mission seem routine, and that helped me to perform simple tasks, like breathing.

But our mission was anything but routine: We were going to meet Bob Pollard for pizza, and then we were being granted the considerable privilege of attending Monument Club, Pollard-speak for going to his house to consume large quantities of beer. We knew going in that we'd be doing the latter—amazing, already, beyond words—but when Matt revealed the news about the pizza, I saw Cory shift anxiously in the front seat. If we had been given this information over the phone away from Matt, we would now be giving each other a high five or fist bump so forceful that it would cause grimacing. But Cory and I had talked about the fine line between caring too much and appearing not to care at all: Cross that line toward caring too much and we'd appear to be chortling fanboys, and no celebrity wants those people around. Whatever occurred, it was better to play it cool—even if Monument Club featured a sex show involving midgets and donkeys. So in the back seat I told myself that this was going to be no big deal: It's just pizza. A few beers at some dude's house. Who's this Bob Pollard guy again?

The drive north on the interstate running through the city reminded me of one of my favorite Guided By Voices songs, a melancholy chugger entitled, appropriately, "Dayton, Ohio—19 Something and 5." [144] Pollard prefaces a live recording by saying, "This is a song about smoking dope, having cookouts, and hanging out on the west side," and then pays tribute to his hometown using uncharacteristically straightforward lyrics, reminisc-

[144] The studio version of this song appears on *Tonics and Twisted Chasers,* a 1996 vinyl release initially available only to members of Postal Blowfish, the official and insanely obsessive GBV e-mail discussion group that launched in 1995.

ing about "children in the sprinkler" and "the smell of fried foods." The tune always summons images of the Grand Rapids of my youth, a place I remember as being a hellmouth of sprinkler-cavorting brats, fried-food whiff, and hazy days. And in so many other ways, Dayton feels like home. The two cities are roughly equivalent in size and population, have seen better days, are ringed by a cluster of affluent and less-affluent suburbs, and play second banana to much larger urban centers elsewhere in the state. Dayton is also just a quick five hours from Grand Rapids via the same flat interstate we were driving on, and it's a very familiar drive: To get there you'd have to pass my mom's hometown of Bowling Green, Ohio, and my two college haunts of East Lansing and Ann Arbor, Michigan.[145] Although I wasn't content to stay, I frequently get nostalgic about Grand Rapids in the way Pollard does in "Dayton, Ohio." Indeed, the G.R. I knew was a place where, as he puts it, "you needn't travel far to feel completely alive," especially with the everyday options of playing cutthroat baseball in a huge backyard and skateboarding furtively on the roof of the church across the street. What I'm getting at is that it's completely inspiring that a force like Pollard could spring up in a place like where I'm from. That comforting thought, brought on by the strip-mall sprawl of the outskirts of Dayton, made me feel closer to Pollard than ever before. And I hadn't even met him yet.

As we pulled into the parking lot of the pizzeria, Matt laid down the golden rule: Upon entering, we would be required to buy a forty-ouncer to drink while waiting for the pizza to come out. I think now is the proper time to inform you that Cory and I have prodigious thirsts for beer. We have little trouble consuming two six-packs each in a sitting; a handful of times, we've tacked

---

[145] Not that Pollard, an ardent Ohio State football fan, needs to know about my University of Michigan affiliation. But come on: Go Blue! (Actually, I'm more a fan of all things Michigan State—but that is subject matter for a different book.)

on a third, plus a shot or two of whiskey.[146] We've been horrible
influences on each other: the instigators of killer hangovers, the
stunters of personal growth. But even we were concerned about
our ability to keep pace with Pollard, who's written songs entitled "Sot," "How's My Drinking?," and "Drinker's Peace," and
who has reportedly gone onstage without alcohol in his system
only one time, and that was because he had the flu. A few days
before we arrived in Dayton, Matt had sent Cory an e-mail warning us not to drink anything before he picked us up. "Monument
Club can take it out of you in and of itself," he wrote.

Even so, Cory and I confidently selected forties of Miller
High Life,[147] joined Matt at a table, and awaited Pollard's arrival.
About ten minutes and fifteen ounces later, he turned up, looking
like an aging hipster. He was wearing an unzipped hooded sweat-
shirt bearing the insignia of the California flag, a T-shirt from a
restaurant out west, blue corduroys, and sneakers; his hair, once
brown and poufy, was now close-cropped and cloud gray. Trail-
ing behind him were Kevin March and Chris Slusarenko, respectively the thirtysomething drummer and bassist of the final
incarnation of GBV. The three of them sat down, poured themselves mugs of beer, and the evening officially began.

According to a promotional Guided By Voices calendar tacked to
the wall of my kitchen, the first meeting of Monument Club occurred on June 5, 1994, three days before Pollard's final day as
an elementary school teacher, and just under three weeks prior to

[146] Opening your first beer of the evening presents a fork in the road:
Will you be sensible or will you be foolish? Each additional beer is another
fork, with the "foolish" direction looking ever more alluring. At the outset
of most drinking nights I usually hold the belief that I'll be in bed at a relatively decent hour with a nice buzz and happy memories. But the great thing
about drinking your first beer—or the bad, depending on your worldview—
is that it's served up with that sliver of risk: You just might wind up blacked
out in a puddle of someone's vomit.
[147] Aka the "champagne of beers."

the release of *Bee Thousand*, the album that would make him the basement genius of indie rock. Monument Club has almost always been held at his house and, as one regular facetiously wrote on an online message board, its members are anyone who can find the place. The Club still meets nearly every week, usually on Wednesdays, whenever Pollard is in town. Kim Deal's been there. Steve Albini's been there. The Strokes have been there. You could say that Monument Club is the indie-rock version of the VIP section at Bungalow 8 or those Puff Daddy/P. Diddy bashes where you're required to wear all white.

By the end of the pizza session, it was clear that things were going well. We'd had a few beers with Pollard and his bandmates, they'd asked us polite questions, they'd accepted us enough to talk about tour expenses in our presence, and we hadn't asked the fanboy questions we knew not to ask. We had figured out the pacing. The afternoon was turning out exactly as Matt had predicted: "Pretty much just sit back and let Bob hold court." Walking (and drinking and eating) amongst giants was exhilarating.[148] We were giddy. On our way out to the parking lot, I sneezed. Cory leaned over and whispered, "You just sneezed five feet away from Bob Pollard." It will forever be the best sneeze of my life. However, the balance was shifting slightly with every consumed beer. I was slowly losing my grip on Midwestern mode, getting a little more outwardly excited (read: louder); Cory was grinning at everybody, probably too much. It's possible that by

---

[148] I was already familiar with this feeling from two lavish steak dinners spent in 2001 across the table from actors Jack Black and Kyle Gass, the portly musical comedians who perform as the self-aggrandizing mock-rock band Tenacious D. The perception of the duo in hipster circles over the years is the prototypical example of indie-rock snobbery: Alt-comedy nerds discover their hilarious, blink-and-you'll-miss-it six-episode series on HBO; start trading dubbed copies on the Internet; turn against them as the band enters the domain of frat boys and when Jack Black appears in the godawful *Saving Silverman;* and, after a five-year hiatus, wax nostalgic for the early D and start buzzing about their first feature film, out at the end of 2006. I will never disown them. They wrote a song about Sasquatch.

becoming too comfortable around Pollard the unthinkable had happened: We had become our true selves again.

That Cory and I would be allowed to mix as relative equals at Monument Club with Pollard, a few band members, and his close friends, most of whom he's known since before he became a full-time musician, was, to put it mildly, a privilege and an honor. Hundreds of other obsessives would kill to be in our place. (No, not literally. Okay, maybe literally.) As a hugely grateful attendee, I am unable to divulge the whereabouts of Monument Club—and any directions would be wholly inaccurate if I tried, because on the drive to Pollard's house, already severely buzzed after the forty and two pitcher pours, I felt not unlike a civilian of Gotham City being blindfolded for a trip to the Batcave except that an eighteen-pack of Miller High Life was on my lap and I was sup-posed to drink all of it. Upon arrival at Pollard's shockingly non-descript home, we dumped our fullskies into a special four-foot high cooler, which, as it was later determined, contained more than three hundred cans of beer. At six o'clock, still broad day-light on a Wednesday evening, twenty middle-aged guys were in attendance at Monument Club.[149] A dozen cars surrounded the house. Crickets were chirping, but ignored. These weeknight par-ties may not have been a factor in the FOR SALE sign being placed in the yard across the street, but you never know.

And let it be said that Pollard knows how to throw a drink-ing bash. A drinking party is different from a regular party. At normal parties, most attendees follow the strange customs of dancing to bad music, bantering with people they don't like, and flirting without discretion; drinking is secondary. At a drinking party, the idea is simply to hang with your buddies and get drunk. I haven't been to that many great drinking parties in my life. In high school there was one held at a hockey rink, where a guy we called Popper puked the alcoholic contents of his stom-

[149] It resembled a scene from the HBO series *Entourage*. Well, maybe a dream sequence in which the characters have aged twenty years and now live in a quaint two-bedroom in Encino.

ach onto the ice. (The vomit froze!) Monument Club was way better than that one. No, there wasn't nudity or barfing (or, darn it, donkey sex shows). But there was a guy riding around on a tiny clown bicycle. The best indication of how much fun was being had? The TV was tuned to game seven of the 2004 American League Championship Series, the instant classic in which Boston Red Sox star Johnny Damon hit a grand slam to break the collective backs of the New York Yankees, helping the Sox move on to the World Series, where they'd finally put an end to "the Curse"—and not one person was watching. Even more telling: In the fifth inning, with the pivotal game not completely out of reach for the Yankees, Pollard started to blast music—and the game was turned off. Sometime around midnight, he rifled through his stunningly large and well-organized record collection,[150] pulled out *Quadrophenia,* and played air guitar to "The Real Me." A little while later he said in his soupy, Dayton drawl to no one in particular, "If you're on a major label, you suck."

Pollard and his crew have been referred to as the Dayton Mafia. (Pollard is obviously the don.) But the few hours we'd spent around Pollard had made me think of him not as a capo but as an uncle of mistaken disrepute. The relative whom your respectable parents usually speak about in hushed tones while exchanging cautious glances. A guy you've been led to believe had wasted his potential—think Bill Murray in *Stripes* before the Army, or Walter Matthau in *The Bad News Bears* before the catch by Lupus. Someone you're scared to answer when he asks you personal questions at Easter dinner because you think he's fucking with you. But who, in your darkest hour, steps in and, with the help of his ragtag gang of misunderstood friends, thwarts the bully and helps you get the girl. These people were pretty welcoming, after all the worry.

[150] The shelving unit housing his records was built by Jim MacPherson, a one-time drummer in GBV but more well-known for his work with the Breeders. "Jimmy Mac," as he was referred to at Monument Club, was insanely friendly to Cory and me for reasons that were unclear. No one could be that nice.

On our way out, Pollard drunk-hugged Cory and me twice each, even though we'd said at most twenty words combined to him all night. We piled back into Matt's designated-driver-mobile and he informed us that we were setting off for the Green Lantern—news that resulted in a lot of hooting and hollering from our mouths. The Green Lantern is a bar outside of which three early GBV pillars Pollard, his brother, Jim,[151] and Tobin Sprout[152] stood in a much-beloved publicity photo; it's Dayton's Salford Lads Club. Earlier in the day we'd told Matt that long before he'd invited us out to meet Pollard, we'd talked often of making a pilgrimage to Dayton just to get drunk at the Green Lantern. Sometime during the evening, without our knowing, Matt had asked Pollard where the bar was, and here at twelve thirty a.m., we were off to look for it. The Green Lantern turned out to look nothing like we expected; in fact, situated as it was in the middle of nowhere, surrounded by dark copses of trees and a gravel parking lot and tragically closed for the evening, it seemed kind of creepy. But Cory and I scampered out of the car and attempted to arrange ourselves outside the bar in precisely the way the brothers Pollard had in the famous publicity still. With the kitschy Green Lantern Bar sign looming over me in the background, I peered coolly downward at the disposable camera held by Matt, channeling Bob. I suppose that photo turned out okay. But the better shots are the ones taken of Cory and me jumping around the parking lot like idiots, releasing the nervousness that had been bottled up inside us all day.

[151] He lingered rather late at Monument Club despite having to get up before dawn to go to his job at a nearby GM parts plant. A high school basketball prodigy in the late 1970s and early '80s (he still holds the all-time points record in the Dayton area), he told us about how he blew out his knee while playing at Arizona State, returned home in shame, joined Guided By Voices, and became a revered indie rock star in his own right. The brothers Pollard led GBV to victory over the Beastie Boys in a pickup game while sharing a bill on Lollapalooza in 1995.

[152] To our disappointment, Pollard's former songwriting foil was a no-show. Boo-hoo!

UNSTABLE JOURNEY

"I'm feeling good and I don't know if that's all right."

Sometimes you wake up and greet the day with a smile. Sometimes you curse it. When I woke up on October 23, 2004, just after noon, I smiled. And then I cursed. Loudly. I had a terrible hangover. A little while later, Cory dry-heaved in our hotel bathroom. But we had to get ourselves in shape. Matt Davis had cheerily called to say he'd be picking us up at three to drive to Columbus for the penultimate Guided By Voices concert in Ohio. Through Advil, coffee, and one of the more arduous bathroom sessions of my life, I managed to resemble a human by the time he arrived. A stop for grease-meat at Burger King further perked me up. But I knew the only thing that would right this ship was more beer to keep company with the sixteen consumed the night before.

On the way to Columbus, Matt played for us a double disc containing some forty songs, many of which would later appear on Pollard's first post-GBV solo album.[153] The sheer quantity of Pollard's output is hard to fathom. Already in 2004 he'd put out thirty-eight songs on three full-length records: *Half Smiles of the Decomposed,* GBV's fifteenth and final album; *Fiction Man,* the

---

[153] Entitled *From a Compound Eye* and whittled down to twenty-six tracks, the album was finally released in January 2006 on Merge Records. Technically speaking, his first post-GBV solo album was 2005's *Relaxation of the Asshole,* a so-called comedy record collecting some of his onstage rants.

fifth LP bearing only the name Robert Pollard;[154] and *Edison's Memos,* a collection of outtakes and demos. And yet he had forty more songs in the can. His write 'em and release 'em methodology has irked some critics, most famously Jim DeRogatis of the *Chicago Sun-Times,* who, in a dismissive 1997 review of *Mag Earwhig!* suggesting that Pollard was too prolific, wrote that "the law of averages was bound to apply sooner or later." [155] What I suppose this meant is that Pollard should put more effort into making his best ideas even better, save up these gems for one and only one mind-blowing album every couple of years, and relegate all of the lesser snippets, half-baked notions, and sonic larks to B-sides, or better yet never release them at all. I can't say that I haven't thought this way myself from time to time. When you've written a practically uncountable number of songs, some of them are bound to disappoint. And there's no denying that a few of his lesser albums could have been combined to create one sterling album. So does Bob Pollard need an editor? Maybe. But I come back to the fact that he's always written and released music at a hyperactive rate. It's what he does. If he'd more stringently edited himself from the beginning, it's possible that we'd have been deprived of some of the best moments on his albums, which come from ideas that aren't fleshed out, or clock in at twenty-three or forty-eight seconds, or sound as if they were added to the track listing at the last second against the counsel of

---

[154] Please don't confuse Robert Pollard the solo artist with the man who fronted Robert Pollard and His Soft Rock Renegades as well as Robert Pollard with Doug Gillard. God knows I have.

[155] To be fair, Pollard could not be stopped from putting out music in 1996 and 1997. Here's my tally of what he released during that two-year span: Four high-quality LPs (*Under the Bushes Under the Stars*—twenty-four songs; *Not in My Airforce*—twenty-two songs; *Tonics and Twisted Chasers*—twenty-four songs; *Mag Earwhig!*—twenty-one songs), two mid-quality EPs (*Sunfish Holy Breakfast*—ten songs; *Plantations of Pale Pink*—six songs) and various kick-ass singles (nine otherwise unreleased songs), containing a total of 116 songs. Not including imports. Plus, both *Propeller* and *Vampire on Titus* were rereleased, and he appeared on Tobin Sprout's first two solo records. The mind reels.

a professional recording engineer. Sure, the rate of output can be overwhelming and confusing even to a die-hard fan like me, but I appreciate being able to decide for myself what's great, what's good, and what's annoying. If his prolific tendencies make casual listeners say, "Again with an album from that guy?" then so be it. And besides, even a lesser Pollard album should stack up favorably when judged on its own merits. Let's use *Half Smiles of the Decomposed* as an example. While it isn't even one hundredth as listenable as the masterful *Bee Thousand* or *Alien Lanes,* it is still a lot better than that the vast majority of non-Pollard crud that gets passed off as music nowadays. And at least two of the songs from *Half Smiles* could have gone to number one if Americans had any damn taste.

What's more, every release offers a promise of a tour, and Guided By Voices is undeniably an excellent live band. Despite missing out on countless opportunities to see them perform over the years, I'm comforted by the fortuitous circumstances of my first GBV show: in front of only fifty people in my hometown of Grand Rapids, Michigan, at the same bar on whose softball team my dad played in the mid-1970s. In the spring of 2003 I read that the band was going to play three warm-up dates in advance of a fall tour supporting *Earthquake Glue,* their penultimate album. To my disbelief, the first was going to be in good old G.R. at the Intersection, my dad's blue-period watering hole. I booked the flight from Brooklyn that same day. When the June date came around, getting to the venue early felt like a requirement of my fanship even though it would mean hanging out by myself in a bar for many hours.[156] That voice, the belligerent one that speaks to me from the root of my obsession, was saying, "To do this right, shithead, you'll need to get as close to the stage as possible." It turned out not to be an issue. When I arrived at five thirty p.m., the café area up front—my father's divey hangout, where

---

[156] Luckily, this is one of my favorite things to do. Why is there a stigma about drinking alone in bars?

I'd seen my first honest-to-God albino at the tender age of six, had relocated, expanded, and trendified; I considered it a quiet tragedy—was staging a free concert by some god-awful John Mayer type, and it was standing-room only. At first I thought everybody was politely enduring this guy's caterwauling as they waited around for GBV, but the coffee-sipping loons were making too many appreciative noises for that to have been the case. By seven, the troubadour and his treacly tunes were long gone; the club had emptied. With exactly six other early birds, I watched in awe as Guided By Voices ran through a sound check. In New York City, this would not have been allowed to happen; you simply do not get to witness the rock 'n' roll equivalent of batting practice unless you are with the band, especially one as well known among the indie rock cognoscenti as Guided By Voices.[157] This was a band that, just a year and a half prior, had coheadlined a New Year's Eve gig with the Strokes, then a major buzz band. It begged questions: Have I entered an alternate universe? Is Guided By Voices not as amazing as I believe them to be? Am I the chump here? And then in a single swig of three-dollar Miller Genuine Draft, I divined the answer to each of these questions: The entire city of Grand Rapids is the problem, not Guided By Voices. By the time GBV took the stage at around ten, the crowd had "swelled" to five rows from the stage. Good old Bland Rapids. But I'm glad so few showed up. It confirmed my suspicion that I was onto something with Guided By Voices that

---

[157] Even bands no one's ever heard of draw crowds in New York City. This is mostly a blessing for the locals, as it ensures that our beloved city will always remain a crucial tour destination; it is also a curse, because there's a real chance that even a show you'd think no one could possibly care about—an acoustic performance by former Ride guitarist Mark Gardener, say—will sell out in less than an hour. In those days before Internet sales, it was a point of pride to join those other obsessives camping out overnight to score tickets, which I've done five times: for R.E.M., New Order, Morrissey, Rush, and U2. Now it's a point of pride to hit the snooze and take my chances.

most people didn't know anything about. It also confirmed my suspicion that most people don't know anything, period.

There are three categories of live performers: Those who want to involve the audience, those who do not, and those who do whatever it is that Chan Marshall (aka Cat Power) does. Guided By Voices is that first, best kind: They make the audience their sixth member. Now, I've been blown away by bands that acknowledge the crowd very little (three Jesus and Mary Chain shows comes to mind) or that pretend no one else is even in the room with them (e.g., the moody Scottish crew Mogwai). If a band rocks, a band rocks. I tend to appreciate shows more and remember them more clearly, however, when the music is augmented by the sensation of being somewhat involved in the process. Yo La Tengo,[158] whom I have seen live four times, has always been good at reeling in a crowd; they're like a band playing at a really good house party. The wonderful thing about Guided By Voices, though, is that they are the party, and they're letting you crash it.

I had learned very little about the history of GBV in the eight months since adopting them as my pet project. And though obsessive listening to their albums had caused me to love their music uncontrollably, my knowledge of their stage persona was restricted to information divulged by my girlfriend, who had seen them in Central Park in 1997 and had been put off by Pollard's blatant drunkenness. That's about all I had to go on. Not that I was expecting much anyway. New York had made me a jaded concertgoer. In college, I'd go to a show and completely let everything out: I'd crowd-surf, mosh, bang my head. But only

---

[158] One always intriguing aspect of living in New York, as it must be in Los Angeles, is the everyday possibility of rubbing shoulders with your pop-culture idols. In early 2005, at a West Village theater that shows revival films, my girlfriend and I spotted bushy-haired Yo La Tengo front man Ira Kaplan and his drummer wife, Georgia Hubley, milling about before show-time. Without telling them, we decided that the four of us were on a double date.

minor outward displays of concert enjoyment are tolerated at alternative-rock shows in New York. By and large they are peopled by hiply dressed twentysomethings standing almost entirely still but for the bobbing of their heads; occasionally some of them might be moved enough to smack their hands against their legs in time to the music. Steve Malkmus said it best to the passive crowd at a Pavement show in 1994:[159] "Congratulations! You are the worst audience we've had on this tour." And he was absolutely right. It made me hate them, too! And then somewhere along the line I became one of these indie-rock pod people. It took GBV to wake me up.

A rock show, if it's any good, should make you feel younger. And if you feel younger, you should act younger. I'm not suggesting that thirty-five-year-olds should demonstrate their indie-rock crushes through stage-diving, or that mosh pits need to consume the timid, reverent audiences at every Shins show. But if you really like the band you're seeing, you should exert some energy—as much as you can muster. Even if it makes you look not as cool as you think you are. I am aware of the many rules of concert etiquette—well aware, as I used to be the world's biggest stickler—and I do still try to exhibit decorum that syncs up with the vibe of the concertgoers I'm standing near. No one needs to make a spectacle of oneself. But I do sometimes find myself envying the abandon with which a stocky, bald guy rocked out a few years ago at a Foo Fighters show.[160] This dude was *into* it. During "Monkey Wrench," he took an aggro stance and violently threw his head around as if he had gotten an unlikely amount of water in his ear. It was a bit of a surprise that his neck didn't snap. It was obvious that he didn't care one whit about anyone around him. We didn't matter—only the music did. It was inspiring.

But yeah, it was also pretty annoying.

My restraint at that first GBV show lasted about twenty min-

[159] Not the remorse-causing one with GBV as the opener.
[160] They played a party thrown by Sony supporting the PlayStation 2. Yes, the Foos are for hire!

utes. The band started off with a few songs from the new album,
and a few others I'd never heard. Nothing too mind-blowing. But
during "Buzzards and Dreadful Crows"—they played their hits!
Or "hits"!—I turned into a hairier, thinner version of that insane
Foo Fighters fan, and stayed that way for the rest of the show,
which lasted a whopping two and a half hours. Pollard was a vi-
sion. He'd fish a Miller Lite out of the cooler he'd brought onstage, pop off the cap and chuck it to the ground, and suck down
the beer during instrumental parts. He'd twirl his microphone
around like Robert Plant and do goofy leg kicks as if he were a
master of drunken-style Kung Fu. Late in the set Pollard, visibly
tipsy yet still somehow able to nail all the lyrics and melodies,
slipped and spent a minute-plus singing from a prone position,
staring at the ceiling. At the end of the song, he sluggishly pushed
himself to his feet—and then pretended like nothing had happened! He simply high-fived a few fans in the front row, ripped
open another beer, and launched into the next song. It was the
coolest thing I'd ever seen.

   That Grand Rapids concert was my official baptism into the
cult of GBV.[161] Mere obsession no longer applied. I had been
pushed over the brink into fanaticism.

❖

We pulled into the parking lot of the Columbus venue[162] at
around six, just as Pollard, wearing exactly the same outfit

   [161] And make no mistake: Hard-core GBV fans would don purple
Nikes and prepare to hitch a ride on Halley's Comet if Pollard asked
them to.
   [162] The show was happening at the Alrosa Villa, a roadhouse surrounded by a black sea of asphalt in a desolate part of Columbus. Six weeks
later a crazed fan would climb onstage here during a Damageplan concert
and shoot to death guitarist "Dimebag" Darrell Abbott, formerly of the
metal band Pantera, in an act of obsession gone horribly awry. As previously mentioned, one of the major selling points of Guided By Voices shows
was the way they involved the crowd—so much so at times that it wasn't
much of a problem to climb right up onstage as the evening wore down, sing

from the day before, was emerging from the club. The last we'd
seen him, at roughly one in the morning, he was still blasting
music. He nodded in our direction as we walked past him and,
intuitively sensing our pain, asked playfully, "How're you guys
feeling?"

The obvious answer: Not well.

"You pussies."

We laughed. It was true.

"I felt pretty good this morning," he said. I asked him how
this was possible. "This is part of my life."

One knock on Pollard is that he drinks too much during performances. He's explained it away by saying that he needs to
drink because he'd be too nervous otherwise. Now that may not
be true; it's entirely possible that he drinks because he likes to
drink. But it doesn't really matter, and here's why: He drinks capably.[163] Pollard seems to know his limit acutely. He pushes that
limit to its fullest extreme, to be sure, but he does obey it. Like, he
never forgets the words to his songs—which is impressive, considering that on any given night he might perform forty-plus
tunes. Also, he has the endurance to last multiple hours on

---

a few bars with the Fading Captain, and then jump back into the crowd un-
molested by security brutes. As long as you obeyed certain unspoken rules,
this behavior was given GBV's blessing. In September 2003, for example, I
attended a New York show at which a woman got up during the gorgeous
stomp of "Smothered in Hugs" and sang with Pollard into his microphone.
(It kind of pissed me off; "Smothered in Hugs" is one of my favorite GBV
songs, and this lady rendered it inert.) A few months later, at a Detroit venue
with a very low stage, at least ten concertgoers clambered up during the anthem "Glad Girls," and no one in charge seemed to care. In light of the
Dimebag Darrell incident, GBV's lax crowd-control policy might have been
a risk to the band members. But it just seems so unlikely that anything violent could occur at a GBV show. Whereas Damageplan and Pantera traf-
ficked in aggression and alienation, GBV is about having a good time, all the
time. Still, there's no accounting for whackjobs.

[163] Most of the time. He reportedly drank so much before and during a
1993 show in Philadelphia that he had to close one eye to acquire the focus
needed just to walk around. Awesome.

stage—while drinking beer the whole way through. Okay, at the Columbus show, the band did play the Beatlesesque "Echos Myron" twice. And during a later stop on the tour, Pollard, who plays guitar on the majority of his albums but seldom live, would strap on a Fender and seem totally unable to remember how the thing was supposed to work. Still, the ten times I've seen him live, his drinking never got in the way of what the crowd had paid to see. In fact, his drinking more likely enhanced the experience.[164]

At any rate, just before showtime in Columbus, Pollard bluntly stated to the twenty or so friends gathered in the band's dressing room, "Anyone who goes on sober is a fucking ass-hole." It's possible that he was already a little buzzed when he said this, given the plentiful beer and tequila options available backstage. Maybe it was a harbinger of doom. As GBV shows go, the one in Columbus wouldn't rank among their best, and I think everyone in the band would back me up on that. They were off the whole night. Avoidable equipment failures. Sloppy play. Too much of a party atmosphere (and, for a GBV show, that's saying something). At one point rhythm guitarist and fan favorite Nate Farley doused his own head in Budweiser. Not surprisingly, the adoring audience didn't seem too bothered by the lowered level of quality. And, at a certain point—like, after our sixth beers—neither did Cory or I.

Then again, we watched much of the action from the stage itself, right next to the drum kit. Such incredible access was difficult to fathom. As I looked down at the reverent faces of those superfans in the front row—especially the ones who would occasionally look in my direction and flash me *(me!)* the devil's horns, as if I were in the band—a great divide was made crystal clear: It was the band vs. the fans. By which I mean us vs. them. Improb-

[164] Fueled by drink, Pollard often launches into comedic rants between songs. (The sort collected on the aforementioned stinker *Relaxation of the Asshole.*) As you might expect, Pollard is no Bono. You'll never hear him railing about relieving third-world debt or enacting laws to provide free condoms in high schools.

ably, Cory and I had been allowed to cross over to the other side: We were with the band. It wasn't until much later that I would see how deluding the access given to us could be. It had started to feel normal to be backstage, like we had a right to be there. As if, because we'd consumed a certain number of beers with these people and hadn't made nuisances of ourselves, we'd passed some sort of initiation ritual. That we had become one of them. But we obviously didn't belong at all. We should have been out there in the audience staring up adoringly at Pollard like everyone else. The delusion had given both of us a continual rush— and it was a powerful one indeed.

I found out just how powerful the next day when I experienced bona fide withdrawal symptoms. We were to see GBV perform in Newport, Kentucky, just across the river from Cincinnati. The difference: Cory and I had been left to fend for ourselves until showtime. As we drove the Elantra across the bridge into Kentucky that afternoon, I saw how it was going to be when we got back home. Very soon we'd be returning to Brooklyn as two ordinary GBV fans. Sure, we'd have memories to trump most other obsessives. But that would be all we'd have. We would no longer have the keys to the Pollard kingdom. We wouldn't have Pollard's ear. We wouldn't have an open invitation to drop by if we were ever in the area. We wouldn't be thanked in any liner notes. In every respect we would cease to be with the band. To know what it was like to walk amongst giants—were we simply supposed to forget about that? As we readied ourselves at our motel, I tried to steer my attention toward having fun. We were doing exactly what we would have done if this were a regular show back in New York: pounding beer, talking shit, eating horribly. Only now we were well aware that we weren't doing so in the presence of our favorite musician. It was impossible to suppress the desire. It was hard not to want that rush. I wanted to have ridden to the show in the van with Pollard and the band. I wanted to have hit the sound check again to see previews of the songs they'd be playing later. I wanted to know things the rest of the audience didn't, even if it was just for one more night.

When we arrived at the venue, a century-old mansion that had been converted into a one-thousand-person-capacity concert hall, Matt Davis was there to greet us with a big, conspiratorial grin.[165] He ushered us upstairs, far from the hoi polloi, to a private dining hall—and they were all there, all the guys we'd met at Monument Club or in Columbus: Jimmy Pollard. Jim Mac-Pherson.[166] The guy who'd ridden the tiny bicycle around. And a burly, jovial man named Mike Lipps, more commonly known in Camp GBV as the Heed, who had regaled us the previous night with a story that involved him and Jimmy Pollard polishing off twenty beers and then playing night golf at an exceptionally high level of skill. And of course there was Bob Pollard himself, sitting at the head of a long table, the king in his court. A short while after we walked in, he flashed us a knowing smile and paid us the ultimate compliment. "You guys are troupers," he said.

Cory and I were allowed to watch the show from the side of the stage once again. This vantage point has many benefits, not the least of which is that you get to see the audience in much the same way the band sees it. You see their upturned, almost holy faces. You get to feel the collective release of euphoria. The only time I'd ever felt anything remotely like it had been a few months before, at the Matador record-release party for *Half Smiles of the Decomposed*, where attendees could sing GBV songs while backed by a cover band. A limited number of fans were allowed to attend, and I luckily managed to get inside. Somehow, when a slip of paper bearing my name was called, I got the exact song I was hoping for: "Tractor Rape Chain," quite possibly my favorite Guided By Voices tune. There were likely only a hundred

[165] Literally. That night we met Matt's wife, Missy, and she literally says "literally," like, every other sentence. It literally became a joke between the four of us.

[166] Somehow he'd remembered our names. It really is possible that someone can be this nice.

people in the crowd; it looked more like a thousand when I took my place at the microphone. But any nervousness about singing in front of strangers left me once the music kicked in. I was feeling it. I didn't do microphone twirls or anything overtly Pollardesque because that would have been lame, but there was this sensation filling me that I had become impervious to harm—or embarrassment. People in the crowd were singing along. Passionately. One guy gave me a thumbs-up, despite my mangling of the chorus the second time around. It was uplifting. But you'd have to multiply that feeling by a gaudy number in order to understand what it must feel like to be Pollard. What a huge surge of adrenaline it must give him to be out there onstage, with all of those loving fans singing along and jamming to the music he wrote. The feeling was so strong that Cory and I were empowered by it too from the side of the stage: adrenaline rush by association. And the feeling was buoyed by a noticeable uptick in musical quality; this was the performance we'd expected when we booked our flights. The band was incredibly tight, almost seamless, as if Pollard had reminded everyone involved that they weren't going to get another shot at this. Why not at least attempt to be perfect?

Which is why I was very surprised when Matt Davis pushed Cory out onstage during the final song of the evening. The gesture implied that Matt viewed Cory as a member of the family— but during the final song? Nice! It was incredibly cool to see my friend up there, with Pollard's arm around his shoulder, belting out a song the crowd was going apeshit over. It was a fitting end to the evening, not to mention our life-changing trip.

And then I got the push. Now, karaoke is one thing. But here I was being told to go out and sing with Pollard in front of a thousand-plus people who had paid a lot of money to see GBV for what might have been their last time. Would it surprise you to learn that I do not have a great singing voice? It's a fact that's been proven many times over on various karaoke outings, most notably this one time when my mike was turned off just a minute into a squawky rendition of "Jesse's Girl." But here's what I thought as I walked toward Pollard: *Who cares? I'm going to sing, and anyone who doesn't like it can suck it!* I passed Cory, who was being dragged off by the stage manager, and we exchanged painfully sharp high fives. Pollard turned and smiled and granted me access to his microphone. And then, together, we plunged dutifully into the final verse of what just might be the most universally revered song in the GBV catalog, "I Am a Scientist." We sang:

> I am a lost soul
> I shoot myself with rock 'n' roll
> The hole I dig is bottomless
> But nothing else can set me free.

And then there was a tug on my shirt informing me that my time onstage was up.

12

GAME OF PRICKS

"I've cheated so long I wonder how you keep track of me."

Hello. *You have two new messages. Message one, from Cory Jones, received November 12, 2004, at 8:41 p.m.:*

"Hey—did you get the e-mail? What should we do? Man, we're fucked. This totally sucks! Call me."

Message two, from Cory Jones, received November 13, 2004, at 10:27 a.m.:

"Holy shit, dude, where the hell are you? Fuck! Check your e-mail and then call me back. Seriously. Do it now!"

You have no more messages in your mailbox.

This was what was lying in wait for me when I woke up just before noon on that fateful day in Ann Arbor, Michigan, just three weeks after the euphoric trip to Ohio, and seven hours after going to bed loaded on a case of beer. I had returned to the old college town to visit my friend Macek,[167] and we'd spent much of the

---

[167] This burly individual now lives in Chicago; the most important thing to know about him is that he's a recovering Grateful Dead addict. Sometimes against my will an image of his big, spherical cranium comes to mind, and when it unfortunately does I am reminded of the summer of 2001, when my friend Sauce and I drove from Seattle to New York City in a rented Ford Ranger. Before setting off, we'd procured from a novelty store a jokester's arsenal—a dashboard hula girl, sombreros, a plastic Pillsbury Doughboy doll, a rubber chicken, and the pièce de résistance, a cardboard cutout of Mr. Spock. All photos from the road trip feature Spock: Spock sticking his head out of the passenger-side window as Sauce guides the truckster through the Tour-Thru Tree; Spock gazing longingly at the Pacific

previous twenty-four hours bar-hopping and trying to restrain ourselves from ogling the shockingly young ladies drinking around us. Groggily deciding that whatever Cory was yammering about could wait until I was good and ready, I lumbered around Macek's town house with coffee in hand, hoping to reverse the wrongs[168] of the previous day. E-mail was finally checked at around three p.m., and it was only then that I understood why a person should always keep his cell phone turned on while on vacation.

This is an excerpt from the first e-mail I read, sent to the Postal Blowfish e-mail discussion group by a beloved member of the GBV camp:

Ocean; Spock in a shopping cart being pushed by Sellers around a Taco Bell parking lot. Ah, memories. And here's another: Somewhere during the endless drive through northern Nevada, en route to Salt Lake City, we decided that the most important thing for us to do in all the world was to stage a footrace in the Bonneville Salt Flats, where land-speed records have repeatedly been established. Both of us knew the race would be no contest: In high school I'd run a 6.2 in the fifty-yard dash to Sauce's 7.8—plus, he'd been outdrinking me three beers to one on the haul across Nevada. But we were men, and men must run. Just before sundown we propped up Spock as a finish line, took our marks on the pale white Utah ground roughly a hundred meters upwind, and readied ourselves for the first bit of exercise either of us had seen in months. And then we ran. I envisioned myself as a mystifying blur, a mix of Carl Lewis and Rickey Henderson, all swagger, and speaking about myself in the third person: *John Sellers gonna win this race! John Sellers got no equal!* But halfway to the finish line, Sauce was still right there next to me. The shock and shame this caused me helped turn what should have been a blowout into a much-disputed photo finish. But in a very real way, victory was mine: I managed to snap the trip's most artistic picture as Sauce puked a bean-burrito-and-beer Picasso onto the white desert floor— although I must say that Spock does not look amused. Anyway, further along in the trip we hit Ann Arbor to hang with Macek for a few nights, and upon our departure we left him a nice parting gift by hiding our gag items in strategic locations around his bachelor pad: the rubber chicken chilling in the fireplace, the Pillsbury Doughboy bobbing in the toilet bowl, and Spock lying suggestively in his bed. It's always good fun to fuck with Macek.

[168] Printed on every Matador CD: ALL RIGHTS RESERVED. ALL WRONGS REVERSED.

From: Rich Turiel
Date: November 11, 2004 10:50:46 PM EST
To: "Postal Blowfish"
Subject: PB: GBV Betrayal

Hey I just wanted to pass something along to you all. A few weeks
ago a couple of folks who do some indie rock writing were invited to
Monument Club via a mutual friend. They stated they were there as
fans, not journalists. It was often expressed that they were not there
writing a story. Well the band came to find out today that one of the
guys has already sold a book and the last chapters deal with his trip.
Obviously we all feel that there is a great betrayal involved. . . .

But wait—there's more! Within minutes of the post by Rich
Turiel, GBV's beloved tour manager and Web guru, the flurry of
e-mails by Postal Blowfish members had begun to fly fast and furious across the GBV universe:

Date: November 11, 2004 11:09:36 PM EST
Subject: Re: PB: GBV Betrayal

That's pretty damn shitty. :(

Date: November 12, 2004 1:56:30 AM EST
Subject: Re: PB: GBV Betrayal

fuckers.

Date: November 12, 2004 9:34:52 AM EST
Subject: Re: PB: GBV Betrayal

I guess this guy must be a "true" journalist.

Date: November 12, 2004 9:39:02 AM EST
Subject: Re: PB: GBV Betrayal

Yeah, it might put him out of the running for a Pulitzer.

Date: November 12, 2004 10:14:10 AM EST
Subject: Fwd: PB: GBV Betrayal

Might get him a job with the NY Times!

Date: November 12, 2004 12:37:43 PM EST
Subject: Re: PB: GBV Betrayal

MAN, that's the suckiest sucker that ever sucked! WHAT a lying sack
of shit!

And that's just about when they found a photo of me online:

From: G. Lynn Burch
Date: November 12, 2004 1:11:51 PM EST
Subject: Re: PB: GBV Betrayal

The wanted poster is at the printers.

From: Jonesy
Date: November 12, 2004 5:56:00 PM EST
Subject: Re: PB: GBV Betrayal

"I have often expressed that I DO NOT look like a peanut dicked
asshat."—John Sellers

Mercifully, the chatter among Postal Blowfish members returned to more pedestrian Pollard matters after that last untop-
pable put-down. But wait—there's more! Over on Disarm the
Settlers, the official GBV message board, the same announcement had been posted under the subject heading "Illegal Sellers."
There, using the full power of the Internet, the Settlers had
swiftly steered the already bitter discussion, complete with calls
for lawsuits and kneecappings, into a forum for posting altered
photos of yours truly. An image that I didn't even know existed
had somehow been tracked down; courtesy the wonders of Pho-

toshop and a particularly evil mind, my head was quickly affixed to the bloated, white body of something I'm guessing is a fat man in a Speedo. This horror was precisely what caused me to shut off Macek's computer and set off for the nearest bar.

❖

Boarding the flight back to New York the next morning, both a mental and physical wreck, I felt as though I'd drawn the GO DIRECTLY TO JAIL! DO NOT PASS GO! card in Monopoly. Only way worse, because this wasn't Monopoly. At that exact moment in Dayton, Bob Pollard, the musician who writes the songs that make my whole world sing, was sitting around cursing my name. All right, it's very possible that after issuing the infamous "GBV Betrayal" proclamation through a faithful henchman, he hadn't been moved to think of me at all. And he might not have been in Dayton at that moment. Either way, and wherever he was, this much was true: I was dead to him. My mind spun through various stratagems for extracting my sorry ass from this unbelievable predicament,[169] but all avenues took me toward the same frightening conclusion: There was no way out.

So, what would you do if you woke up one morning knowing that your hero hated your guts? And not just any hero but a hero made human by the generosity he extended to you? Would you lie down on your bed and decide never to move again? Because that's what I did upon arriving back at my apartment from the airport. My obvious mental anguish—Bob Pollard hated my guts!—had been joined by searing pain in my gut, and that pain was saying, *You are the biggest fucking loser in the entire universe.* And the pain was absolutely right.

Let me be clear: Cory had nothing to do with our Pollard problem. The crisis entirely stemmed from terrible communication on my part—namely, that there was zero communication,

[169] One of these ideas had me renting a U-Haul, cramming it with Miller Lite, and unloading it on Pollard's doorstep. This is something I seriously considered for more than ten minutes.

either preceding our trip to Dayton or in the three weeks afterward, about my intention to write a book that greatly concerned Robert Ellsworth Pollard Jr., the driving force behind Guided By Voices. How could this be possible? My proposal had been sold the day before I headed out to Dayton. Why not inform Pollard when I was hanging out with him? And, for the love of God, why hadn't I done so in the three weeks following the trip?

The perfect answer: "You have shit for brains."

These are the first words Matt Davis said to me when he finally consented to take my call later that afternoon. Cory had brokered the conversation. When I'd spoken to Cory in those breathless minutes after reading the e-mails and message boards that first time, he'd sounded as if his cat had just died. Worse, that he'd run over his cat. Worse still, that he'd run over his cat, adopted a new cat, and then run over that one, too. I'm not sure I've ever heard a person sound more distraught than the Cory Jones of November 13, 2004. But the following day, as I lay on my bed intent on never rising again, the phone rang, and the voice on the other end had a renewed vigor to it. He had spoken to Matt: Good news—things weren't entirely bleak. For one thing, Cory wasn't being held in contempt by Pollard for my mistake. My anguish lessened considerably upon hearing that. Still, that Cory had to endure any of this was ridiculous. There was nothing I could do to make that right. Or was there? I dialed Matt's number and took a deep breath.

Needless to say, the conversation that took place over most of the next hour wasn't filled with cheerful reminiscences about the beers we'd drunk together or how awesome the Ohio shows had been. Nor was there talk of future beers or shows we might be taking in. It's not a conversation I'd ever want to have again. But it went about as well as that kind of phone call could go. Matt patiently let me explain my side of the story, made sure I understood the many flaws in my decision not to tell Pollard about my book, and described in crystal-clear detail the first step I'd have to take if I hoped ever to square things with Pollard. A long, apologetic letter was sent off to Dayton the following morning—the print version of donning sackcloth and ashes.

And then I waited. And waited another day. And waited some more. Eight long days after disappointing Pollard and his crew to the extreme, and four panic-filled days after overnighting the apology, with each day peeling off like the slowest Band-Aid ever, I still had no word on whether he'd accepted my side of the story. And the not knowing was killing me. Work was impossible to consider. I barely ate. My girlfriend [170] was being driven nuts by my constant fretting—fretting that was exacerbated by my reading and rereading the anti-Sellers e-mails and message-board posts. New people had come forth on Disarm the Settlers to call into question my integrity, looks, and manhood. So convincing was the anger of the GBV mob that I was almost moved to denounce myself anonymously: *What a douchebag this John Sellers is! And I know where he lives!*

---

[170] Precisely two years after she'd given me the gift of Guided By Voices, my girlfriend had quite obviously grown good and tired of my Pollard obsession. When we first started dating, my musical diet was supplied mostly by bands no longer in existence: Pavement, My Bloody Valentine, Sebadoh, Dinosaur Jr., the Replacements, Soundgarden, Nirvana, Joy Division, the Pixies, Hüsker Dü. I was a corpse shagger. But here came a sweet-tempered, restless, always inquisitive girl asking me to rejoin the living. While she'd been reared on the Smiths, Liz Phair, and Belle & Sebastian, she was ashamed of or fed up with the bands that reminded her of her younger years. As a monthly record reviewer, she heard a lot of new music and embraced much of it, but never to the point of folly: She rejected electroclash outright, fled a theremin concert a few songs in, and, like me, agreed that mash-ups were a waste of everyone's time. It was easy and satisfying to concede to her tastes. "Here," she'd say, holding out an advance copy of an upcoming CD, "you'll like this band." And very often I did. She turned me on to the New Pornographers, Ted Leo, the Shins, the White Stripes, Interpol, and the Walkmen, among others. But my GBV obsession, which she unwittingly introduced into our relationship like one of those Asian swamp eels that are ravaging the Florida Everglades, became a wedge between us; it was something I had to hide from her. So many times she'd hear me whistling absentmindedly and make a harmless inquiry as to the song's origin, and I would lie and say that it was Cheap Trick. It makes me wonder how I would have made out if we'd ever moved in together. Alas, we broke up for good in 2006.

On the Friday before Thanksgiving, needing to commiser-
ate with the only other person in the world who knew exactly
what I was going through, I phoned up Cory for drinks. And man,
what a bitch session that night was, the two of us whining and
pouting like two brats who'd been banished to the principal's office by our favorite teacher. Near the end of the night, eight unsat-
isfying beers in but sober as a cat, Cory had come to a conclusion.

"It's over."

"What do you mean, 'over'?" I asked.

"It's over. Even if he accepts your apology, which he won't,
he'll never forget what happened. We'll never be able to hang out
with him again. And even if we do, it wouldn't be the same." He
took a long pull on his beer. "It's over."

With only a couple of weeks until the three shows in New
York City and a little over a month until that final show in Chicago and nothing but silence coming from the direction of Dayton, Cory's pessimism did feel warranted. And that shook me.
For some reason, I hadn't consciously considered during the or-
deal that we wouldn't be able to attend the final Guided By
Voices shows. Maybe it was blind faith brought on by fanatical
devotion, but I had always expected Pollard to understand and
accept my apology, and that everything would turn out okay. It
was always my belief that I'd be able to rock out at these final
shows with the sense that I still belonged. But Cory's announcement left me reconsidering that assumption. Might I have to
sneak into the venues in order to say good-bye to my favorite
band? The idea that I might have to wear a wig and sunglasses to
mix with kindred spirits was preposterous.

"Should we sell the tickets?" I asked. On eBay, tickets for the
sold-out final show were going for $400 and up—but this
wouldn't be about profit. Profit wouldn't take away the sting of a
failure of this magnitude. Profit wouldn't make up for my recent
lack of interest in playing Pollard songs, or music of any kind, for
that matter. But selling the tickets would be *something*. It would
allow us to be men of action. And action seemed to be what we

needed, even if that action would have seemed unfathomable to the people we were just a month before. Maybe it was time to give in and give up.

It's good that we waited out the weekend. On Monday afternoon when I returned from lunch resigned to unloading the tickets, this e-mail was waiting in my inbox:

From: Rich Turiel
Date: November 22, 2004 12:44:13 PM EST
To: "Postal Blowfish"
Subject: PB: Update on the John Sellers situation

John wrote a letter of apology to Bob. Bob read the letter and accepts John's apology and so end of story.

SMOTHERED IN HUGS

"But I believe you. No need for further questioning."

End of story? Not quite.

As 2004 entered its final day, I still hadn't talked to Bob Pollard. Matt Davis: yes. The Heed: yes. The guy on the tiny bicycle: yes. But Bob Pollard? No.

In that intervening month, during which I'd felt just comfortable enough with my status in Pollardland to attend one of the New York shows,[171] I went back and forth on whether having a personal connection to him mattered to me. It still amazed me that I'd got to talk to him at all—let alone the circumstances under which I'd met him and over how many beers. And it's not like we'd had much of a heart to heart: The entire time we were in Dayton, Cory and I said at most fifty words to him combined. So it really didn't seem like a big deal not to have talked to Pollard again. But I still felt the pull. I wanted to be the guy who knew his favorite musician. I wanted to be another Jim Greer, the *Spin* writer who championed Guided By Voices in the early days, befriended Pollard as a result, was assimilated into the band as bassist, and whose official GBV history was published in 2005. Sometimes when I listened to the band's music, I'd hear a song

---

[171] Despite the absolving e-mail, Cory and I were deathly afraid of the face-to-face reaction we'd get from Matt Davis et al. In fact, we almost skipped the show. But buoyed by at least six pints of Harp we entered Irving Plaza prepared for the worst. Not only did Matt Davis greet each of us with a man-hug and sportingly chide me for my douchebaggery, he let me buy him a couple of $7 beers. Yeah, I pretty much owe him for life.

that reminded me of the trip (mostly "I Am a Scientist," for obvious reasons) and I'd start to think: *Maybe I should be trying to get invited to Monument Club again.* You know, call up Matt and say that I'll be in the Dayton area and that I was hoping to return to Bob's house to finish off those two Miller High Lifes I'd left in the cooler.

Most of the time I wasn't the guy who drank sixteen beers at the house of the man who's written lyrics about bright paper werewolves, navigable flood regions, and flings of the waistcoat crowd. I was just a guy blasting the music of his favorite band alone in his room. A guy air-guitaring during the same awesome parts he always had. A guy analyzing Pollard's songs as if they were the Bible and discovering meaningful new passages he'd somehow overlooked—like the majestic, wandering "Will You Show Me Your Gold?" from the 1999 side project Lexo and the Leapers, or the pretty, petite Robert Pollard track entitled "Snatch Candy." In other words, I was still a huge geek of a fan—the fan I hoped to be for life.

Cory and I did end up going to Chicago for the final Guided By Voices show. In defiance of the end of something it didn't want to end, my mind had staged a mild protest in the days leading up to my flight out of New York. I started having premonitions that something ugly would happen in Chicago that would cause me to miss the show altogether. Like, I'd get into a horrific accident in a taxi. Or I'd lose the tickets. Or a mugger would steal the tickets at knifepoint. Or a mugger would steal my pants. (This is a chronic neurosis.) And what happened on my flight out on the 29th did appear to be a harbinger of some form of doom. Before takeoff, I pretended to read a newspaper—a smoke screen that belied the usual anxiousness about who would fill the two empty seats next to me.[172] It was mildly relieving when a couple showed up, meekly said, "Excuse us," and sat down without jostling my person. Dur-

---

[172] Why must I always get stuck next to that oversize guy whose sole carry-on item is an hours-old KFC dinner or that mother and in-flight breast-feeder of a screaming infant? Plane Rule No. 1: No fried-chicken whiff! Plane Rule No. 2: No suck-tots!

ing the runway taxiing, however, I glanced over toward the window seat and noticed that the man had placed a stuffed monkey on each knee. My initial reaction was along the lines of, "Oh, ha ha! This dude bought some cute stuffed monkeys for his kid back home and is showing them to wifey." I soon deduced that this was not the case. Clue one: Neither the man nor the woman was laughing or talking about the monkeys. Clue two: The monkeys were both facing him, and he had carefully placed them on his knees in a way that ensured they wouldn't fall off—that is, he'd done this before and the plush toys were going to stay that way for the entire two-hour flight. Clue three: Right before takeoff, the guy pulled a muffin from a small paper bag, tore a piece off, and pretended to feed it to the monkeys. Now, I'm no primatologist, but I was pretty certain that those stuffed monkeys weren't hungry. And yet, as he blathered to his companion about a recent PowerPoint presentation he had suffered through, he continued to "feed" his faux simians what appeared to be their daily dose of bran.[173] I decided that if the opportunity and a parachute presented themselves I would jump out of the plane, even if it meant being stranded in a red state.

But it was no ill omen. We arrived at the final show without incident. Plastic cups of beer in hand, Cory and I entered the sweating, jockeying mass of true believers, and promptly met some of our peers in Pollard. Next to us, three college students roughly half my age told us they'd driven fifteen snowy hours from Chapel Hill, North Carolina, to attend the concert. Nearby, a thirty-three-year-old graphic designer named Scott, wearing a

---

[173] My best guess is that the man had a pathological fear of flying—one that very well might have manifested itself in an urge to defecate on the service cart. The monkeys must have been psychological crutches prescribed by a highly paid professional to prevent him from doing the unprintable. A harder theory to consider was that the couple had recently lost a child or children, or were unable to have kids, and that they were using the monkeys to fill whatever void had opened up in their sad lives. But that latter scenario seems unlikely. At the conclusion of the flight, the man unceremoniously stuffed the monkeys into his bag as if they were tattered copies of *The Da Vinci Code*.

self-created T-shirt riddled with band-related images, was passing out commemorative refrigerator magnets; he claimed to be attending his fifty-seventh GBV show, a number that surely rivals a forty-year-old Deadhead's (including Macek's). Were an outsider to meet these obsessives, they might be seen as overly eccentric, or even marginally sad. But to fellow GBV fans like Cory and me, these people were entirely worthy of high fives. It was an honor to be standing next to them. Indeed, everyone in the house was a friend, all of us united in a common purpose: to say goodbye as passionately as possible.

Three weeks before the final Guided By Voices show, I'd gleefully caught the Pixies on their reunion tour and had encountered a different sort of fan: the nostalgia-seeker. Other than a waifish early-twentysomething girl wearing a rubber backpack that bounced annoyingly around as she danced in front of me (it's not a rave, lady!), the one thousand or so attendees were entirely sedate. People in the balcony, which had seating, decided not to stand during the performance—even during "Broken Face," arguably the hardest song written by the band. Elsewhere, two pregnant women leaned heavily against their graying baby-daddies. It was hard not to be moved by the noise the Pixies unleashed that night; they played hit after hit after hit.[174] It was also hard not to hate the aging fans at the show. Are crowds at the various reunion tours of the Who and Pink Floyd that passive? But saying "hello again" to a band is a lesser cause for extreme exuberance than the one final good-bye. Still, it's a sentiment longtime indie-rock fans need to get used to as we enter the era of the alt-rock reunion.

Sorry to flash forward here, but in March 2005 I went to see the influential Kentucky math-rock band Slint, re-formed after a hiatus of more than a decade. Each of the six tracks on their second and final album, *Spiderland* (1991), begins slow and soft, builds to an electrifying crescendo, and then returns to land.

---

[174] The Pixies never wrote a bad song, unless you count 2004's "Bam Thwok," which you can't.

During the quiet parts of their songs at the show I took in, Slint made so little noise that you could hear every polite cough, every clink of glass. Except for a drunk guy who kept yelling, "Fuck yeah!" at strategic moments, the crowd did its part by staying reverential and silent; as such, the ninety-minute set had the feeling of a détente. Which is why, when guitarist David Pajo (also of Tortoise and, briefly, the Billy Corgan–led Zwan) capped off the loping, sinister guitar line that runs through *Spiderland*'s finale, "Good Morning, Captain," by producing furious bolts of sound at the same moment vocalist Brian McMahan belted out the phrase "I miss you!," it was more cathartic than anything that occurred at the Pixies show. Far more invigorating, though, was a July 2005 show put on by the original lineup of Dinosaur Jr. J Mascis and bassist Lou Barlow, he of Sebadoh fame, had parted as bitterly in 1989 as Frank Black and Kim Deal had in 1993. But they'd also mended their sizable rift and, with bald-headed Murph on drums, the Massachusetts-born power trio [175] tore through nearly everything they'd produced together during the late 1980s, including virtually all of 1987's explosive *You're Living All Over Me*. Mascis now resembled a Cousin Itt with glasses; his long silver hair obscured his entire face and flopped all over as he banged on the guitar. Barlow, sixteen years after fleeing the band, looked ecstatic to be playing Dinosaur Jr. songs again. In this case, maybe the "hello again" theory doesn't apply, because the show was one of the best I've ever witnessed in eighteen years of concert-going. It's tough to blow the roof off a roofless venue (they played in Central Park)—but they did it.

But few reunions could ever top a well-planned-out farewell tour for emotion, and no good-bye show will ever touch that last Guided By Voices concert. Fans were whipped into a frenzy as Pollard and various current and former band members trudged

---

[175] Ah, the power trio. Rush. Hüsker Dü. The Police. The Jam. The James Gang. Motörhead. Nirvana. Primus. Sleater-Kinney. Sebadoh. ZZ Top. So where does the original lineup of Dinosaur Jr. rank amid these illustrious triumvirates of rock? Find out in Appendix A.

through sixty-four of the band's best-loved songs. After four consistently rewarding hours, GBV sent everyone home wistful, tired, mind-blown, and more likely than not, pleasantly drunk. The last song, perfectly selected, was "Don't Stop Now," a should-have-been-a-hit anthem off *Under the Bushes Under the Stars* that Pollard called "the official theme song of Guided By Voices." Roughly three minutes later, the music finally stopped.[176]

Did indie rock die when Guided By Voices quit, as Pollard

---

[176] In the cab after the show, Cory and I yet again griped about Pollard's place in the pantheon of rock. As usual, we brought up the five main reasons why he's virtually unknown outside of indie circles—and refuted each of them in turn:

1. **He's never actively courted mainstream audiences.** Believe it or not, he has repeatedly tried and failed to make a crossover. In 1995, GBV recorded with alt-rock hitmaker Steve Albini at arguably the height of their buzz; nothing came of the sessions. They moved in 1999 from Matador to a bigger label, TVT Records, and enlisted Weezer and Hanson producer Ric Ocasek to refine their power-pop sound; no hits. Pollard has been quoted as saying he made a conscious effort on *Isolation Drills* to write a mainstream hit; not a single song charted on the Billboard Hot 100.
2. **His songs are too short.** Bullshit. This is just another way of saying that short songs suck. How many of the early Beatles hits clock in at more than three minutes? How many early Kinks hits? Pollard packs more into two minutes and change than other bands put into a radio-approved four minutes. Most songs these days are too damn long. Like, you don't need that fifth repetition of the chorus. We get it. Less is more, people.
3. **His best songs aren't radio friendly.** This is an untruth. "Game of Pricks" would have sounded just fine on the radio. But what mainstream station could get away with playing a song named "Game of Pricks"? Or "Tractor Rape Chain"? Still, a dozen other Pollard songs would have knocked mainstream-radio junkies onto their coal-mining asses had they been given the chance.
4. **He lives in Dayton.** Nope. Björk comes from Iceland. 'Nuff said.
5. **GBV isn't attractive enough to market.** Name one attractive member of AC/DC. Pink Floyd. U2, circa 2007. Anyway, my ex-girlfriend thinks Pollard is kind of hot.

So why isn't Robert Pollard more famous? The only answer: People are stupid.

suggested it would back in April 2004? Obviously not.[177] Steve Malkmus sagely pointed out way back in 1994 on "Cut Your Hair" that "bands start up each and every day." Then has indie rock died for me? Uh, no—although I am increasingly dismayed that none of the groups that I'm currently obsessed with are still in existence. (It's too much of a stretch to think of the Pixies and Dinosaur Jr. as active bands just yet.) Then what has changed? And where's the character development? (And, darn it, why can't I stop asking questions and answering them myself?) It would appear that those growth-stunting music-listening habits are still with me. But therein lies the change. Two years after the demise of my favorite band, I have become adamant that the only way to listen to music is the way I've always done it. The euphoric end of the extremes is what matters: It is simply wrong to love music halfway. My friends and family should be able to accept the foolishness brought on by my many obsessions, even if they can't ignore it completely. Indeed, sometimes I feel like Daffy Duck in that Bugs Bunny cartoon where a genie gets perturbed at Daffy's singular snottiness and shrinks him to the size of a walnut. ("Consequences, schmonsequences," says Daffy when warned about the dangers of messing with a magic-user.) The last we see of the greedy duck, he's inside an oyster holding onto a pearl for dear life, quacking, "Mine, mine, mine!" While I have hope that another band will come along to blow me away—and in fact my new girlfriend has been pushing me toward Superchunk, that seminal, super-influential North Carolina band I'd felt totally fine ignoring for the past seventeen years but whose music is now making me regret that decision—it's equally likely that I've reached the end of the line as a music listener. And maybe it's fitting that my road also terminates at a Bob. But you know what? My Bob is better than my dad's.[178] Yeah, you heard me.

[177] And in fact Pollard began touring as a solo artist in 2006, and his set includes a few Guided By Voices favorites. Some things aren't meant to die.

[178] At the very least he's nicer. In November 2005, Pollard descended on Manhattan with Matt Davis and some other friends for a Jim Greer

Just after midnight during a festive onstage drinking break at the final Guided By Voices show—2005!—someone nudged me in the arm. As the revelers surrounding us hooted in approval at Pollard's showmanship, I looked over to find Cory talking on his cell phone with a healthy grin on his face. He turned around and pointed to the VIP balcony that ringed the venue, and there on high was Matt Davis waving to us, beckoning us upward. Cory nodded, said something into the phone, and hung up. As we pushed our way through the crowd to get to the balcony stairs, I looked back at the stage and saw Pollard getting smaller and smaller.

---

book signing. A year after the incident that caused my banishment from the kingdom of GBV, Cory and I found ourselves being invited to a bar to watch the Ohio State–Michigan football game and to drink large amounts of beer with our one true hero. Out of extreme gratitude for the inclusion, not to mention fear of being banished again for supporting my alma mater, Michigan, I rooted without shame for Ohio State, the archrival of the Wolverines. These are the things a guy has to do to satisfy his obsessions. But damn, Michigan lost.

APPENDIX A

THE LISTS

MY TOP TEN FAVORITE ALBUMS

1. The Smiths, *The Queen Is Dead*
   Best song: "I Know It's Over"
   Worst song: "Vicar in a Tutu"
2. Pavement, *Slanted and Enchanted*
   Best song: "Here"
   Worst song: "Chesley's Little Wrists"
3. Joy Division, *Closer*
   Best song: "Twenty Four Hours"
   Worst song: "Heart and Soul"
4. My Bloody Valentine, *Loveless*
   Best song: "What You Want"
   Worst song: "Touched"
5. Guided By Voices, *Bee Thousand*
   Best song: "I Am a Scientist"
   Worst song: "Her Psychology Today"
6. The Pixies, *Doolittle*
   Best song: "Tame"
   Worst song: "Silver"
7. Sonic Youth, *Daydream Nation*
   Best song: "Teenage Riot"
   Worst song: "Rain King"
8. Dinosaur Jr., *You're Living All Over Me*
   Best song: "The Lung"
   Worst song: "Poledo"

9. Guided By Voices, *Alien Lanes*
    Best song: "Watch Me Jumpstart"
    Worst song: "The Ugly Vision"
10. Pavement, *Crooked Rain, Crooked Rain*
    Best song: "Gold Soundz"
    Worst song: "Hit the Plane Down"

THE EIGHT DINGERS (SEE PAGE 50)

Guns N' Roses, *Appetite for Destruction*
Nirvana, *Nevermind*
The Pixies, *Surfer Rosa*
The Shins, *Chutes Too Narrow*
The Silver Jews, *American Water*
The Smiths, *The Queen Is Dead*
The Strokes, *Is This It*
U2, *The Joshua Tree*

TOP FIVE MOST DISAPPOINTING ALBUMS (SEE PAGE 97)

1. The Stone Roses, *Second Coming*
2. Morrissey, *Kill Uncle*
3. Def Leppard, *Hysteria*
4. Van Halen, *5150*
5. Ride, *Carnival of Light*

TOP FIVE ALBUMS OFTEN CITED AS INDIE-ROCK BENCHMARKS THAT I SOMEHOW NEVER LISTENED TO BEFORE WORKING ON THIS BOOK, WITH A NOTE AS TO WHY I MISSED OUT AND A FIVE-WORD REMARK UPON HEARING THEM

1. Wire, *Pink Flag* (1977)
    Why I missed it: No excuse other than I'm really lazy.
    Favorite song on first listen: "Ex-Lion Tamer"
    Verdict: Great songs trump thick accents.
2. Mission of Burma, *Signals, Calls & Marches* (1981)
    Why I missed it: I was ten when it came out; ignored many recommendations thereafter.

Favorite song on first listen: "That's When I Reach for My Revolver"

Verdict: I also love *Vs.* (1982).

3. The Fall, *This Nation's Saving Grace* (1985)

Why I missed it: I heard Pavement sounded like the Fall—that seemed to be enough.

Favorite song on first listen: "Paint Work"

Verdict: Sounds like bad Pavement; sorry.

4. Liz Phair, *Exile in Guyville* (1993)

Why I missed it: I graduated from college and didn't care about new music.

Favorite songs on first listen: "Fuck and Run" and "Girls! Girls! Girls!" (tie)

Verdict: Cute lo-fi chicks rock! Sorta.

5. Elliott Smith, *Either/Or* (1997)

Why I missed it: I was deep in a heavy-metal-nostalgia phase at the time.

Favorite song on first listen: "Say Yes"

Verdict: His debut album is better.

TOP NINE WORST NAMES OF ALTERNATIVE BANDS I USED TO SORT OF LIKE

1. Tears for Fears
2. INXS
3. Ned's Atomic Dustbin
4. Toad the Wet Sprocket
5. The Information Society
6. Orchestral Manoeuvres in the Dark
7. The Violent Femmes
8. Bettie Serveert
9. Edie Brickell and New Bohemians

TOP THREE WORST NAMES OF BANDS I NEVER LIKED

1. Carter the Unstoppable Sex Machine
2. Alien Sex Fiend
3. Miranda Sex Garden

TOP FOURTEEN MUSICIANS ELIGIBLE FOR THE ROCK AND ROLL HALL OF FAME WHO, AS OF NOVEMBER 2006, HAVE NOT BEEN INDUCTED, BECAUSE THE ROCK AND ROLL HALL OF FAME IS A JOKE

1. Van Halen (first year of eligibility: 2003)
2. Iggy Pop (1994 with Stooges; 2002 solo)
3. Kiss (1999)
4. Rush (1999)
5. The Cure (2004)
6. Peter Gabriel (2002)
7. Lou Reed (1997 solo; Velvet Underground is already inducted)
8. The Jam (2002)
9. Leonard Cohen (1992)
10. The Cars (2003)
11. Devo (2003)
12. Roxy Music (1997)
13. Black Flag (2005)
14. Joy Division (2004)

TOP THREE NEWLY ELIGIBLE BANDS THAT WOULD HAVE BEEN ON MY NOMINATION LIST HAD I BEEN ABLE TO VOTE FOR THE 2006 INDUCTION (ARTIST'S DEBUT ALBUM IN 1981)

1. Hüsker Dü
2. New Order
3. Minutemen

TOP TEN MOST EXCELLENT ALT-ROCK GUITARISTS

1. J Mascis
2. Bob Mould
3. Joe Strummer
4. Lee Ranaldo
5. Thurston Moore
6. Kim Thayil
7. Kurt Cobain

8. Jack White
9. Mitch Mitchell
10. Corin Tucker

TOP FIVE MOST AWESOME-TO-WATCH FEMALE BASSISTS (NOT INCLUDING SUPERCHUNK'S LAURA BALLANCE, BECAUSE I SUCK)

1. Kim Gordon
2. D'Arcy
3. Melissa Auf Der Maur
4. Kim Deal
5. Sean Yseult

TOP THREE COOLEST ALT-ROCK DRUMMERS

1. Dave Grohl
2. Gary Young
3. Murph

TOP NINE ALTESQUE MUSICIANS I COULD DO WITHOUT EVER SEEING AGAIN

1. Moby
2. Carlos D
3. Dave Navarro
4. Conor Oberst
5. Billy Corgan
6. Bez
7. Flea
8. Wayne Coyne
9. Evan Dando

TOP SEVEN POWER TRIOS (SEE PAGE 180)

1. Rush
2. Nirvana
3. Dinosaur Jr.
4. Hüsker Dü
5. The Police

6. Sleater-Kinney
7. The Jam

TOP FOURTEEN SONGS THAT APPEAR LAST ON ALBUMS I HAVE IN MY CD COLLECTION (* DENOTES LAST SONG ON BAND'S LAST ALBUM—OOH!)

1. The Pixies, "Gouge Away" *(Doolittle)*
2. Pavement, "Fillmore Jive" *(Crooked Rain, Crooked Rain)*
3. Slint, "Good Morning, Captain" *(Spiderland)*
4. Joy Division, "Decades" *(Closer)*
5. Guided By Voices, "Huffman Prairie Flying Field" *(Half Smiles of the Decomposed)*
6. Black Sabbath, "Jack the Stripper/Fairies Wear Boots" *(Paranoid)*
7. Robert Pollard, "Their Biggest Win" *(Fiction Man)*
8. Nirvana, "All Apologies" *(In Utero)*
9. Guided By Voices, "Captain's Dead" *(Devil Between My Toes)*
10. Rush, "Cygnus X-I" *(A Farewell to Kings)*
11. Pavement, "Carrot Rope" *(Terror Twilight)*
12. Guided By Voices, "Trust the Wizard (Radio Show)" *(Self-Inflicted Aerial Nostalgia)*
13. Interpol, "Leif Erikson" *(Turn on the Bright Lights)*
14. Guns N' Roses, "Rocket Queen" *(Appetite for Destruction)*

TOP NINE SONGS THAT ARE IN NO WAY INDIE ROCK

1. Van Halen, "Unchained" *(Fair Warning)*
2. Ozzy Osbourne, "Flying High Again" *(Blizzard of Ozz)*
3. Van Halen, "Ain't Talkin' 'bout Love" *(Van Halen)*
4. Van Halen, "Everybody Wants Some!!" *(Women and Children First)*
5. Mötley Crüe, "Come on and Dance" *(Too Fast for Love)*
6. Rush, "Red Barchetta" *(Moving Pictures)*
7. Mötley Crüe, "Bastard" *(Shout at the Devil)*
8. Journey, "The Wheel in the Sky" *(Infinity)*
9. The Who, "The Seeker" (single)

TOP EIGHT WILDLY POPULAR ARTISTS WHO I DON'T THINK ARE AS GOOD AS MOST PEOPLE DO, WITH COMMENTS AS TO WHY

1. The Rolling Stones
   Mick Jagger is not my kind of lyricist. Puerto Rican girls are never dying to meet me.
2. Elton John
   I hate his glasses fetish, and I'm not a lover of piano-based music.
3. Pink Floyd
   I've never taken acid.
4. The Grateful Dead
   Ditto.
5. Jimi Hendrix
   Love the guitar-on-fire gimmick; hate the songs.
6. AC/DC
   I've never been able to get beyond the schoolboy outfits.
7. Coldplay
   Too wimpy; too same-y; lead singer's daughter's name is Apple.
8. The Beatles
   Admit it: *Sgt. Pepper's Lonely Hearts Club Band* is an embarrassing album.

TOP FOUR INDIE-ROCK ARTISTS WHOM EVERYONE LIKES BUT WHOM I AM LUKEWARM TO, AND WHY

1. Elvis Costello
   "Alison" ruined everything else for me.
2. R.E.M.
   Loved this band up through *Green,* but Michael Stipe has bugged the shit out of me ever since.
3. The White Stripes
   Terrible drummer. Plus: Renée Zellweger.
4. The Flaming Lips
   I don't like the name of the band. Even worse are the animal costumes.

TOP FIVE SONGS THAT I AM MOST ANNOYED BY IN ALL THE WORLD

1. Don McLean, "American Pie"
2. The Allman Brothers Band, "Jessica"
3. Aerosmith, "Rag Doll"
4. Dan Fogelberg, "Longer Than"
5. James Taylor, "You've Got a Friend"

TOP NINE INDIE LABELS

1. Matador (best artist ever on its payroll: Guided By Voices)
2. SST (Black Flag)
3. Creation Records (My Bloody Valentine)
4. Merge (Superchunk)
5. 4AD (Pixies)
6. Sub Pop (Nirvana)
7. Drag City (Pavement)
8. Touch and Go (Big Black)
9. Homestead Records (Dinosaur Jr.)

TOP FIVE MUSICAL THINGS I HOPE HAPPEN NOW THAT THE ORIGINAL LINEUPS OF THE PIXIES AND DINOSAUR JR. HAVE REUNITED

1. Ian Curtis is resurrected.
2. The Smiths reunite for a private party at my favorite bar.
3. There is a new My Bloody Valentine album.
4. A new Nirvana comes along to blow away all of these fey Duran Duran emulators.
5. Radiohead stops listening to Pink Floyd and starts listening to Black Sabbath.

TOP TWELVE INDIE BANDS I COULD HAVE WRITTEN ABOUT AT LENGTH BUT FAILED TO DO SO, THEREBY FAILING THE BANDS I LOVE

1. Built to Spill
2. Archers of Loaf
3. The Pixies
4. Yo La Tengo
5. Sonic Youth
6. Superchunk
7. Queens of the Stone Age
8. The Replacements
9. The Jesus and Mary Chain
10. The Cure
11. Silkworm
12. Unrest

ONE HUNDRED AND SEVENTY-THREE INDIE ARTISTS I NEGLECTED TO MENTION ELSEWHERE, GIVEN A SIMPLE SHOUT-OUT HERE SO AS TO WARD OFF ANGRY LETTERS

Ryan Adams
Ambulance LTD
American Music Club
. . . And You Will Know Us by the Trail of Dead
Animal Collective
The Apples in Stereo
Arab Strap
Art Brut
At the Drive-In
Band of Horses
Beat Happening
Beck
Belly
Ben Lee

Beta Band
Big Audio Dynamite
The Birthday Party
Black Rebel Motorcycle Club
Bloc Party
Bonnie "Prince" Billy
Brian Jonestown Massacre
Broadcast
Broken Social Scene
Butthole Surfers
Cake
Calexico
Camper Van Beethoven
Neko Case
Catherine Wheel
Billy Childish
Chisel
Cibo Matto
Clinic
The Cocteau Twins
Codeine
Come
Julian Cope
Cowboy Junkies
The Cramps
The Dandy Warhols
Dead Can Dance
The Dead Milkmen
The Dears
Death from Above 1979
Deerhoof
Destroyer
Detachment Kit
Dismemberment Plan
Doves
Dr. Dog

Editors
18th Dye
Electrelane
Eleventh Dream Day
Faith No More
Feeder
The Feelies
The Fiery Furnaces
fIREHOSE
Fishbone
The Folk Implosion
Fountains of Wayne
The Futureheads
Galaxie 500
Godspeed You! Black Emperor
Gomez
The Go! Team
Grandaddy
Guadalcanal Diary
Half Japanese
Helium
Helmet
Robyn Hitchcock
Hole
The House of Love
The Housemartins
I Love You But I've Chosen Darkness
The (International) Noise Conspiracy
Iron & Wine
James
Jawbox
The Jesus Lizard
Jimmy Eat World
Jon Spencer Blues Explosion
Killdozer
Killing Joke

Kings of Convenience
Kings of Leon
Kyuss
Lambchop
LCD Soundsystem
Le Tigre
The Lemonheads
Les Savy Fav
Jenny Lewis
The Libertines
Lightning Bolt
Low
Luna
The Magic Numbers
Magnetic Fields
Mates of State
Meat Puppets
The Mekons
The Melvins
Mercury Rev
Mission U.K.
The Mountain Goats
My Morning Jacket
Morphine
Mother Love Bone
Mudhoney
Nada Surf
Neutral Milk Hotel
A.C. Newman
Nine Inch Nails
Nitzer Ebb
OK Go
Will Oldham
Beth Orton
Panic! at the Disco
Pere Ubu

The Pernice Brothers
Pinback
Portastatic
Portishead
The Presidents of the United States of America
Pretty Girls Make Graves
Archer Prewitt
Quasi
Red House Painters
The Rentals
Rocket from the Crypt
Rogue Wave
Rollins Band
Royal Trux
The Sea and Cake
The Screaming Trees
Secret Machines
Shonen Knife
Sigur Rós
Slowdive
Social Distortion
Spacemen 3
Sparklehorse
The Spinanes
Spiritualized
Spoon
Stereolab
Sugar
Sunny Day Real Estate
Super Furry Animals
Superdrag
Supergrass
Matthew Sweet
Tad
Tapes 'n Tapes
10,000 Maniacs

Thee Headcotes
Throwing Muses
Tones on Tail
Tool
Treepeople
TV on the Radio
Uncle Tupelo
Unsane
Versus
The Wedding Present
Ween
Wilco
The Wonder Stuff
The Wrens
Xiu Xiu

APPENDIX B

THE FORMULA

Is it possible to devise an equation that will perfectly rank your musical preferences? I suspect so, but that one airtight formula remains tantalizingly out of my grasp. What follows is another imperfect attempt, as concocted on September 30, 2006 (with a nod to Tim Midgett of Silkworm).

x = .65(quality of music) + .25(band's image) + .10 (X factor) (where x = value of band)

SECTION ONE: QUALITY OF MUSIC
quality of music = $[\{10[(a + b^b) \div c] + 5d + e + f^2 - 2g\} (\sqrt{h})] + 3i + j - k - 10l$

KEY:
a = number of good full-length studio albums
b = number of brilliant full-length studio albums
c = number of full-length studio albums in total
d = number of killer EPs
e = percentage of good songs
f = percentage of brilliant songs
g = percentage of awful songs
h = number of years from band's first album to present or, if defunct, final album
i = sound better when turned up very loud? (if *yes*, value = 3; otherwise −1)

j = good guitar solos? (if *yes*, value = 2; otherwise 0)

k = keyboards more often than not heavily involved? (if *yes*, value = 5; otherwise 0)

l = percentage of songs using only acoustic guitar and/or harmonica (aka the Dylan Negation)

SECTION TWO: BAND'S IMAGE
band's image = $m + n + o - p$

KEY:

m = 10 points if they look like someone you'd want to have a beer with; if not, – 47

n = on a scale of 1 to 100, how awesome is the front man?

o = sum of values resulting from the following situations (*yes* = 2 and *no* = 0, where applicable):

Is it a power trio?

Are there fewer than six members in the band?

Female bassist?

British?

Canadian?

From an American city with a population of 500,000 or less?

How hard does the band party, on a scale of 1 to 10?

p = sum of values resulting from the following situations:

If the band members have costumes, – 10 points, unless that band is Kiss (in which case, + 75).

For each male member of the band not named Robert Smith who has ever worn eye makeup, – 17 points.

For every nose ring, goatee, and fauxhawk, – 7 points.

For every member of the band regularly pictured without a shirt on or in a wifebeater, – 2 points.

If artist is a harpist with a childlike voice who uses the lyric "thee" unironically, – 99 points → 0

SECTION THREE: X FACTOR
(*yes* = 2 and *no* = 0, unless otherwise noted)

Tour often?

Live show, get money's worth?

Does the band move around onstage?

Do they play obscure songs?

Drink onstage?

Heavily?

Break shit onstage?

Videos generally clever?

Pornographic? *(– 5 points)*

Pretentious? *(– 10 points)*

Did lyricist go to college?

A good college?

Ivy League? *(– 5 points)*

Is Morrissey involved? *(+ 25 points)*

Every lyric equal to or better than "My love's a pony"?

Silly feud with another band? *(– 5 points)*

Silly feud between band members? *(– 10 points)*

Lead singer commit suicide? *(+ 8 points)*

Any tragic deaths or disfigurements?

Any albums appearing in Billboard Top 10? *(– 2 points each)*

Any songs appearing in Billboard Top 20? *(– 3 points each)*

Can they be funny without always being funny?

PROOF ONE

Test of theory using Radiohead:

SECTION ONE: QUALITY OF MUSIC

a = number of good full-length studio albums $\rightarrow$ 5 (all except *Pablo Honey*)

b = number of brilliant full-length studio albums $\rightarrow$ 3 *(The Bends, OK Computer, Kid A)*

c = number of full-length studio albums in total $\rightarrow$ 6

d = number of killer EPs $\rightarrow$ 0

e = percentage of good songs $\rightarrow$ 83

f = percentage of brilliant songs $\rightarrow$ 11

g = percentage of awful songs $\rightarrow$ 9

h = number of years $\rightarrow$ (2007 – 1993) = 14

i = sound better when turned up very loud? $\rightarrow$ Yes = 3

j = good guitar solos? $\rightarrow$ No = 0

k = keyboards more often than not heavily involved? $\rightarrow$ No = 0

l = percentage of songs using only acoustic and/or harmonica (aka the Dylan Negation) $\rightarrow$ 3

$$[\{10[(5 + 9) \div 6] + 0 + 83 + 121 - 18\} (\sqrt{14})] + 9 + 0 - 0 - 30$$

or $(209) (3.7) - 21 = 752$

SECTION TWO: BAND'S IMAGE

band's image = $m + n + o - p$

m = 10 points if they look like someone you'd want to have a beer with, if not, $- 47 \rightarrow 10$

n = on a scale of 1 to 100, how awesome is the front man? $\rightarrow$ 72

o = sum of values resulting from the following situations:

Is it a power trio? $\rightarrow$ 0

Are there fewer than six members in the band? $\rightarrow$ 2

Female bassist? $\rightarrow$ 0

British? $\rightarrow$ 2

Canadian? $\rightarrow$ 0

From an American city with a population of 500,000 or less? $\rightarrow$ 0

How hard does the band party, on a scale of 1 to 10? $\rightarrow$ 1

Total = 5

p = sum of values resulting from the following situations:

If the band members have costumes, $- 10$ points $\rightarrow$ 0

For each male member of the band not named Robert Smith who has ever worn eye makeup, $- 17$ points $\rightarrow$ 0

For every nose ring, goatee, and fauxhawk, $- 7$ points $\rightarrow$ 0

For every member of the band regularly pictured without a shirt on or in a wife beater, $- 2$ points $\rightarrow$ 0

If artist is a harpist with a childlike voice who uses the lyric "thee" unironically, $- 99$ points $\rightarrow$ 0

Total = 0

$m + n + o - p = 87$

SECTION THREE: X FACTOR
(*yes* = 2 and *no* = 0, unless otherwise noted)

Tour often? → 2

Live show, get money's worth? → 2

Does the band move around on stage? → 2

Do they play obscure songs? → 0

Drink onstage? → 0

Heavily? → 0

Break shit onstage? → 0

Videos generally clever? → 2

Pornographic? → 0

Pretentious? → –10

Did lyricist go to college? → 2

A good college? → 0

Ivy League? → 0

Is Morrissey involved? → 0

Every lyric equal to or better than "My love's a pony"? → 2

Silly feud with another band? → 0

Silly feud between band members? → 0

Lead singer commit suicide? → 0

Any tragic deaths or disfigurements? → 0

Any albums appearing in Billboard top 10? → –6

Any songs appearing in Billboard top 20? → 0

Can they be funny without always being funny? → 2

Total = – 2

Radiohead = .65(752) + .25(87) + .10(– 2) = 510

PROOF TWO

Test of theory using the Strokes:

SECTION ONE: QUALITY OF MUSIC

a = number of good full-length studio albums → 1 *(Is This It)*

b = number of brilliant full-length studio albums → 1 (ditto)

c = number of full-length studio albums in total → 3

d = number of killer EPs → 0

e = percentage of good songs → 38

f = percentage of brilliant songs → 8

g = percentage of awful songs → 24

h = number of years → (2007–2001) = 6

i = sound better when turned up very loud? → Yes = 3

j = good guitar solos? → Yes = 2

k = keyboards more often than not heavily involved? → No = 0

l = percentage of songs using only acoustic and/or harmonica (aka the Dylan Negation) → 0

$$[\{10[(1 + 1) \div 3] + 0 + 38 + 64 - 48\}\, (\sqrt{6})] + 9 + 2 - 0 - 0$$

or $(61)\,(2.4) + 11 = 157$

SECTION TWO: BAND'S IMAGE

m = 10 points if they look like someone you'd want to have a beer with, if not, – 47 → 10

n = on a scale of 1 to 100, how awesome is the front man? → 24

o = sum of values resulting from the following situations:

Is it a power trio? → 0

Are there fewer than six members in the band? → 2

Female bassist? → 0

British? → 0

Canadian? → 0

From an American city with a population of 500,000 or less? → 0

How hard does the band party, on a scale of 1 to 10? → 8

Total = 10

p = sum of values resulting from the following situations:

If the band members have costumes, – 10 points → 0

For each male member of the band not named Robert Smith who has ever worn eye makeup, – 17 points → 0

For every nose ring, goatee, and fauxhawk, – 7 points → 0

For every member of the band regularly pictured without a shirt on or in a wife beater, – 2 points → 0

If artist is a harpist with a childlike voice who uses the lyric "thee" unironically, – 99 points → 0

Total = 0

$m + n + o - p = 44$

SECTION THREE: X FACTOR

Tour often? → 2

Live show, get money's worth? → 2

Does the band move around on stage? → 2

Do they play obscure songs? → 2

Drink onstage? → 2

Heavily? → 0

Break shit onstage? → 0

Videos generally clever? → 0

Pornographic? → 0

Pretentious? → 0

Did lyricist go to college? → 2

A good college? → 0

Ivy League? → 0

Is Morrissey involved? → 0

Every lyric equal to or better than "My love's a pony"? → 2

Silly feud with another band? → 0

Silly feud between band members? → 0

Lead singer commit suicide? → 0

Any tragic deaths or disfigurements? → 0

Any albums appearing in Billboard top 10? → 0

Any songs appearing in Billboard top 20? → 0

Can they be funny without always being funny? → 0

Total = 14

The Strokes = .65 (157) + .25(44) + .10(14) = 114

VALUES OF OTHER NOTABLE BANDS

Guided By Voices = 1,369

The Smiths = 1,193

Pavement = 1,036

Yo La Tengo = 82

Joanna Newsom = −203

Dave Matthews Band = −445

APPENDIX C

THE VERDICTS

Hear ye! Hear ye! After lengthy deliberation in that most private and porcelained of chambers where I conduct much of my serious thinking, I, the judge, the jury, and the prosecution, render verdicts on each of the following defendants, all musicians who came to prominence in the first decade of the twenty-first century:

THE KILLERS have been found GUILTY of the charges that they have sold more records than bands with considerably more talent and that they are way too concerned about looking cute. The evidence is clear-cut and needs no explanation. In rendering its decision, however, the court acknowledges that the single "All These Things That I've Done" is actually pretty good, although it goes on at least a minute too long. THE GAVEL HAS SOUNDED!

THE STROKES have been found NOT GUILTY of the charge that they are lame. The court, in striving for fairness, set aside the band's contrived hipsterness, the Barrymore affiliation, and the fact that one or more of the band members outbid the court's friend Miranda on a town house in Brooklyn. Instead, the court rested its entire decision on the memory of a road trip taken the day it ditched those hateful crutches, six dull weeks after a painful 2002 knee operation. The band's debut album, *Is This It,* was playing as the court drove across the Verrazano Bridge, and it felt liberating. THE GAVEL HAS SOUNDED!

THE ARCADE FIRE has been found GUILTY of the charges that there are too many members in the band. To determine precedent, the court looked at *Sellers v. Bez, Shaun Ryder, Paul Ryder, et al., aka the Happy Mondays,* wherein this court ruled that the cutoff number is five for a rock band, particularly if one of the excess members is employed only to dance while E'd out of his mind. Fact: The Arcade Fire has seven full-fledged members, at least two of whom seem to be doing nothing more than annoying the world with antic drum banging and xylophone plinking. However, the court declares the band to be found NOT GUILTY of the charge that they are too weird, after being shown evidence of their Montreal residency. THE GAVEL HAS SOUNDED!

FRANZ FERDINAND has been found GUILTY of the charge that their song "Take Me Out" was played to death in the winter of 2004. While the court recognizes that this wasn't entirely the band's fault, the heart of the matter is that the defendant wrote the song that the court heard on the radio every two seconds in November of that year. THE GAVEL HAS SOUNDED!

DEATH CAB FOR CUTIE has been found GUILTY of the charge that they are entirely too wimpy and O.C. friendly. This was a tough decision because the court was on board near the beginning, having bought the first album with the light-blue cover and the unrememberable name, and having liked a few of those songs more than a little bit. But ultimately: the voice. The court suggests that you grow some, Mr. Gibbard. THE GAVEL HAS SOUNDED!

TED LEO has been found NOT GUILTY of the charge that he's too derivative. The court found crucial the evidence of Leo's 2004 single "Tell Balgeary, Balgury Is Dead," which it played seven times in a row during deliberations. The song does sound a bit like Elvis Costello, but in the court's opinion such innuendo is merely that, because the Leo track rocks harder than anything that bespectacled Irishman ever did. THE GAVEL HAS SOUNDED!

THE YEAH YEAH YEAHS have been found GUILTY of the charge that they are mentioned at least once in every issue of *Spin* magazine. This may seem to be an indictment of *Spin* more than the band, but the court could find no evidence suggesting payola, and thus can render no judgment against the magazine. Although it has no bearing on this case, it is the court's opinion that the Yeah Yeah Yeahs are simply not good enough to warrant so much coverage, despite the easy application of Siouxsie Sioux–wannabe Karen O's lyric "Wait—they don't love you like I love you" to everyday life. THE GAVEL HAS SOUNDED!

THE SHINS have been found NOT GUILTY of the charge that they deserved the fate that befell them in the overhyped movie *Garden State*. The evidence: two albums, each solid all the way through, the first of which includes the band's 2001 single "New Slang," which, as has been suggested by the prosecution and duly noted, was nearly ruined by a scene in the aforementioned movie. When the court challenged the prosecution to find a prettier, more listenable song written this century, the prosecution was not able to do it. THE GAVEL HAS SOUNDED!

SUFJAN STEVENS has been found GUILTY of the charge that he did not include a song about the court's native Grand Rapids on his *Greetings from Michigan* album. THE GAVEL HAS SOUNDED!

CONOR OBERST, aka BRIGHT EYES, has been found GUILTY of the charge that he is really fucking annoying. No supporting evidence is needed. THE GAVEL HAS SOUNDED!

RHETT MILLER, formerly of the band the Old 97's, has been found GUILTY of the charge of having married an entirely too skinny model. After seeing a photograph of the model in question, the court was not amused (or aroused). She does not please the court. THE GAVEL HAS SOUNDED!

THE NEW PORNOGRAPHERS have been found NOT GUILTY of the charge that they are dumb. Primary evidence considered: the contribution of their song "Your Daddy Don't Know" to the sound-track for *FUBAR,* a winning mockumentary about beer-swilling Canadian headbangers that the court's friend Paul Spence cowrote and costarred in. A quote from that movie that the court submits as evidence that it was a worthy cause for the New Pornographers to have supported is, "Turn up the good, turn down the suck." Another highly quotable one, to be said while toasting one's cancerous testicle, is: "To my left nut—see you later, fella." The final piece of evidence used is the video for the aforementioned song, as it features the court's friend Cory Jones, he of the Dayton road trip, wearing a helmet and acting like a total douchewad—in a good way. THE GAVEL HAS SOUNDED!

COLDPLAY has been found GUILTY of the charges that they got too much mileage out of that bland song "Yellow," that they sound entirely too similar to U2 and Radiohead, and that Chris Martin's voice is warbly. Not crucial to the verdict but still influential to the decision was the court's review of the Paltrow file. THE GAVEL HAS SOUNDED!

SNOW PATROL and RILO KILEY have had their cases DISMISSED due to lack of interest. THE GAVEL HAS SOUNDED!

JACK WHITE has been found GUILTY of the charge that he bears a disturbing resemblance to Michael Jackson. Too-pale skin, big hat, odd-looking stubble: The court says, "Hmm." However, the defendant has been found NOT GUILTY of the greater charge that he is an overrated guitarist. "Black Math" was the only song considered in rendering the verdict. THE GAVEL HAS SOUNDED!

THE WALKMEN have been found NOT GUILTY of any charges that will ever be filed in the future against the band, on the grounds that they wrote "The Rat." The reason: When the court used to go out, it would know everyone it saw; now the court goes out alone if it goes out at all. THE GAVEL HAS SOUNDED!

CARLOS D, aka the Interpol bassist, has been found GUILTY of the charge that he looks like a dick with ears. The court considered several photographs of the defendant, and the verdict was rendered after the court determined that it was unable not to deface each and every one of them with a pen, often by scrawling the word POSEUR! on Mr. D's forehead. THE GAVEL HAS SOUNDED!

INTERPOL has been found NOT GUILTY of the charge that it is a Joy Division knockoff. While the defendant's first album had at least three songs that the court warmed to specifically because they sounded like Joy Division, it is the opinion of this court that Interpol has successfully shied away from the seminal postpunk band altogether on its sophomore album, *Antics*. The court also thanks Christ for that. THE GAVEL HAS SOUNDED!

ACKNOWLEDGMENTS

LONG LIVE THE KINGS OF DAYTON!

It goes without saying that *Perfect From Now On* wouldn't have been possible without the considerable access granted to me by Bob Pollard and the other members of the band Guided By Voices. I will never have a better time than I did hanging out with them during the Electrifying Conclusion Tour in the fall of 2004. And so, ice-cold Miller Lites go to:

Bob Pollard: Thank you for calling me a pussy.

Matt Davis: You and your wife, Missy, are literally two of the nicest people I've ever met. Thanks for all the beer, smokes, access, and understanding. Literally.

The Heed and Jim Pollard: You absolutely rule. But, please, no more drunken night golfing.

Rich Turiel, Nate Farley, Chris Slusarenko, Kevin March, and Doug Gillard: May you each always find a Puke/Piss bucket when you need it most.

Thanks also to David Newgarden for liaising; to Joe Goldberg for GBV karaoke; to Jim MacPherson for remembering our names two nights after Monument Club, at which we spoke to you for only twenty minutes; to Darrell Strine for being extremely cool; and to that dude who rode around on a tiny bike at Monument Club. And thanks to anyone else in the GBV camp who had to put up with a drunk John Sellers in Dayton; Columbus; Newport, Kentucky; New York; or Chicago. Also, to the well-meaning and like-minded GBV fans on Postal Blowfish and Disarm the Settlers: You guys know how to insult a person better than C.P.O. Sharkey—I'm truly impressed. (And I'm grateful one of you didn't follow through on that threat to slice my throat with your "valuable hunting knife.") Finally, thanks to Mitch Mitchell, Tobin Sprout, Greg Demos, Kevin Fennell, Jim Greer, and all those countless others who helped make Guided By Voices a force for good in this evil world.

LONG LIVE THESE PEOPLE TOO!

NAME	SONG THEY SHALL RECEIVE (FIGURATIVELY)
Carlene Bauer	Joe Jackson, "Is She Really Going Out with Him?"
Leigh Belz	Pavement, "Unseen Power of the Picket Fence"
Jane Clapp	Neil Diamond, "America"
Art Chung	John Fogerty, "Centerfield"
Jonathan Coulton	Rush, "Cygnus X-1 Book II"
Larissa Dooley	Jonathan Coulton, "Code Monkey"
Greg Emmanuel	Joe Dolce, "Shaddap You Face"
Georgia Gaveras	Kelis, "Milkshake"
John Hodgman	The Beatnik Filmstars, "Now I'm a Millionaire"
Dave Jargowsky	Frank Black, "Los Angeles"
Cory Jones	Ned's Atomic Dustbin, "Happy"
Rob Kemp	Black Sabbath, "Fairies Wear Boots"
Phil Kim	Love and Rockets, "Dog-End of a Day Gone By"
Nicole Kim	Echo and the Bunnymen, "Monkeys"
Geoff Kloske	Tenacious D, "Wonderboy"
Krystian Kukulski	The Walkmen, "The Rat"
Jud Laghi	Nirvana, "Rape Me"
Matt Larson	Mötley Crüe, "Bastard"
Megan Lynch	The Stone Roses, "I Wanna Be Adored"
Tom Macek	Buffalo Tom, "Birdbrain"
Brett Martin	Shelly Palmer, "Let's Go Mets!"
Anthony McErlain	George Thorogood, "One Bourbon, One Scotch, One Beer"
Pauline O'Connor	A. C. Newman, "Come Crash"
Katy Parry	Yo La Tengo, "Barnaby, Hardly Working"
Whitney Pastorek	Lionel Richie, "Hello"
Sam Potts	Superchunk, "Slack Motherfucker"
Andrew Reale	The Allman Brothers Band, "Jessica"

Brant Rumble	The Replacements, "Color Me Impressed"
Karin Schulze	Van Halen, "Drop Dead Legs"
Joel Stein	James Taylor, "How Sweet It Is (To Be Loved By You)"
Emily Stone	Men at Work, "Down Under"
Thunderegg	The Smithereens, "Too Much Passion"
Kelly Welsh	The Smiths, "Paint a Vulgar Picture"